Studies in Rhetorics and Feminisms

Series Editors, Cheryl Glenn and Shirley Wilson Logan

Rhetorical Education

IN TURN-OF-THE-CENTURY
U.S. WOMEN'S JOURNALISM

◆————————————————◆

GRACE WETZEL

Southern Illinois University Press
Carbondale

Southern Illinois University Press
www.siupress.com

Copyright © 2023 by the Board of Trustees,
Southern Illinois University
Printed in the United States of America

26 25 24 23   4 3 2 1

Cover illustration: Photograph of Winifred Black Bonfils, courtesy of Good
Housekeeping/Hearst Magazine Media, Inc.; Photograph of Gertrude
Bustill Mossell from the University of Pennsylvania Archives; Photograph
of Susette La Flesche, courtesy of History Nebraska (RG2026-5).

Library of Congress Cataloging-in-Publication Data
Names: Wetzel, Grace – author.
Title: Rhetorical education in turn-of-the-century U.S. women's journalism /
Grace Wetzel.
Identifiers: LCCN 2022044189 (print) | LCCN 2022044190 (ebook) |
ISBN 9780809338672 (paperback) | ISBN 9780809338689 (ebook)
Subjects: LCSH: Women journalists—United States—History—19th century. |
English language—Rhetoric—Study and teaching—United States—
History—19th century. | Minority journalists—United States—History—
19th century. | Journalism—Social aspects—United States—History—
19th century. | Women teachers—United States—History—19th century. |
Rhetoric—Social aspects—United States.
Classification: LCC PN4888.W66 W488 2023 (print) |
LCC PN4888.W66 (ebook) | DDC 071/.3082—dc23/eng/20221121
LC record available at https://lccn.loc.gov/2022044189
LC ebook record available at https://lccn.loc.gov/2022044190

Printed on recycled paper ♻

SIU
Southern Illinois University System

Contents

List of Illustrations

Newspaper Abbreviations

BDET	Boston *Daily Evening Traveller*
BDS	Beatrice *Daily Sun*
CA	*Colored American*
CR	*Christian Recorder*
FJ	*Freedom's Journal*
GH	*Good Housekeeping*
IC	*Indian Chieftain*
IW	*Indianapolis World*
NYF	*New York Freeman*
NYT	*New York Times*
NYW	*New York World*
OMWH	*Omaha Morning World-Herald*
PI	*Philadelphia Inquirer*
SFE	*San Francisco Examiner*
WE	*Woman's Era*

Foreword

Shari J. Stenberg

As I met Winifred Black Bonfils, Gertrude Bustill Mossell, and Susette La Flesche Tibbles in the pages of *Rhetorical Education in Turn-of-the-Century U.S. Women's Journalism*, I was reminded that historiography not only deepens our understanding of the past and its inflections on the present—it connects us to community. It invites us into cross-generational conversation and offers companionship in the process. I felt just that community as I encountered the work of Black, Mossell, and La Flesche, who refused a divide between the rhetorical and the pedagogical and who entered a male-dominated public sphere in order to transform it. As Grace Wetzel so artfully reveals, Black, Mossell, and La Flesche understood that rhetoric teaches, both in its argument and its approach, and their instruction was collaborative, reciprocal, and inviting. Long before the fields of composition studies and feminist rhetoric were established, Black, Mossell, and La Flesche enacted social and pedagogical commitments that are every bit as vital today as in the late nineteenth century and that we continue, as rhetors and teachers, to build on in our contemporary classrooms.

By profession, Black, Mossell, and La Flesche were primarily journalists, not teachers. But these late nineteenth-century writers made the newspaper their site of teaching; they actively invited their audiences—particularly those often ignored and devalued by the mainstream press—to be writers and collaborators along with them. They sponsored their readers' contribution to prominent social issues and taught them practices of critical literacy. Situated in the era of the Harvard Entrance Exam, when writing instruction privileged correctness and conformity to standards over rhetorical engagement, Black, Mossell, and La Flesche offered an alternative path. They serve as early exemplars of the "difference" in pedagogical approach and values that we ascribe to composition studies today.

As Sharon Crowley so aptly describes, "composition pedagogy focuses on change and development in students rather than transmission of a heritage. Composition studies encourages collaboration. It emphasizes the historical, political, and social contexts and practices associated with composing rather than concentrating on texts as isolated artifacts" (3). In the three case studies that Grace offers, you'll find seeds of contemporary composition pedagogy—both its socially conscious visions and its invitational instructional acts—sown in reciprocal engagement between each journalist and her readers.

So, too, will you find in the contributions of Black, Mossell, and La Flesche the visions, values, and practices that we would characterize as feminist rhetoric over a hundred years later. Grace's compelling and comprehensive analysis of the life and work of each journalist highlights the rhetor's importance, both for her very presence—each of them writing in a profession then dominated by white men—and for the innovative principles, methodologies, and strategies she employed. *Rhetorical Education in Turn-of-the-Century U.S. Women's Journalism*, then, not only gifts feminist rhetoric with the recovery and recuperation of three important rhetorical figures, providing us a new set of rhetorical ancestors, it underscores the "difference" of Black, Mossell, and La Flesche's rhetorical practice, prompting us to revise and expand understandings of our (white, masculine) rhetorical past and offering us promising approaches aligned with contemporary notions of "rhetorical feminism." As Cheryl Glenn characterizes it, rhetorical feminism is a theoretical stance that is "dialogic and transactional rather than monologic and reactional"; attends to "marginalized audiences that may or may not have the power to address or resolve the exigence"; "employs and respects vernaculars and experiences, recognizing them as sources of knowledge"; "shows us ways to reshape rhetorical appeals, including a reshaped logos based on dialogue and understanding, a reshaped ethos rooted in experience, and a reshaped pathos that values emotion"; and "uses and respects alternative delivery systems, especially those long considered feminine, such as silence and listening" (4). As you'll see in the chapters ahead, Black, Mossell, and La Flesche enact rhetorical feminism by repurposing the masculine tradition of journalistic writing to facilitate a dialogic exchange with marginalized groups, allowing their experience and knowledge to be centered, heard, and valued.

Grace first introduces us to Winifred Black, a middle-class white reporter who is most known for her work as a "stunt girl" and "sob sister"
journalist, despite her long and illustrious career beyond these roles. Grace
highlights Black's often-overlooked work, wherein Black remade her ethos
into that of a wise mother and female teacher, one of few available roles
of authority that were granted to women at the time, in order to sponsor
social activism in children. This ethos was a far cry from the writing-
teacher-as-disciplinarian role that emerged in the late nineteenth century,
a figure whom Susan Miller describes as "at once powerless and sharply
authoritarian, occupying the transgressive, low-status site from which
language may be arbitrated" (139). Instead, Black crafted a mother-teacher
ethos as a nurturer, intellectual, and public leader (Rothermel 40) who
invited her readers-turned-writers to challenge the status quo rather than
conform to it.

This pedagogical-rhetorical practice is most vivid in Black's "Little Jim"
campaign, where Black tells her readers the story of a young, lower-class
boy with a disability who was denied care at the San Francisco Children's
Hospital owing to a lack of space. She turns to her readers for help: "What
is going to become of little Jim?" Children write her with ideas, which
Black has published in the *Examiner*; in response, she highlights the letters' moral principles and rhetorical effectiveness, which she always privileges over grammatical correctness and polished prose. In their letters,
published without editing, children describe a plethora of fund-raising
activities they engaged in to help "Little Jim" by building a new children's
ward, from raffles to baseball fund-raisers to benefit performances. In
one case, Black juxtaposes the humanitarianism and public action of the
children with the "brisk, self-confident air" of a (presumably wealthy) man,
who offers financial support to the campaign yet who declares, "I am a
man of business, my time's worth money. How big of a commission will
you give me?" She contrasts his self-important approach with that of the
children, who express authenticity and concern for others and so become
an example to her adult readers.

Having spent the last several years gathering twenty-first-century wom-
en's rhetorics for the anthology *Persuasive Acts: Women's Rhetoric in the
Twenty-First Century*, I thought about how efforts like Black's to sponsor
the rhetorical potential and possibility of young writers yield social benefit
across generations, as we see powerfully demonstrated by young activists

today. Indeed, it is often young rhetors who take the lead in arguing for and insisting upon remedies to social problems that adults can't, or won't, address. I think, for instance, of the rhetorical leadership demonstrated by the Parkland students regarding gun control through their Everytown movement, of Malala Yousafzai's advocacy for access to education, and of Greta Thunberg's fiery polemic on the environmental crisis created by generations before her. In an address to My Brother's Keeper Alliance after the murder of George Floyd by police in 2020, former president Barack Obama upheld the importance of youth activism, reminding listeners that "historically so much of the progress that we've made in our society has been because of young people." He continues, "If we can give them a hand up, if we can give them mentorship and tools and interventions and resources and love and support, not only can they succeed for themselves, but our communities and our country will be stronger for it" ("Town Hall"). This is the ethos Black enacted with her young readers, one that reminds us of the importance of inviting our students into social engagement and of the value of their rhetorical contributions.

Grace's next case study introduces us to Gertrude Bustill Mossell, an African American journalist who engaged in a dialogic and reciprocal relationship with the readership of the *New York Freeman*. Using her column "Our Woman's Department" as an extracurricular site of learning, Mossell invites her readers to contribute letters and what Grace calls "raw material" to the newspaper, including letters describing their experience and clipped articles on topics from parenting to politics. Mossell's primary pedagogical aim was to sponsor racial uplift by providing education and literacy practices to mothers, preparing them, in turn, to instruct their daughters. To do so, Mossell espoused an ethos of "true womanhood." This ethos should not be conflated with the white articulation of true womanhood, a cult of domesticity whose focus was on submissiveness and piety. For Black women, true womanhood centered on women's moral leadership and agency.

In the late nineteenth century—a time not unlike our own—African American communities experienced both a greater range of educational and political opportunities and an increase in discrimination and brutality. Mossell, like many of her contemporaries, addressed this tension by encouraging a form of uplift that fostered "moral purity"; she instructed mothers to raise their children in ways that challenged stereotypes of African Americans. For mothers raising daughters, this required an emphasis on sexual purity and individual responsibility in order to protect the daughters from stereotypes and sexual violence perpetrated by white people. For mothers of sons, Grace explains, Mossell advised "rhetorical intervention" for averting "types of young men's behaviors that could be used by whites as an excuse for lynching."

Grace traces a striking contrast between Mossell's rhetorical tactics and those of her colleague Ida B. Wells, who placed responsibility for lynching and sexual assault squarely on white men. Wells's approach may feel more resonant with contemporary rhetorical approaches to confronting racism and violence, particularly at a moment when Black Lives Matter protesters have recently occupied the streets of cities across the country and the #MeToo movement has called out perpetrators of sexual harassment and assault. But rather than create a binary of resistant versus accommodationist rhetoric, Grace invites us to listen closely to cultural and historical context, as she observes that "[t]his individualized, mother-oriented response may have possibly appealed to Mossell and . . . readers because it created empowerment within Black female communities—particularly for those women who may have often felt politically powerless to change systemic inequalities—through its focus on preventive action." By placing her analysis of Wells and Mossell side by side, Grace creates space for her readers to grapple with timely questions about protest, history, and power. How have Black communities been required to teach their children assimilation, or even invisibility, in order to survive? How is Mossell's attention to teaching Black boys to avoid being lynched akin to conversations that Black parents must have with their children today to protect them from police brutality? What are the costs of directly challenging racism, and for whom? Who is allowed to speak and be heard about the racist brutality? Mossell's work on racial uplift is an essential part of the history of Black activism and instruction—a history that deserves careful attention today as we embark on national conversations about police brutality and systemic racism.

Grace's final case study features Susette La Flesche Tibbles, a Native American journalist who enacted "rhetorical sovereignty" (Lyons; King) in her writing by claiming "the right to determine communicative need and the right to participate in the process of public image making and meaning making" (King, "Sovereignty" 26). Through rhetorical practices that Grace describes as "relationally based logic," storytelling, and contextualizing facts, La Flesche intervened in dominant modes of newspaper reporting that dangerously mischaracterized Indigenous peoples as savage and monstrous. These media depictions fueled and justified colonialist practices; they stoked in white readership a fear of Indigenous people and suppressed opportunities for relationship. Grace highlights how La Flesche powerfully challenged this "discursive recklessness" through rhetorical practices that featured a "relationally based logical style" and "strategies of alliance building" (Powell; King).

Locating La Flesche in a long tradition of Indigenous rhetors, Grace shows us how La Flesche's reporting exemplified an Indigenous research paradigm centered on relationality (S. Wilson). La Flesche's research practices involved dialogue and relationship building with the Indigenous people whose subjectivity she represented with depth and nuance in her writing. Her relational methodology provided her white readership of the *Omaha Morning World-Herald* a richer, and more accurate, understanding of the conditions that Indigenous people endured, and it fostered a humanizing alliance between her subjects and her readers. This is La Flesche's pedagogy at work, as she both modeled ethical, accurate reporting and, in Grace's words, taught "wise forms of reading and writing intended to encourage more ethical representations of Indigenous peoples and, by extension, more just policies."

Indeed, Grace shows us how La Flesche's journalism not only propelled readers toward more critical reading practices; it also urged social action spurred by new understanding. Critical literacy, she seemed to argue, should compel critical action. In fact, La Flesche's call to readers to critically examine the news they consume and how they respond to it feels urgent 130 years later. If we read news through La Flesche's journalistic lens of relationality and sovereignty, for instance, we might ask why most mainstream media coverage of the Keystone XL oil pipeline, planned to run through tribal lands, focused primarily on corporate, economic, and environmental interests—with only cursory attention paid to the impact on Indigenous peoples, even though Indigenous societies are deeply intertwined with the land and environment. Or as news outlets report discoveries of mass graves of Indigenous children removed from their families and taken to boarding schools, La Flesche would have us pay close attention to the stories of those who were harmed and ask ourselves what it means to restore justice for the centuries of cultural devastation inflicted by these atrocities.

To be sure, La Flesche's rhetoric reminds us that propaganda and news designed to elevate the already-powerful is far from unique to our times.

As historian Yuval Noah Harari observes, across history "[w]e spend far more time and effort on trying to control the world than on trying to understand it." La Flesche does otherwise, centering the stories of those that dominant culture marginalizes and teaching readers to see through a more relational lens—a pedagogical approach that remains deeply resonant for our twenty-first-century classrooms.

In this remarkable contribution to rhetorical and pedagogical history, Grace deepens our understanding of women's contributions to civic literacy and ethical journalism and rhetoric; in so doing, she models a methodology of rhetorical, cross-cultural listening that works in communion with her subjects. Our field's rhetorical and pedagogical conversations are sure to be enriched by Grace's rhetorical study, which has much to teach twenty-first-century readers about the power and possibility of extracurricular sites of instruction.

WORKS CITED

Crowley, Sharon. *Composition in the University: Historical and Polemical Essays*. U of Pittsburgh P, 1998.

Glenn, Cheryl. *Rhetorical Feminism and This Thing Called Hope*. Southern Illinois UP, 2018.

Harari, Yuval Noah. "Are We Living in a Post-truth Era? Yes, but That's Because We're a Post-truth Species." *TED Conferences*, 7 Sept. 2018, ideas.ted.com/are-we-living-in-a-post-truth-era-yes-but-thats-because-were-a-post-truth-species/.

King, Lisa. "Sovereignty, Rhetorical Sovereignty, and Representation: Keywords for Teaching Indigenous Texts." *Survivance, Sovereignty, and Story: Teaching Indigenous Rhetorics*, edited by Lisa King et al., U of Utah P, 2015.

Lyons, Scott Richard. "Rhetorical Sovereignty: What Do American Indians Want from Writing?" *College Composition and Communication*, vol. 51, no. 3, 2000, pp. 447–68.

Miller, Susan. *Textual Carnivals: The Politics of Composition*. Southern Illinois UP, 1993.

Powell, Malea. "Down by the River, or How Susan La Flesche Picotte Can Teach Us about Alliance as a Practice of Survivance." *Rhetorics from/of Color*, special issue of *College English*, vol. 67, no. 1, 2004, pp. 38–60.

Rothermel, Beth Ann. "A Sphere of Noble Action: Gender, Rhetoric, and Influence at a Nineteenth-Century Massachusetts State Normal School." *Rhetoric Society Quarterly*, vol. 33, no. 1, 2003, pp. 35–64.

Stenberg, Shari J., and Charlotte Hogg, editors. *Persuasive Acts: Women's Rhetorics in the Twenty-First Century.* U of Pittsburgh P, 2020.

"Town Hall with Former President Obama on Racial Justice and Police Reform." *C-SPAN*, 3 June 2020, www.c-span.org/video/?472749-1/town -hall-president-obama-racial-justice-police-reform.

Wilson, Shawn. *Research Is Ceremony: Indigenous Research Methods.* Fernwood Publishing, 2008.

Preface

◆————————————————————————————————◆

This study situates turn-of-the-century women's journalism as a dynamic and underexplored site of rhetorical education and social change. I illuminate the work of three female newspaper writers—white middle-class reporter Winifred Black Bonfils, African American column editor Gertrude Bustill Mossell, and Omaha journalist and activist Susette La Flesche Tibbles (Inshta Theamba)—whose innovative set of rhetorical practices together point to journalism's vital role in the extracurriculum of rhetoric and composition studies. At a time when "thousands of teachers were working with thousands and thousands of children" in schools across the United States, Black, Mossell, and La Flesche were functioning in a similar capacity through the highly influential medium of the mass-circulating newspaper (Schultz 151). Unlike school teachers, these journalists addressed "thousands and thousands" at once, yet they nonetheless cultivated close dialogic relationships with their readers or local communities as a conduit for various forms of literacy learning and social change. *Rhetorical Education in Turn-of-the-Century U.S. Women's Journalism* explores this process through a close examination of the newspaper writings of Black, Mossell, and La Flesche—three extraordinary journalists, social advocates, and teachers.

At the close of the nineteenth century, all three of these newspaperwomen used journalism as a site of important pedagogical work. Each wrote and taught in a distinct context; as such, their teacherly ethe assumed different shapes. Yet Black, Mossell, and La Flesche share a commitment to fostering the rhetorical capacities, discursive public participation, and social action efforts of their readers and local communities. To better understand the pedagogical and rhetorical dimensions of their work, I ask questions such as these: How did white middle-class women, African American women, and Native American women use mass-circulating newspapers as a site of extracurricular literacy instruction at the end of the nineteenth century? What similar and different (as well as explicit and implicit) pedagogical strategies did they employ? In doing so, how did they negotiate and challenge various power asymmetries present within the field of journalism and within their respective contexts? How did their teacherly practices build relationships and enable members of provisionally yet systematically marginalized groups to pursue social change?[1] Finally, how have the rhetorical careers of Black, Mossell, and La Flesche continued to influence the extracurricular literacy practices of diverse individuals and groups by way of public memory—decades after these journalists penned their powerful work?

To explore such questions, I situate the writing of these journalists within multiple contexts, including rhetorical historiography, rhetorics and feminisms, rhetoric and composition's extracurriculum, and school-based curriculums and textbooks. I draw on library and archival research methods I had employed in my initial exploration of Black's *San Francisco Examiner* writing—the origin for this project. Reviewing her work on microfilm alerted me to the intricate ways in which Black inspired writing development and social activism among children readers. I then viewed microfilm holdings of both Mossell's "Our Woman's Department" column (published in the *New York Freeman*) and La Flesche's writing for the *Omaha Morning World-Herald*, which broadened my understanding of how women's journalism contributed to public rhetorical education during this period. Archival work supplemented these microfilm explorations with speeches, clippings, and other surviving texts. I analyze this rich body of work through multiple lenses including rhetorical theories, feminist theory, feminist rhetorical research, and public memory studies in rhetoric. In the introduction to this study, I discuss my methods and methodologies in greater detail and provide nuanced context for my argument.

The case studies begin with an analysis of journalist Winifred Black, who inspired and taught young writers while offering encouraging feedback on their writing. Chapter 1, "Winifred Black's 'Little Jim' Campaign: Children's Extracurricular Writing for Social Action," explores a children's public literacy project inspired by Black's 1894 story of "Little Jim," a boy whom the San Francisco Children's Hospital turned away for lack of space. After concluding her article with a question—"What is going to become of little Jim?"—Black received answers from children whose letters she had published in the *Examiner* and often commented on in print. Ultimately, the collaborative efforts of Black, the *Examiner*, and

San Francisco children propelled a vigorous statewide campaign to fund a hospital ward for lower-income children. Scores of previously politically inactive California children wrote letters, formed fund-raising clubs, and composed a newspaper special edition to benefit "Little Jim."

I demonstrate how Winifred Black constructs an ethos capable of inspiring the writing and social action efforts of children from various socioeconomic classes. Specifically, Black revises the rhetorical tradition of the "stunt girl reporter" in order to craft a teacherly ethos anchored in a "symbolic motherhood"—an effective rhetorical strategy because of close cultural links between teaching and mothering (Tonn 2). Combined with aspects of what Karlyn Kohrs Campbell terms a "feminine style," this ethos allows Black to promote not merely social change but also a particular kind of rhetorical education that (1) privileges moral principles over prescriptive grammar and mechanics and (2) blurs gender and class lines. The "Little Jim" campaign is an important subject of study because it illustrates how a "subaltern counterpublic" of children found channels into public participation through inspiration from Black, whose teacherly ethos initiated their public sphere discourse and social activism (Fraser 67).

Chapter 2, "Gertrude Bustill Mossell's 'Helpful Sisterhood': Racial Uplift, Raising Girls, and Reader-Centered Pedagogy," turns to Mossell, editor of the column "Our Woman's Department," an intimately collaborative column that calls to mind a student-centered classroom. I examine how one of the first woman's columns published in a Black newspaper, the *New York Freeman*, orchestrated dialogic literacy instruction among African American women. More specifically, Mossell published and responded to many readers' letters while practicing a pedagogy that actively incorporated African American women into her writing process. Readers helped to research articles, compile knowledge, and shape column content by identifying issues of common concern.

One central issue that emerged during Mossell's time as column editor was the purity of African American girls. Column discussions of this issue settled on the vital role of motherly influence and educational self-improvement in mitigating sexual threats to these girls. By publishing readers' letters and inviting African American women into her writing process, Mossell practices a type of reader-centered pedagogy intended to edify mothers so they might effectively rear their daughters. Positing idleness as a source of immorality and intelligent, moral mothers as the model through which daughters can flourish, Mossell provides her mother-readers with extensive reading lists, writing tasks, and research assignments. This pedagogical strategy allows Mossell to (1) prepare mothers to serve as moral and intellectual guides for their daughters and (2) contribute to the larger African American project of racial uplift.

Chapter 3, "Susette La Flesche's Relational Journalism and Literacy Teaching: Collaborative Practices of Survivance," considers La Flesche, a reporter for the *Omaha Morning World-Herald* whose teaching practices invited relational ways of being and knowing as means of cultivating ethical writing (S. Wilson). Stationed at Pine Ridge Agency during the weeks surrounding the 1890 Wounded Knee Massacre, La Flesche sought to intervene in commercial press discourses that "assert[ed] control of" Indigenous peoples through a "rhetorical imperialism" upholding colonialization (Lyons 452). As an Omaha writer addressing a primarily white audience while living and working in close relation to Lakota people, La Flesche challenges such rhetorical imperialism as well as U.S. governmental opposition to the Ghost Dance movement that had been growing among the Plains tribes.. She pens relationally based newswriting as a practice of "survivance" to reshape narratives about Lakota people and teach wiser forms of reading and writing (Vizenor, *Manifest Manners* vii).

Specifically, La Flesche uses three interrelated strategies to advocate for Indigenous rights, teach critical literacy, and model for fellow journalists a more responsible form of news research and reporting. She (1) collaborates with her husband, Thomas Henry Tibbles, a *World-Herald* journalist and Native American rights activist; (2) works to "build alliances" with her primarily white audience using relationally based logic and storytelling among other techniques (King, *Legible Sovereignties* 7); and (3) engages in conversation and relationship building, especially with Lakota people, as a key methodology (S. Wilson 79). I analyze her writing to demonstrate how La Flesche both promoted critical reading among her *World-Herald* audience and modeled relationally based news reporting in claiming "rhetorical sovereignty" and enacting survivance (Lyons, "Rhetorical Sovereignty" 449; Vizenor, *Manifest Manners* vii).

The conclusion considers the sustained extracurricular influences of Black, Mossell, and La Flesche. I describe various forms of extracurricular literacy learning and rhetorical education involving diverse individuals and groups that have engaged in processes of remembering these three newspaperwomen or their influential work decades after this work was published. First, I analyze Black's enduring influence on extracurricular writing among clubwomen, junior high school students, children hospital patients, nursing students, musicians, and other San Franciscans decades after "Annie Laurie's Appeal" introduced "Little Jim" to the public in 1894. I next consider collection-based, spatial, and digital literacy practices relevant to public memory of Mossell by exploring the collection practices of librarian Jessie Carney Smith, author of *Notable Black American Women* (1992), and the African American historical marker program headed by Dr. Charles Blockson in Philadelphia during the 1990s, which memorialized Mossell with a marker placed outside her former home and which has since sparked notable digital extracurricular literacy practices. Third, I give an account of extracurricular literacy endeavors related to La Flesche and her inclusion in the Nebraska Hall of Fame, including self-sponsored newspaper advocacy of La Flesche's induction and a "Nebraska Story" composed by Princella Parker (Omaha Nation) that celebrates La Flesche as a role model. Ultimately, this account points to ways in which public memory of La Flesche has been both enmeshed in the "continuing rhetorical legacy of colonialism" and delinked from this legacy through Indigenous-led rhetorical practices of remembering (Kelly and Black 5; Mignolo, "Delinking"). Finally, I propose takeaways for future scholarship at the intersection of women's rhetorical historiography, public memory, and rhetoric and composition's extracurriculum.

Overall, *Rhetorical Education in Turn-of-the-Century U.S. Women's Journalism* illuminates and analyzes the vibrantly dialogic extracurricular teaching of Black, Mossell, and La Flesche. Their pedagogical practices highlight ways that turn-of-the-century journalism offered women new opportunities not only to enter public discourse but also to extend to readers and community members of diverse racial, ethnic, and socioeconomic backgrounds a unique role in shaping such discourse through their literacy practices. The following chapters chart how women's newspaper writing contributed to dynamic forms of relationship building, social action, and public rhetorical education at the close of the nineteenth century.

Acknowledgments

My heartfelt thanks to the many people who have supported and guided me through the course of this book's development. First, I owe my sincerest appreciation to Christy Friend and Cynthia Davis. Your wise and patient guidance on many drafts of this project in its formative stages was essential, and I am deeply grateful for your mentorship. Shevaun Watson and John Muckelbauer also provided many meaningful insights on this project—thank you both. I am additionally grateful for the warm encouragement of Anne Boyle and for dedicated support and valuable feedback received from Ann Green, Melissa Goldthwaite, Peter Norberg, Thomas Brennan, Owen Gilman, Richard Haslam, and Rich Fusco.

I am especially grateful for rich, encouraging, and discerning insights from series editors Cheryl Glenn and Shirley Wilson Logan on multiple drafts of this manuscript. I thank them both immensely for their meaningful guidance. The anonymous reviewer for this project also provided constructive and highly attentive feedback for which I am greatly appreciative. Kristine Priddy has meanwhile been a wonderfully supportive acquisitions editor, and I am tremendously thankful for her support and patience.

This project is also indebted to many others whose influence was instrumental. During my time in Minnesota, Nathan Nakoma and Marcia Nichols helped me think more complexly about my chapter on Susette La Flesche Tibbles, and I am grateful to them both. Ann Daugherty and I shared memorable conversation about "Little Jim" in San Francisco, and Cristina D. Ramírez inspired much productive reflection on this project. My friend and colleague Rachel N. Spear was an incredible support throughout this project's development. I am also grateful for Lucilla Tan's wonderful ability to help me persevere. Finally, I thank Shari Stenberg for her generous and insightful collaborative work.

The Northeast Modern Language Association and Saint Joseph's University provided support for writing time, research, and travel related to this project, for which I am very appreciative. I also thank the many librarians, archivists, and special collections staff members at the University of California Bancroft Library, the San Francisco Public Library, the University of California San Francisco Library Archives and Special Collections, the Boston Public Library, the Library of Congress, the Smithsonian Institution's National Museum of the American Indian, and the Nebraska State Historical Society—all of whom lent their assistance to this project.

My family has provided sustaining love and encouragement throughout my academic career and especially as I worked to complete this project through many drafts over many years. I extend to them my loving gratitude for their enduring support.

Parts of chapter 2 previously appeared in my article "Winifred Black's Teacherly Ethos: The Role of Journalism in Late-Nineteenth-Century Rhetorical Education," published in *Rhetoric Society Quarterly*, vol. 44, no. 1, 2014, pp. 68–93. Archival materials appear courtesy of the University of California Bancroft Library, the San Francisco Public Library, the University of California San Francisco Library Archives and Special Collections, the Boston Public Library, the Library of Congress, the Smithsonian's National Museum of the American Indian, and the Nebraska State Historical Society.

RHETORICAL EDUCATION IN TURN-OF-THE-CENTURY U.S. WOMEN'S JOURNALISM

Introduction

◈———————————————————————————◈

In a chapter titled "American Newspapers" from his book *America and the Americans* (1897), French visitor Price Collier observed that to "a greater extent than in any other country, the newspapers of America are read and talked about" (267). He continued: "The Americans are such voracious readers of their own newspapers, that the newspapers must be taken into account as an important—not to say the chief—factor in what may be termed the secondary education of the mass of the people" (268). Collier's remarks underscore a crucial link between newspapers and education in the United States at the close of the nineteenth century. Indeed, an enormous number of people across various socioeconomic backgrounds, races, ethnicities, and geographic regions read, recirculated, and in various ways used newspapers for educational purposes during this period. The biggest urban dailies boasted "half a million readers each by 1900,"[1] while affordable weekly, monthly, and other paper types also bolstered newspaper-reading culture. This literacy landscape extended far and wide, reaching "[e]ven impoverished readers [who] received papers second- or thirdhand" (Garvey 6–7). Turn-of-the-century newspapers thus fostered widespread literacy development as Collier suggests and, moreover, presented valuable opportunities for rhetorical learning and public writing—all while forging connections among learners across considerable distances.

This capacity of newspapers to foster such mass education was affirmed by a range of editors and journalists during the period. Ida B. Wells, recipient of a 2020 Pulitzer Prize citation, declared in 1892 that "there is no educator to compare with the press" (42); two years later, reporter and textbook author E. L. Shuman asserted that "as an educator the press can never be overrated" (9).[2] E. M. Camp similarly deemed the newspaper "a great educator" in an 1888 lecture at the University of Pennsylvania: "It is a pedagogue to more people every day than are all the college professors in a year" (5). Colonel A. K. McClure of the *Philadelphia Times* asserted during the same year that "[j]ournalists are the greatest of our teachers," and New York press giant Joseph Pulitzer referred to the journalist as "everybody's critic and teacher" in a 1904 article for the *North American Review* (qtd. in Camp 11; Pulitzer 663).

Today, in the third decade of the twenty-first century, journalism's endurance as an educational instrument is crucial. Almost one in four newspapers in the United States closed between 2004 and 2019; meanwhile, "news deserts" (areas with no local newspaper or minimal reporting) are emerging throughout the country (Luo; Abernathy, *Expanding News Desert* 8, 16). Yet independent, rigorous journalism is vital to literacy development, civic engagement, community building, and a healthy democracy. It circulates information essential to individual, community, and national decision-making; it can powerfully instigate social action; and it acquaints readers with diverse voices and viewpoints—helping to illuminate "how we are still connected politically, economically, and socially to neighbors we know and those we don't" (Abernathy, *Saving Community Journalism* 130). Journalism is thus, as Wells, Pulitzer, and many others observed, historically and contemporarily, a valuable educator and teacher.

Rhetorical Education in Turn-of-the-Century U.S. Women's Journalism explores an important piece of this long-standing correlation between journalism and teaching by examining how newspaperwomen contributed to the educational work of the late nineteenth-century press. Specifically, I analyze the writings of three journalists—white middle-class reporter Winifred Black; African American column editor Gertrude Bustill Mossell; and Omaha writer, speaker, and activist Susette La Flesche Tibbles (Inshta Theamba)—to situate U.S. women's journalism of the period as a powerful site of rhetorical education, literacy learning, discursive public participation, and social change. These journalists each employed distinct teaching strategies and methods in pursuit of their goals—yet all three used the press as the medium for their important pedagogical work.

During the latter nineteenth century, teaching was both an exceedingly popular and ideologically endorsed occupation for women. As Jessica Enoch explains in *Refiguring Rhetorical Education: Women Teaching African American, Native American, and Chicano/a Students, 1865–1911*, "it was almost taken for granted that women were best suited for the work of the teacher" due to prevailing associations between mothering and teaching (2). Yet unlike those many women who taught inside classrooms, the journalist-pedagogues I examine in this study assumed their teaching roles within a glaringly public and male-dominated profession. Their pedagogies also embodied commitments that differed significantly from prevailing prescriptions for classroom teachers. As Enoch explains, classroom teachers during this period were largely invested with the responsibility of "prepar[ing] students for citizenship"—a responsibility most often understood as "reproducing in students those preexisting norms, language practices, and behaviors already firmly entrenched in dominant American society" (3).

The teacherly work of the newspaperwomen in this study, though, departs from such prescriptions—much like the subversive instructional practices of the five teachers Enoch explores in *Refiguring Rhetorical Education*.[3] Through the medium of the mass-circulating newspaper, Black, Mossell, and La Flesche orchestrated various forms of literacy teaching and rhetorical education for social change that challenged "preexisting norms" for language use or that promoted new ways of (or reasons for) writing. Moreover, their widely broadcast journalism was anchored in close and active dialogue with a diverse range of readers and community members—especially children, African American women, and Indigenous peoples, respectively. By cultivating a personal, dialogic form of newspaper discourse, these journalist-pedagogues sought to both educate readers and call them to social action, in response to vital issues in the United States at the time.

Rhetorical Education in Turn-of-the-Century U.S. Women's Journalism situates the journalism of Black, Mossell, and La Flesche as a dynamic form of rhetoric and writing teaching that involved and inspired meaningful forms of learning, relationship building, and discursive public participation. This study furthers historiographic work in rhetoric and composition by contributing to our complex understandings of rhetoric and writing instruction in the United States and the more specific operations of the extracurriculum at the turn of the century—particularly as it was shaped by women rhetors. Indeed, statements by Wells, Pulitzer, and McClure (characterizing the press as an educator and comparing journalists to teachers) invite us to see Black, Mossell, and La Flesche as pedagogues who utilized turn-of-the-century newspapers as vehicles for dynamic instructional practices. Put differently, print culture opened up new possibilities for women to forge professional identities not only as journalists but also as innovative, socially driven teachers of rhetoric and writing.

This study thereby furthers scholarship that has "complicate[d] the narrative of reductivism and decline associated with rhetorical instruction in the late nineteenth and early twentieth centuries" (Gold 4). As David Gold summarizes, this narrative holds that robust instruction in rhetoric fell to the demands of a changing historical moment marked by such factors as the rise of print culture, industrialization, and broadening student populations. In the academy, this yielded "a system of instruction in writing that narrowly construed the possibilities for public discourse," overemphasized prevailing standards of correctness, and "perpetuated class inequities" (2–3). Gold, Enoch, Susan Kates, and other scholars have challenged this narrative through their diverse and intricate accounts of socially and politically oriented rhetoric teaching and learning during the period.[4] My study reveals further limitations with "the narrative of reductivism and decline associated with rhetorical instruction" at this time precisely because Black, Mossell, and La Flesche taught *through* the medium of mass-circulating newspapers—a major part of the "shift from oral to print culture" that was deemed a precipitating factor in rhetorical instruction's purported "decline" (Gold 4, 2). These journalists used print culture for vibrant forms of rhetorical teaching that promoted practices and values such as sincerity, social consciousness, collaboration, and cross-cultural dialogue for social justice—all while upholding belief in the transformative "possibilities for public discourse" (Gold 3).

This study thus aims to expand our continually growing understandings of rhetoric and composition's extracurriculum. Since Anne Ruggles Gere first called for us to recognize a broader "range of teachers" by "separat[ing] pedagogy from the traditional pedagogue" and by attending to robust sites of literacy instruction outside the academy, a rich array of scholarship has emerged on this subject ("Kitchen Tables" 80). Pamela VanHaitsma has catalogued the breadth of such extracurricular literacy sites illuminated by scholars over the past twenty years. They include "African American literary societies; white and black women's clubs; conduct, elocution, and letter-writing manuals for women; diaries and letters by female as well as male students; black periodicals and Spanish-language newspapers; and farm journals, grocery lists, and recipes" ("Romantic Correspondence" 183).

Amid this broad landscape of extracurricular teaching and learning, an exploration of turn-of-the-century women's journalism enriches our understanding of how periodicals operate in the extracurriculum. This work is already well under way. Enoch's *Refiguring Rhetorical Education*, for instance, features a chapter on *La Crónica*, a Spanish-language newspaper that served as "a diverse pedagogical space that welcomed the work of teachers" (121). Enoch demonstrates how three Mexican teachers worked to "educate their readers toward a cultural citizenship that replicate[d] neither Mexican nor Anglo society but instead propose[d] a new kind of cultural and political practice" for residents of the border city of Laredo, Texas (123). In *Liberating Language: Sites of Rhetorical Education in Nineteenth-Century Black America*, Shirley Wilson Logan spotlights the Black press as one of many key extracurricular sites of African American rhetorical instruction. Focusing primarily on antebellum newspapers, Logan shows how these periodicals provided rhetorical training, "educated readers in sound rhetorical principles," and critiqued a range of rhetorical performances (97).

Recently, Elizabeth Leahy's article "'Their Voice Should Be Allowed to Be Heard': The Rhetorical Power of the University of New Mexico's Bilingual Student Newspaper" analyzes student journalists' "extra-curricular writing" and argues that "[b]y incorporating Spanish into their English-language newspaper," these student journalists "challenged monolingual notions of literacy and advocated for a multilingual understanding of American citizenship" (138, 127). Work by Coretta M. Pittman and Cristina D. Ramírez—although less explicitly focused on the extracurriculum—has relatedly explored the influential journalistic practices of twentieth-century African American blues artist Alberta Hunter and Mexican women journalists such as Laureana Wright de Kleinhans, Juana Belén Gutiérrez de Mendoza, and Hermila Galindo. First, Pittman's "To Labor with Dignity: Alberta Hunter's Respectability and Resistance Rhetoric" demonstrates how Hunter's entertainment columns "help[ed] black entertainers increase their wages, argue for better workplace conditions, receive equal opportunities for jobs on the stage in the United States, and maintain the jobs they already had abroad" (146). Second, Ramírez's *Occupying Our Space: The Mestiza Rhetorics of Mexican Women Journalists and Activists, 1875–1942* analyzes how a range of Mexican women journalists influenced discourses about both feminine identities and "emerging national politics of the late nineteenth and early twentieth centuries" (9).[5] Finally, Alicia Brazeau has analyzed the extracurricular functions of turn-of-the-century magazines. Brazeau's *Circulating Literacy: Writing Instruction in American Periodicals, 1880–1910* explores how farm journals and women's magazines "sought to supplement the writing instruction offered in schools by teaching readers new practices that editors argued were meaningful in readers' lives" (15–16).

I build on this body of work by heeding Brazeau's call for scholars to attend more fully to "popular periodicals and their place in the literate lives" of individuals in the turn-of-the-century United States (1). Indeed, as Brazeau affirms, "newspapers and periodicals at this time . . . represent a complex site of study in that they offered multiple perspectives on literacy and, more important, articulated their own definitions of literacy for their readers" (2).[6] My study of late nineteenth-century women's journalism fills an important gap by showing how a diverse set of women used three mass-circulating newspapers—the *San Francisco Examiner*, the *New York Freeman*, and the *Omaha Morning World-Herald*—as unique sites of extracurricular literacy learning, relationship formation, and rhetorical education for social change. By analyzing their writings, I extend historiographic work that illuminates the innovative and varied ways in which women's voices have shaped rhetoric and composition's extracurriculum.

In the first of three case studies, I consider *San Francisco Examiner* journalist Winifred Black, whose teacherly work involving rhetorically oriented feedback on features of young people's writing may appear to be the most explicitly pedagogical. As a journalist-pedagogue, Black (known by her pen name "Annie Laurie") forged close ties with children and initiated their public sphere discourse. By printing children's letters and positing features of their writing as useful for civic participation, Black promoted social change and a particular kind of rhetorical education that privileged moral principles over prescriptive grammar and spelling while simultaneously blurring gender and class lines.

Second, I turn to *New York Freeman* columnist Gertrude Bustill Mossell, whose "Our Woman's Department" demonstrates the value of intimate collaboration in writing and literacy teaching. I show how Mossell orchestrated writing instruction and rhetorical education among African American women readers by collaborating with her audience and inviting readers into her writing process. Assigning both research and writing tasks, Mossell inspired informed and collective conversations about education, sexuality, and other issues vital to racial uplift.

Third, I discuss *Omaha Morning World-Herald* contributor Susette La Flesche Tibbles (Inshta Theamba), whose (perhaps more implicit) pedagogical practices encouraged relational ways of being and knowing as means of cultivating wise writing (S. Wilson, *Research Is Ceremony*). In modeling relationally based news research and reporting during the weeks surrounding the Wounded Knee Massacre, La Flesche's writing powerfully asserted "rhetorical sovereignty" and "survivance" (Lyons, "Rhetorical Sovereignty" 449; Vizenor, *Manifest Manners* vii).[7] Her work ultimately functioned as a pedagogical platform for critical literacy instruction in community-embedded journalism as a means of advocating for Indigenous rights.

Together, these case studies establish how Winifred Black, Gertrude Bustill Mossell, and Susette La Flesche Tibbles used the press as an educational instrument for change by (1) mobilizing readers or local communities in the service of vital social causes; (2) inviting members of provisionally yet systematically marginalized groups into a dialogic form of discursive public participation;[8] and (3) contributing to the rhetorical education of various publics in a range of ways. Ultimately, the teaching practices of these three journalists exemplify ways by which newspaperwomen writing in the 1880s and 1890s orchestrated innovative forms of extracurricular learning for social change.

Turn-of-the-Century Female Journalists and Their Contexts

The press powerfully shaped the United States at the turn of the century. Carl F. Kaestle asserts that "American culture from 1880 to 1940 was increasingly a 'culture of print,' that is, a culture that was knit together and defined by the printed word" (24). The closing decades of the nineteenth century witnessed an especially rapid proliferation of newspapers—a print medium that "defined the world for the reading public" (Gray xiii). From 1880 to 1900, the number of daily newspapers printed in English rose from 850 to 1,967 while total daily circulation increased from 3.1 to 15.1 million (Kaestle and Radway 12).

Table 1. Growth in daily U.S. newspapers in English from 1880 to 1900.

	1880	*1900*
Number of English-language dailies	850	1,967
Number of cities with dailies	389	915
Total daily circulation, in millions	3.1	15.1

Source: Adapted from Kaestle, Carl F., and Janice A. Radway. "A Framework for the History of Publishing and Reading in the United States, 1880–1940." *Print in Motion: The Expansion of Publishing and Reading in the United States, 1880–1940*, edited by Carl F. Kaestle and Janice Radway. *A History of the Book in America*, vol. 4, U of North Carolina P, 2009, p. 12. Kaestle and Radway drew these data from Emery, Edwin. *The Press and America: An Interpretive History of the Mass Media*. 3rd ed., Prentice-Hall, 1972, p. 443.

Alongside this growth in daily newspapers was a dramatic expansion of many additional types of periodicals. As Randall S. Sumpter explains, "[t]he big changes ... were in the numbers of triweeklies, semiweeklies, monthlies, and quarterlies being published. Semiweeklies, for instance, soared 228.3 percent between 1890 and 1900 for a total of 637 publications" (50).

Fueling the growth of newspapers of all kinds were advances in printing technology, "[c]heaper paper," and a national railway system facilitating efficient production and distribution of newspapers (Chambers et al. 17). No longer dependent on subscriptions and sales revenue alone, newspapers also now benefited from widespread advertising that "alongside cheap paper and fast presses ... enabled publishers to dramatically expand their papers." As Julia Guarneri notes in *Newsprint Metropolis: City Papers and the Making of Modern Americans*, "[i]n 1880, American companies spent thirty million dollars on advertising. By 1910, that number increased twentyfold to six hundred million dollars, a full 4 percent of the national income." As a result, "larger papers, bigger presses, and more skilled staffs" emerged (Guarneri 19, 21). Illiteracy meanwhile "dropped by half (to 10.7 per cent of the population) between 1870 and 1900" (Chambers et al. 17). Newspaper reading thus became a remarkably widespread activity across the country.

Newspaper print culture also became increasingly diverse—facilitating a range of expressions of "social protest, racial and ethnic pride, or artistic experimentation" (Lutes, "Beyond" 337). Guarneri observes that "African American papers, religious weeklies, neighborhood weeklies, and suburban newsletters all thrived in the turn-of-the-century metropolis." Papers printed in English as well as in other languages flourished; "collective circulations" of the latter "rivaled those of English-language papers in several cities, and African American weeklies' circulations usually reached across several states" (10). Tribal, nontribal, and intertribal newspapers meanwhile formed "a rich journalistic tradition" composed by Indigenous peoples (Peyer 108).

Such publications frequently forged strong connections among (oftentimes) geographically separated readers. Kaestle and Radway affirm that "[s]pecialized, targeted print forms gathered people together from across the nation on the basis of interests not directly tied to where people resided. In this way the larger culture of print proliferated new, cross-cutting possibilities for the construction of identities and the creation of communities" (21). Overall, newspaper-reading practices spread rapidly among a diverse and massive array of individuals of varying socioeconomic, racial, and ethnic backgrounds during the last decades of the nineteenth century.

Women journalists such as Black, Mossell, and La Flesche played important roles in this flourishing newspaper-reading culture; they also inspired powerful forms of writing and other communicative practices among diverse readerships and communities. Their ability to do so reflects new opportunities that began emerging for women in journalism toward the end of the nineteenth century. Jean Marie Lutes summarizes the emergence of such opportunities:

> in 1870, the first year in which the U.S. Census distinguished journalists by sex, women made up fewer than 1 percent of working journalists. As the turn of the century approached, women as a group began to make a significant mark in newsrooms. The 1880s saw the launch of the first women's press associations, and by the early 1900s, some two dozen such groups had been established in seventeen states. The new respectability of reporting as a profession, expanding educational opportunities for women, and newspapers' growing interest in female readers, who were highly desirable to department store advertisers, all fueled the trend. (*Front-Page Girls* 8)

As a result, the U.S. Census identified that "the percentage of women journalists more than doubled between 1880 and 1900 and climbed steadily after that. Women made up 16 percent of all working journalists by 1920 and 23 percent by 1930" (Lutes, *Front-Page Girls* 8–9). These changes offered unprecedented professional opportunities for late nineteenth- and early twentieth-century women across various intersectional positions. Yet the shape and extent of these opportunities—as well as the aims and exigences of women's newspaper writing—differed widely.

For white middle-class women, their journalism was met with a combination of qualified support and lingering conservative attitudes. In *Steps into Journalism* (1894), for instance, E. L. Shuman asserted that newspaper journalism

> is still decidedly in the hands of men, and the very nature of the work demands that it remain so, to a large extent. Yet even on the newspaper the women have a strong foothold and are making a larger place for themselves every year. Especially in the journalism of the smaller towns, where the stress and strain are not so heavy as in the cities, women are

doing a good deal of unostentatious but successful work at the desk, and many of our largest country weeklies owe their bright paragraphs to the faithful labors of ambitious women.

But on the large metropolitan daily the outlook for women is not so bright. Much of the work is too arduous, too exhausting, and for the most part too rude in its requirements for the gentler sex. (146–47)

A *New York Evening Post* editor meanwhile suggested to journalist Rheta Dorr that men were "permanent industrial factors, women mere accidents" in the field (Dorr 98). Even considerably after the century's turn, when women's participation in journalism had risen tremendously, prominent reporter Ishbel Ross still characterized the newsroom as "that sound haunt of masculinity" in her 1936 history *Ladies of the Press: The Story of Women in Journalism by an Insider* (2).

Expressing a more optimistic outlook on women's journalism, suffragist and journalist Abigail Scott Duniway declared in an 1897 speech that

[t]hose women who take editorial and reportorial positions, stand side by side, if not shoulder to shoulder, with the men with whom they compete on daily newspapers . . . Recent as is their debut into this world of power and responsibility, women are now a recognized factor in daily journalism; and, having won their place by honorable effort and filled it with consummate tact, there is no more likelihood of their being driven from it than there is of a mother chicken returning to her original shell. (Duniway)

During the same decade, Winifred Black attempted to rebut claims about metropolitan journalism's unsuitability for women by maintaining that "[a]ny woman that is a woman carries her sphere with her wherever she goes—be it in a ballroom or a newspaper office" ("Annie Laurie's Experience").

Yet even reluctant white male editors often capitulated to "the pressing demands of commerce" in recognizing the value of an alleged feminine angle (Fahs 4). Driven by the commercialization of cities, the flourishing of shopping districts, and the corresponding use of advertising to appeal to female readers, metropolitan newspapers increasingly turned to white middle-class women for their seemingly feminine point of view. In 1906, for instance, journalist Charles H. Olin wrote of women's newspaper writing that "the field is restricted usually to the gathering of society news, the editing of a woman's page, which may also include the conducting of a woman's club column and the selection of items of interest to her sex from the exchanges." In regard to "subjects which are not ordinarily congenial to women," he reasoned, "[h]er story is not supposed to add anything of importance to the report of her brother journalists, its whole value lying in the fact that it is written from a wholly feminine standpoint, in a bright feminine manner, with little touches of feminine sympathy, pathos and sentiment" (Olin 51–52).[9]

Such attitudes helped justify white women's public participation in mass journalism while simultaneously perpetuating strict gendered labor divisions. Mary Twombly accordingly commented in 1889 that "[t]he easiest, and, as a rule, the only, way through which a woman can make a beginning on the press is through writing on what men regard as distinctively feminine topics" (qtd. in Fahs 4). A year later, Winifred Black similarly reflected: "The first real trouble that a sensitive woman will have in newspaper work is this: When she first goes into any office she will be expected to do 'woman's work' exclusively" ("Annie Laurie's Experience"). Yet articles on many supposedly feminine topics, such as family budgeting, were rarely bereft of economic and political dimensions. Moreover, newspaperwomen such as New York *Evening Journal* contributor Marie Manning and two colleagues engaged in general reporting and book reviews while also penning the *Journal*'s 1890s woman's page; still other white middle-class female journalists including Nellie Bly, Nell Nelson, and Ada Patterson were at this time exposing urban and institutional injustices and rallying for social change through the popular genre of stunt reporting (Fahs 5–7, 200; Lutes, *Front-Page Girls* 31, 33).

Pioneered by Joseph Pulitzer, the stunt girl reporter emerged as a major role for white middle-class female journalists at the end of the nineteenth century. Often defined by elements of disguise and exposé, stunt girls went undercover in opium dens, fainted on crowded city corners, explored sewers, and posed as chorus girls. They rolled tobacco, visited dissecting rooms, and raced one another around the world (Lutes, *Front-Page Girls* 13; Adams and Keene 31; *Life* Dec. 17, 1896). Lutes has characterized stunt reporting as a thoroughly corporeal genre—one that "involved not just reporting the news but *becoming* the news" (*Front-Page Girls* 5). This is famously evident in Nellie Bly's self-imposed confinement in Blackwell's Island Asylum, for which she feigned insanity to gain access to the largely abusive New York institution. Headlines such as "Who Is This Insane Girl?" and passages such as the following (in which Bly describes a forced bath) emblematize how stunt girls "used their bodies . . . as the very source of [news]" (Lutes, *Front-Page Girls* 14):

> My teeth chattered and my limbs were goose-fleshed and blue with cold. Suddenly I got, one after the other, three buckets of water over my head—ice-cold water, too—into my eyes, my ears, my nose and my mouth. I think I experienced the sensation of a drowning person as they dragged me, gasping, shivering and quaking, from the tub. (Bly)

As this genre grew, West Coast newspapers such as William Randolph Hearst's *Examiner* also adopted stunts during a fiercely competitive age of "new journalism." Winifred Black was to this end instructed to "faint" on a crowded city street ultimately to expose deficient hospital treatment of indigent San Franciscans and the "BRUTALITY OF PUBLIC SERVANTS" (*SFE* Jan. 19, 1890). Stunt reporting by Black and others shared several conventions of new journalism: attention-grabbing headlines, "bold-faced type," plentiful illustrations, and "vivid accounts" (Fahs 3–4; Britton 27; Lutes, *Front-Page Girls* 14). Yet elements of dramatic performance and corporeality do not adequately characterize the careers of all stunt girls. As one example, Black—initially a purported stunt girl—shifted attention away from sensational corporeal reporting and toward children's writing and rhetorical education during the 1894 "Little Jim" campaign, a literacy-driven civic project I discuss in chapter 1.

The types of metropolitan daily newspapers to which Black and Bly contributed largely, although not entirely, excluded African American journalists. This occurred across a range of white periodicals, causing Gertrude Bustill Mossell to comment: "we have long wondered why we could not secure space for good work in white journals" (*WE* May, 1895). Amelia Johnson meanwhile protested her experience of discrimination by *Youth's Companion*, to whom she had "identified herself as 'a colored woman, and proud of it'" (qtd. in Wagner 99).[10] These examples of "[t]he historical lack of status and privilege" afforded to African American women indicate why—as Jacqueline Jones Royster has explained—"their uses of language would not typically be within 'mainstream' communities of discourse but within . . . 'counter' discourses" (60).

Royster, Logan, and many other scholars have shown how the Black press functioned as a primary site for the circulation of such discourses during the late nineteenth century. With a foundation in *Freedom's Journal*, established in 1827 and considered to be the first African American periodical, the Black press proceeded to "gr[o]w at an astonishing rate following the Civil War"—particularly toward the end of the century. "While a dozen new publications were established in the nine months following the War's end, from the late 1880s through the early 1890s, the black press experienced unprecedented and astonishing growth," relays Teresa Zackodnik, drawing on work by Hazel Dicken-Garcia (204). Indeed, "by 1890 more than 600 black papers had been started. Many failed, but more than 150 were operating in 1900, asserting citizenship rights long deferred" (Shott 2). These newspapers constituted a chief means of defense against libel, a venue for "reconstructing individual and group definitions," and a powerful platform for advocacy and activism (Foster 716). Such advocacy work extended into more "mainstream" periodicals (Mossell, for instance, contributed to the Philadelphia *Press* and *Inquirer,* while Wells called the white press "the medium through which I hoped to reach the white people of the country"); yet it was the Black press that more often enabled African American female journalists to establish a public voice at this time (Royster 60; Wells 75).

African American women entered the newspaper profession in both the North and South during the 1880s and 1890s "in unprecedented numbers" (Zackodnik 204; Lutes, *Front-Page Girls* 45). They included Wells, Pauline Hopkins, Frances Ellen Watkins Harper, Alice Dunbar-Nelson, Victoria Earle Matthews, Mary E. Britton, Mary V. Cook, and Delilah Beasley (Lutes, *Front-Page Girls* 45; F. Wilson 93). Writing alongside female poets, fiction and nonfiction authors, and biographers, these journalists used the African American press as "the platform from which they could speak and be heard" (Royster 221). Championing their work were male contemporaries such as prominent editor and *New York Freeman* owner Timothy Thomas Fortune, who expressed great support for Black women writers: "We have some very bright women contributors to the colored press," Fortune commented. "I think our women are going to outstretch our men in the variety of their information, the purity of their expression and in having the courage of their convictions" (qtd. in Lutes, *Front-Page Girls* 47). Female writers such as Lucy Wilmot Smith confirmed this robust male support. In 1889, she wrote that

> [t]he educated negro woman occupies vantage ground over the Caucasian woman of America, in that the former has had to contest with her brother every inch of the ground for recognition; the negro man,

having had his sister by his side on plantations and in rice swamps, keeps her there, now that he moves in other spheres. As she wins laurels, he accords her the royal crown. This is especially true of journalism. (qtd. in McMurry 89)

Additional writers such as Mossell made similar remarks. In an 1889 article for the *New York Age*, she celebrated the inclusiveness of the African American press, writing, "[t]hey do not even debar us from their Press Associations. For [that] we are truly thankful, and each editor will bear witness to the noble women who have strengthened his work" (qtd. in Lutes, *Front-Page Girls* 47–48). Later, she adopted reasoning different from Smith's but still assured Black women journalists that "so far I have found nothing to discourage an earnest worker." As she explained in *The Work of the Afro-American Woman* (1894), "[o]ur men are too much hampered by their contentions with their white brothers to afford to stop and fight their black sisters, so we slip in and glide along quietly. We are out of the thick of the fight. Lookers-on in Venice, we have time to think over our thoughts, and carry out our purposes; we have everything to encourage us in this line of effort" (100).

Overall, African American female journalists, together with clubwomen, speakers, and activists, constituted a powerful force for change during what Mossell called "the Women's Century."[11] As 1903 Fisk graduate Grace Hadnott affirmed, "The future of the Negro race lies in the hands of its women . . . She alone has the power to uproot ignorance, break down prejudice and solve for us this great race problem" (qtd. in F. Wilson 91). More specifically, and as Royster has demonstrated, it was often elite, well-educated African American women who assumed this central role in social change leadership. These women "were perceived and perceived themselves to be hard-working, socially conscious, and ideologically committed to activism and advocacy"; they had both "access to power and influence" and "the luxury, the class privilege, and the time to use this access in their own interests and in the interests of others" (6–7).

As a member of the influential Bustill family and wife of prominent Philadelphia physician Nathan F. Mossell, Gertrude Bustill Mossell used her elite status to do exactly this—exhibiting the type of educated leadership that W. E. B. Du Bois would come to promote through his concept of the "talented tenth," referring to those Black intellectuals and race leaders whose own educational and cultural development would "guide the Mass" (qtd. in Gooding-Williams 33). Mossell and other Black female journalists such as Wells "constructed careers and public lives as community and national leaders" while operating alongside an array of additional race leaders including social scientists engaged in Black labor studies, club-women and educators, and members of new national organizations such as the Bethel Literary and Historical Association and the Society for the Collection of Negro Folklore (F. Wilson 93, 17). Chapter 2 explores ways in which Mossell's "Our Woman's Department" column in the *New York Freeman* modeled and promoted Black female leadership while fostering vibrant extracurricular literacy development and discursive civic partic-ipation among readers.

During the nineteenth century and beyond, Native Americans used the press for various expressions of rhetorical sovereignty and as one form (among many) of survivance (Lyons, "Rhetorical Sovereignty" 449; Vizenor, *Manifest Manners* vii). Scott Richard Lyons defines *rhetorical sov-ereignty* as "the inherent right and ability of *peoples* to determine their own communicative needs and desires in [the pursuit of self-determination], to decide for themselves the goals, modes, styles, and languages of public discourse" ("Rhetorical Sovereignty" 449–50). In expressing rhetorical sov-ereignty through the press, Indigenous writers asserted "an active sense of presence" through *survivance stories*, which functioned as "renunciations of dominance, tragedy, and victimry" (Vizenor, *Manifest Manners* vii). Survivance stories in this way reshaped settler colonial discourses that sought to control, define, and dehumanize Indigenous peoples (Lyons, "Rhetorical Sovereignty" 452).

Describing this dehumanization, Linda Tuhiwai Smith writes that

> [o]ne of the supposed characteristics of primitive peoples was that we could not use our minds or intellects. We could not invent things, we could not create institutions or history, we could not imagine, we could not produce anything of value, we did not know how to use land and other resources from the natural world, we did not practice the 'arts' of civilization.

"By lacking such virtues," she continues, "we disqualified ourselves, not just from civilization but from humanity itself. In other words we were not 'fully human'; some of us were not even considered partially human" (25). Thus, as "[t]he logic of coloniality" underlined and drove colonizing mea-sures ranging from land theft and removal to forced assimilation, violence, and genocide, many Indigenous writers used journalism as one vehicle for survivance and sovereignty (Mignolo, "Delinking" 477, 486). "Every issue has been approached by indigenous peoples with a view to *re*writing and *re*righting our position in history," Linda Tuhiwai Smith stresses (28).

Beginning with publications such as the *Cherokee Phoenix* (first published in 1828 and still printed today by the Cherokee Nation of Oklahoma), Native Americans have used journalism as one powerful form of written expression—a way, among other forms of writing, "to advance their interests, to promote an idea, to rethink (or reclaim) their values" (Peyer 108; Gubele 112; Lyons, Foreword xiv). The tribally owned *Cherokee Phoenix*, for instance, "was created, in part, to foster rhetorics opposing removal" (Gubele 100). It constituted a vital space for the expression of Cherokee ideas in both English and the Cherokee syllabary and was notably followed by the publication of the *Cherokee Advocate* in 1844 and "over fifty tribal, nontribal, or intertribal newspapers and periodicals [that] were either founded, edited, or maintained by American Indians and Alaskan Natives" in subsequent decades (Gubele 106–07; Peyer 108).[12] In addition to the *Cherokee Phoenix* and *Advocate*, tribally run newspapers also included the *Indian Champion* (Choctaw Nation) and the *Progress*, a weekly publication initiated in 1886 on the White Earth Reservation by Chippewa tribal members Augustus Hudon Beaulieu and Theodore Hudon Beaulieu (Peyer 108; Vizenor, "Aesthetics" 10). Despite being "seized capriciously by federal agents" after its first issue, the publication resumed in 1887 and "created a singular sense of native presence and survivance" (Vizenor, "Aesthetics" 10, 5).[13] Moreover, intertribal papers such as the *Indian Journal* and other nontribal papers such as the *Indian Chieftain* took shape during this period (Peyer 109).

"[D]evoted to the Interests of the Cherokees, Choctaws, Chickasaws, Seminoles, Creeks, and All Other Indians of the Indian Territory," the *Indian Chieftain* contained news, literature, and subscriber letters among other features (qtd. in Rogers 88). Discourses about sovereignty were highlighted in this weekly newspaper's coverage of allotment during the 1890s (Rogers 88). As Principal Chief Isparhecher stated in a message to the Creek Council, published in the *Chieftain* regarding the Creek-Dawes Commission treaty: "It will be observed by you that [the treaty] provides for the allotment of our lands and the extinguishment of our tribal title. I regard this feature of the treaty as being very dangerous, and therefore very objectionable. Allotment of lands to Indians has heretofore proven disastrous in every instance and is sure to result likewise with us when we try it." He continued later in the message:

> I am aware that the U. S. government is urging us to change our relations with her and has expended considerable money in surveying our country and in maintaining a commission for the past three years, but all of this has been done at the option of that government and not at our request. We have not asked for any of these things, but they have been asked for by grasping, unsatiable boomers, who are always on the trail of the Indian, until every foot of his land is opened up. (*IC* Oct. 14, 1897)

Chief Isparhecher then called for careful deliberation: "It therefore remains for you to decide whether or no you will make yourselves a party to this scheme of the boomers" (*IC* Oct. 14, 1897).

Expressions of rhetorical sovereignty also appeared in the white press during this period. In 1877, for instance, chiefs of the Ponca Tribe—White Eagle, Standing Buffalo, Standing Bear, Smoke Maker, Frank La Flesche, Little Chief, Big Elk, and Gahega—issued a statement, "published at their desire" in a Sioux City newspaper,[14] recounting their abuse and abandonment by a U.S. government agent "in a strange country" after refusing to relocate the Ponca Tribe to an uninhabitable reserve (La Flesche, Letter). The statement begins: "We the Ponca Chiefs and principal men of the tribe desire to make the following statement of facts concerning ourselves, in all good faith, hoping it may come to the ears of the President of the United States." Proceeding to document their staunch objection to forced relocation and their punishing thirty-day journey back to their homeland from the newly proposed territories, the Ponca chiefs conclude:

> There we were left in a strange country among a people of a strange language, without money, to find our way back. We have been thirty days in getting as far as the Omahas, <u>weary</u> & <u>footsore</u> <u>and sick at heart</u>. Why are we so treated, we wish to know, and to know if the man who took us down South was told to leave us there. It seems to us that the man deceived us.
>
>   White Eagle
>   Standing Buffalo
>   Standing Bear

> Smoke Maker
> Frank La Flesche
> Little Chief
> Big Elk
> Gahega.
>> Chiefs of the Ponca Indians
>> (La Flesche, Letter)

In 1879, following the subsequent forced relocation of the Ponca, Chief White Eagle again issued a statement for newspaper circulation, of which portions were published. His statement—intended to "be read by all the White people"—recounts the abandonment of the ten Ponca chiefs, the violently enacted relocation, and the devastating death toll resulting from an uninhabitable reserve. In concluding, Chief White Eagle calls on readers to "save the living" (White Eagle).[15]

Native American women also contributed in powerful ways to a range of turn-of-the-century periodicals. Cherokee journalist Ora V. Eddleman Reed contributed to *Twin Territories: The Indian Magazine*, for instance, and also served as editor beginning in 1898 (Littlefield and Parins 207). Indigenous women writers including Angel DeCora, Zitkala-Ša, and Susette La Flesche Tibbles, moreover, carved out a place for themselves in white newspapers and magazines—writing alongside male contemporaries such as Charles Alexander Eastman, who published articles in *Harper's Monthly Magazine, Nicholas*, and other periodicals (Powell, "Rhetorics of Survivance" 417). DeCora served as both writer and illustrator of two 1899 stories for *Harper's*; Zitkala-Ša penned an autobiographical series for *Atlantic Monthly* (Gere, "Art of Survivance"). A form of subversive pedagogy as described by Jessica Enoch, Zitkala-Ša's essays challenged white narratives that concealed the destructiveness of Carlisle School's assimilationist educational program by relaying its "devastating effects" on Native children (*Refiguring* 75). As chapter 3 demonstrates, Susette La Flesche Tibbles similarly "claimed her rhetorical sovereignty" by "us[ing] English to speak *to* her white audience" and "teac[h] them a new story" (Enoch, *Refiguring* 119). Rewriting commercial newspaper portrayals of the Ghost Dance movement and exposing and challenging "marginalizing, colonial narratives and policies," La Flesche promoted critical reading and offered instruction in relationally based journalistic ethics through her *Omaha Morning World-Herald* reporting (King et al. 7).

Despite the differing intersections of race, ethnicity, class, and material circumstances from which turn-of-the-century newspaperwomen wrote, the field of journalism offered them valuable opportunities for cultivating professional writerly identities, fostering rhetorical and literacy development, and promoting discursive public participation and change. Other female newspaper journalists who engaged in such practices during this period, aside from Black, Mossell, and La Flesche, include stunt reporter Nellie Bly and anti-lynching activist Ida B. Wells—both of whom are likely more familiar to rhetoric and composition scholars today.

First, stunt reporter Bly not only captivated the mass readership of the *New York World* (and beyond) but inspired readers' public discourse as well. The trumpeted last stages of Bly's seventy-two-day, round-the-globe journey, for instance, prompted well-wishers such as Will C. Ferrill to telegram the reporter. His message was included—along with other supportive expressions from citizens eagerly following her progress—in Bly's January 24, 1890, article, "Almost Home." "Good luck to Nellie Bly. May you have a safe and rapid journey along the Arkansas River," he begins. "Great interest in Denver over your race against time. Again good luck to you, Nellie Bly," Ferrill concludes (*NYW* Jan. 24, 1890). Such contributions indicate how Bly's activities stimulated not only reader interest but also audience response.

Aside from circling the globe, Bly also famously exposed institutional abuses at Blackwell's Island Asylum in 1887. Her writing spurred significant social changes—most notably the allotment of "$1,000,000 more than was ever before given" for the care of patients (Bly, *Ten Days*). This series (which prompted from readers "hundreds of letters in regard to it") and Bly's subsequent compilation of her exposé articles in *Ten Days in a Madhouse* documented the disturbing alacrity with which many women were sentenced to institutional life, relayed misuses and abuses of medical authority, and revealed the particularly appalling treatment of poor and non-English-speaking women by New York institutional systems (Bly, *Ten Days*).

A second journalist whose work has been widely analyzed, Ida B. Wells, embraced the educational affordances of the late nineteenth-century press through her "excellent career as an outspoken investigative reporter" (Royster 221). As Wells contends in *Southern Horrors: Lynch Law in All Its Phases* (1892), "the press contains unreliable and doctored reports of lynchings, and one of the most necessary things for the race to do is to get these facts before the public. The people must know before they can act, and there is no educator to compare with the press" (Wells-Barnett 42). Wells here articulates an educational philosophy premised on collecting and disseminating facts. This is evident throughout *Southern Horrors*—a pamphlet that arose from Wells's *New York Age* journalism following her exile from Memphis on account of her editorial challenging "the old thread-bare lie that Negro men rape white women" (Wells-Barnett 146). The pamphlet functioned powerfully as an "educator" by providing "a true, unvarnished account of the causes of lynch law in the South" through factual compilation and critical reading of white newspapers (14).

One example of this critical reading is Wells's discussion of the *Memphis Ledger*, which published an account of a young white woman's "disgrace[d]" childbirth. "The truth might reveal fearful depravity or it might reveal the evidence of a rank outrage," the *Ledger* pronounced, but "[s]he will not divulge the name of the man who has left such black evidence of her disgrace" (qtd. in Wells-Barnett 22). In response, Wells conducts a close reading of the *Ledger* that exposes the recklessness of its discourse and its promotion of unsubstantiated characterizations of African American men: "Note the [*Ledger*'s] wording. 'The truth might reveal fearful depravity or rank outrage.' If it had been a white child or . . . a pitiful story of Negro outrage, it would have been a case of woman's weakness or assault." But the woman decides "to withhold its father's name and thus prevent the killing of another Negro 'rapist.'" (23)

In addition to conducting such critical readings, Wells also—as Daniel Libertz, drawing on Aja Y. Martinez, has observed—compiles facts amplified by counterstory to "problematiz[e] majoritarian narratives and commonplace stories of race that typically go forth unchecked" (315). Wells in this way exposes both the fallacy and brutal consequences of characterizing African American men as "rapist[s]." She discusses the case of Edward Coy, for instance, who "died protesting his innocence" in Texarkana, Texas (Wells-Barnett 24). To corroborate his innocence, Wells cites evidence from the *Chicago Inter-Ocean* indicating that the alleged victim "was publicly reported and generally known to have been criminally intimate with Coy for more than a year previous" and was moreover "compelled by threats, if not by violence, to make the charge against the victim" (qtd. in Wells-Barnett 24). These examples—two of many included in *Southern Horrors*—debunk claims of African American male "barbarism" and "bestial perversion" recklessly promulgated by white Southern newspapers such as the Memphis *Daily Commercial* and *Evening Scimitar* (qtd. in Wells-Barnett 31–33).

The three women journalists in this study, while sharing important similarities with their contemporaries, nevertheless produced work that differs from that of Bly and Wells. As one comparative point, Bly's success at inspiring discursive public participation from readers bears some resemblance to the extracurricular teaching practices of the newspaperwomen studied here. Black and Mossell, for instance, inspired myriad reader letters that were often published—like the message from Ferrill in Bly's "Almost Home"—alongside their own words. La Flesche meanwhile called on her *Omaha Morning World-Herald* readers to pursue discursive public participation in support of Indigenous rights. The work of these three journalists is distinguished, however, by the centrality of active dialogue with readers or community members who intimately and integrally shaped their newspaper writing—marking a key difference from contemporaries such as Bly. In "Almost Home," for example, Bly does not respond to Ferrill (at least not in print), nor does his message appear to significantly influence the shape of her article. The newspaperwomen featured in this study, on the other hand, penned a strongly dialogic form of journalism closely interconnected with the communicative practices of readers or community members.

The work of these three journalists also differs from that of Ida B. Wells. As scholars such as Francille Rusan Wilson and Ellen Gruber Garvey have emphasized, Wells anchors her anti-lynching journalism in dialogue with the white press—critically reading white newspaper discourse, collecting facts, and exposing the complicity of commercial white newspapers in the subjugation of African Americans (F. Wilson 94; Garvey 150). In comparison, the pedagogical work of Black, Mossell, and La Flesche foregrounds—and is significantly informed by—the discursive practices of children, African American women, and Indigenous peoples. The newspaper pages of Black and Mossell form a tapestry of such commingled voices: Black's writing interacts with children's letters, while the voices of Mossell's readership populate the column and often drive its content. La Flesche meanwhile employs conversation and relationship building, especially with Lakota people, as a key methodology guiding her research and news reporting (S. Wilson 79).[16]

Overall, then, Black, Mossell, and La Flesche compose in close relation with diverse voices for the purposes of social action. This distinguishing commonality is not intended to deter important comparisons with their contemporaries (nor elide crucial differences among the three journalists). The work of Wells and La Flesche, for instance, is particularly aligned in aiming to curb vicious mischaracterizations of Black and Indigenous peoples in white newspaper discourse—a parallel that highlights ways in which both groups were dehumanized by the commercial white press during this period. Lynching coverage often portrayed "the black lynch victims . . . as savage," echoing commercial news misrepresentations of Indigenous peoples (Bederman 51). bell hooks has likewise recognized "the degrading representations of red and black people" that have permeated U.S. media (186).[17] I discuss this important point of comparison—and other parallels between Black, Mossell, and La Flesche and their contemporaries—more extensively in the following chapters.

Definitions and Scholarly Contexts

In situating these three journalists as extracurricular teachers and social advocates in conversation with members of provisionally yet systematically marginalized groups, I posit several central features of their journalism that require further definition and scholarly grounding. I argue that the newspaper writing of Black, Mossell, and La Flesche—a rich array of work underexamined by rhetoric and composition scholars—was (1) dialogic: privileging intimate and active conversation within a mass-market medium; (2) democratic: promoting inclusive and highly collaborative forms of extracurricular literacy learning and rhetorical education (oftentimes through the creation of specific counterpublics); and (3) socially responsible: working to mobilize readers or community members in the service of vital social causes. As such, their journalism joins a rich and diverse body of rhetorics by women who have powerfully "inhabited the public sphere of rhetoric, where they deliver their spoken and written messages, often fusing their own unique style with their delivery" to influence the shape and direction of public discourses and to drive social action (Glenn, *Rhetorical Feminism* 80).

First, the newspaper rhetoric of these writers was dialogic—constituted by various forms of discursive interplay among the journalists and their readers or communities. As I illustrate in the following chapters, this interplay was often intimate in nature. My use of the term *intimate* here refers to the innovative ways in which Black, Mossell, and La Flesche orchestrated close-knit extracurricular learning through personal dialogue and mutuality—often across geographic separation. Readers and community members did not merely respond *to* but rather integrally shaped the work of these journalists, who in turn advanced forms of rhetorical education for social change relevant to the lives of their readers and communities.

There has been little focus on the dialogic dimensions of newspaper journalism in this specific sense. Instead, many have argued that newspapers generated "imagined communities" (B. Anderson). The imagined nation community, for instance, emerged in large part due to the newspaper, according to Benedict Anderson. Jean Lutes—building on work by Michael Warner—made a similar argument about nineteenth-century women's journalism, namely, that female reporters contributed to the creation of a publicity-centered media cycle that "addressed itself to the mass public, an imagined community of readers that, as Warner has argued, includes everyone in general but no one in particular" (*Front-Page Girls* 6). In *"Doers of the Word": African-American Women Speakers and Writers in the North (1830–1880)*, Carla L. Peterson has meanwhile drawn on both Anderson and Alexis de Tocqueville to characterize the newspaper as a cultural form that "helps create 'imagined community'" (11).[18]

Turning to other types of extracurricular venues—including women's clubs, epistolary correspondence, and debate teams—we often find scholarly discussions of the intimate nature of literacy development and learning occurring therein. In *Intimate Practices: Literacy and Cultural Work in U.S. Women's Clubs, 1880–1920*, Anne Ruggles Gere charts the close relationships lying at the heart of clubwomen's extracurricular activities. At the border of the academy and the extracurriculum, the "intimate relationships" cultivated between Wiley College professor Melvin B. Tolson and members of his enormously successful debate team—described by Gold in *Rhetoric at the Margins*—offer another example of intimacy within an extracurricular site (43).

More recently, Pamela VanHaitsma's *Queering Romantic Engagement in the Postal Age: A Rhetorical Education* has illuminated pedagogies of "romantic engagement" reflected in "intimate texts" exchanged by same-sex letter writers (9, 21). In charting "relations between intimate and political life" that are not principally tied to citizenship, VanHaitsma "join[s] queer as well as feminist scholars in troubling normative, hierarchical distinctions—between public and private, political and personal, civic and romantic—that often frame histories of Western rhetoric and rhetorical education" (6). Following their lead, I also attend to important interrelations between the "public and private," the "political and personal," and the professional and relational in this study. Such interrelations particularly guide my understanding of the intimacy undergirding the mass-circulating newspaper writing of Black, Mossell, and La Flesche.

Few rhetoric and composition scholars have joined discussions of intimacy and the newspaper extracurriculum. One near exception is Brazeau, who has argued in *Circulating Literacy* that nineteenth-century women's magazines and farm journals—both rich venues for extracurricular learning—"sought to reflect the experiences of their audiences and to build an intimate relationship among readers" (8).[19] A compelling example from the *Maine Farmer* compared printed discussions among readers about farming practices to intimate conversation between neighbors: "a good farmer leans over the fence to rest and talk with his neighbor, and they tell each other the what and how of their crops . . . [W]hen it is in print it is only that talk over the fence dressed up a little for a larger audience" (qtd. in Brazeau 127). For "contributors and editors," Brazeau recaps, "reading and contributing to the journal are merely responsible extensions of the educational 'talk over the fence'" (127). This example highlights the intimate nature of dialogic learning that occurred within the *Maine Farmer*. I build on Brazeau by spotlighting related practices in mass-circulating newspapers at the turn of the century. My focus notably extends work by children's literature and journalism scholar Paige Gray, whose book *Cub Reporters: American Children's Literature and Journalism in the Golden Age* (2019) includes a chapter on the Chicago Defender Junior—the vibrant youth section of an influential early twentieth-century Black newspaper that enabled "young African Americans to learn about and engage with other children" (78). The Defender Junior not only solicited children's letters and creative writing but also "gave readers a means to reach out to one another" by facilitating pen pal correspondence (80–81). I expand this type of attention to intimate dialogic aspects of newspaper journalism by exploring close-knit discursive interactions fostered by turn-of-the-century women journalists.

Work by Black, Mossell, and La Flesche thereby reveals how newspapers such as the *San Francisco Examiner*, the *New York Freeman*, and the

Omaha Morning World-Herald offered spaces for creating intimate (versus merely imagined) communities. These three newspaperwomen reshaped intimate practices within an expansive public venue—calling attention to journalism as a vital setting for a personal, dialogic quality. "[E]nact[ing] goals that are dialogic and transactional rather than monologic and reactional," all three journalists thus fashioned unique possibilities for intimacy within the commercial press while adopting a central tactic of what Cheryl Glenn terms "rhetorical feminism"—a stance through which rhetorical women have across time "disidentifi[ed] with hegemonic rhetoric" through their discursive actions (*Rhetorical Feminism* 4).

Second, the newspaper rhetoric of Black, Mossell, and La Flesche was democratic. By listening for, valuing, and actively incorporating into their writing the voices of people of diverse racial, ethnic, and socioeconomic backgrounds, these journalists engage in "growth-fostering relational connections" (Flynn et. al 12).[20] That is, they function less as authority figures dictating to readers or community members and more as relational members of various "counterpublics" (Fraser 67). This revisionist understanding of the public sphere is premised on scholarly critiques of Habermas, who argues that in the eighteenth-century, a bourgeois public sphere emerged when "private people c[a]me together as a public" by way of "public use of their reason" (27). Nancy Fraser and Gerald Hauser, among others, have identified limitations with this idealized notion of the public sphere.

To begin with, Fraser complicates "the assumption that it is possible for interlocutors in a public sphere to bracket status differentials" in order to engage as "social equals." Instead, members of provisionally yet systematically marginalized groups form what Fraser calls "subaltern counterpublics" in which to "invent and circulate counterdiscourses" (62, 67). Gerald Hauser agrees that Habermas's model "conceals the ways in which particular, often marginalized public arenas form and function" but claims that such alternative publics arise as a result of rhetorical interactions involving "ongoing dialogue on public issues" (46, 6). Hauser hence establishes public spheres as rhetorical—emerging when "social actors" are "engaged by issues that bear on their lives" (108).

This study explores both newspaperwomen's rhetorics and the particular counterpublics that their writing created at the turn of the century. As Hauser suggests, Black, Mossell, and La Flesche facilitated the formation of counterpublics around particular issues: children's medical care, sexual threats facing African American girls, and U.S. government policies undermining Lakota sovereignty. Yet the ethe of these rhetors was strongly relational and "reflect[ed] the characteristics and qualities . . . valued by their audience, culture, or community" (Glenn, *Rhetorical Feminism* 84). As such, they connected meaningfully with the audiences or communities they cared deeply about—a means of fostering collaborative participation for social change. As one salient example, dialogue in "Our Woman's Department" about female purity was initiated by a reader whose inquiry sparked a sustained column conversation. This counterpublic (part of what Peterson terms "the ethnic public sphere") solidified around a specific issue that was closely linked to the shared community identity of those discussing it (10).[21] African American women readers were invested in, and united by, this issue because of its relevance to racial uplift and their shared sense of community—described by Mossell as "a helpful sisterhood" (*NYF* July 10, 1886). In such ways, the journalists in this study promoted democratic forms of extracurricular literacy development and rhetorical education.[22]

I root my understanding of the term *extracurricular literacy* in both the robust body of scholarship on rhetoric and composition's extracurriculum and Alicia Brazeau's more specific discussion of the extracurricular role of turn-of-the-century periodicals. I define *extracurricular literacy* as those communicative practices—including reading, writing, speaking, and listening—that are developed outside formal school settings and that provide participants a "tangible voice within a community, or communities, of their choosing" (Brazeau 165). In investigating women's journalism as a site of such extracurricular literacy, I follow the lead of scholars including Gere, Schultz, Enoch, Logan, and VanHaitsma, whose work on the extracurriculum (focused on women's clubs, children's amateur writing, Spanish-language newspapers, African American extracurricular literacy sites, and the queer extracurriculum) has attended specifically "to the instruction of culturally marginalized learners . . . because of how they have been denied full access to the formal curriculum of higher education" (VanHaitsma, "Romantic Correspondence" 183). Building on Schultz, I also understand the extracurriculum as frequently enabling opportunities "for self-expression and for resistance that w[ere] not ordinarily available" in classrooms (134).[23]

As journalist-pedagogues, Black, Mossell, and La Flesche forged outlets for a range of diverse or resistant communicative practices. In doing so, they enacted various forms of rhetorical education that take their very shape from the literacy practices of provisionally yet systematically marginalized groups. Black, for instance, highlights the sincerity and social consciousness of children writers from various socioeconomic classes to teach a form of rhetorical education for *Examiner* readers that privileges moral principles over prescriptive grammatical and mechanical standards. Mossell and the readership of "Our Woman's Department" meanwhile embody values of collaboration and community responsibility—values that Mossell promotes as essential characteristics of meaningful communication. La Flesche, finally, advances a form of rhetorical education for journalists strongly informed by Indigenous expressions of rhetorical sovereignty and survivance—one grounded in relationship building that imparts lessons in critical literacy to her broader *Omaha Morning World-Herald* audience.

In analyzing turn-of-the-century women's journalism as an extracurricular site, I thereby illuminate ways in which Black, Mossell, and La Flesche dynamically "influenc[ed] how people understand and practice effective communication" (Logan, *Liberating Language* 3). Building on Logan, then, I understand *rhetorical education* in this study as the teaching or advocacy of effective and intimately driven communication for social, political, or civic transformation. In considering these journalists as rhetorical educators, I ask: How did they develop ethe through which to advocate or cultivate specific skills and values useful for meaningful communication within their respective contexts? And by extending to children, African American women, and Indigenous peoples a central role in their pedagogical practices, how did they promote inclusive forms of literacy and rhetorical learning while mobilizing people for social change?

Third, by exploring these questions, I show how the rhetorical pedagogies of Black, Mossell, and La Flesche emerge from and foreground close-knit discursive relationships to drive social action efforts aimed at ameliorating various inequalities and injustices. As such, I term them *socially responsible*. Black, for example, conversed with and united young people through a social reform project that spurred both the provision of medical care for lower-income children and a special *Examiner* issue in which young people identified and questioned structural reasons for poverty. Mossell and La Flesche orchestrated collaborative and relational sites of rhetorical education to further racial uplift and to call for justice for Lakota people. These women journalists therefore heightened both public awareness of, and public discursive involvement in, crucial issues at the turn of the century. The chapters that follow discuss these processes in greater detail as I explore the extracurricular literacy and rhetorical education orchestrated by Black, Mossell, and La Flesche in their respective contexts.

Methods, Methodologies, and Further Contributions

I accessed the newspapers quoted in this study by using library, archival, and digital research methods—means of unearthing empirical evidence of female journalists' pedagogical activity during this period. I examined a set of underexplored primary sources that broaden our histories of writing instruction and rhetorical education in the United States. Enoch, drawing on Gere, has noted that while traditional histories of writing instruction mine "lecture notes, course descriptions, department meeting minutes, and so on," histories of extracurricular writing and rhetorical instruction turn to a "more varied collection of materials, such as conduct books, club papers, newspapers, and parlor rhetorics" ("Changing Research Methods" 50–51). I focused on mass-circulating newspapers as sites of extracurricular literacy instruction at the turn of the century because of their far-reaching influence on a diverse array of readers. It is therefore fortunate that so many nineteenth-century newspapers are available for study, whether in digital or microfilm form. To recover the work of Black, Mossell, and La Flesche, I relied primarily on microfilm and archival investigation, as the newspapers to which these writers contributed had not yet been sufficiently digitized until the concluding stages of this project.[24]

I consulted microfilm copies of the *San Francisco Examiner*, the *New York Freeman*, and the *Omaha Morning World-Herald*. I also examined Mossell's "Our Woman's Department" column for the *Indianapolis World*—an offshoot of her *Freeman* column. Additionally, I combed through a range of journalism bibliographies, histories, and biographies while acquiring through interlibrary loan and newspapers.com many supplemental articles from periodicals, including the Boston *Daily Evening Traveller*, Lincoln *Journal Star*, *Nebraska History Magazine*, *Nebraska State Journal*, Billings *Gazette*, Missoula *Missoulian*, Pittsburgh *Sun-Telegraph*, and Sacramento *Record-Union*.

I supplemented my digital and microfilm research with visits to archives. From the University of California Bancroft Library, I gathered primary documents by Black housed in several collections including the Fremont Older Papers and the James D. Phelan Papers. These documents included letters and other materials relevant to the "Little Jim Club" and Black's 1924 reflective piece "How Little Jim Helped the Children." The San Francisco Public Library shared newspaper clippings published after Black's death that highlighted her rhetorical skills and widespread influence. Additionally relevant were copies of the *Little Jim* annual published by student nurses of the Children's Hospital of San Francisco—now housed in the University of California San Francisco Library Archives and Special Collections. I also visited the Boston Public Library, where I viewed Mossell's "The Open Court" column published in the *Woman's Era* (edited by Josephine St. Pierre Ruffin and Florida Ruffin Ridley). Finally, the Nebraska State Historical Society and the Smithsonian's National Museum of the American Indian (which houses the Thomas Henry Tibbles papers) provided primary documents written by, and related to, La Flesche. These included her signature book and speeches from a lecture tour following the Standing Bear habeas corpus trial in 1879.

To analyze this body of primary texts, I applied methodologies derived from feminist rhetorical studies, public memory studies in rhetoric, and understandings of archival engagement as a "lived process" (Kirsch and Rohan). I first followed Cheryl Glenn's suggestion to "continue to intervene in rhetorical histories, especially when . . . interpolations invigorate our understandings of rhetoric's capacities and infinite instantiations across time and space" (*Rhetorical Feminism* 105). Indeed, twenty-five years after Glenn observed that "the neglect of women in the past has been so complete that the opportunities for exploration and experimentation are rich and plentiful," the process of "[r]ewriting rhetorical history" remains "an endless task" (*Rhetoric Retold* 178; *Rhetorical Feminism* 105). Participating in this process moreover carries implications for the present day. As Kirsch and Rohan write, "historical lives can shape the present as researchers work with and publish their data" (6). I chose to study the historical lives and journalistic work of Black, Mossell, and La Flesche because their rich body of writing powerfully reflects "rhetoric's capacities" to foster dynamic, inclusive, and personally oriented forms of rhetorical education and literacy learning relevant to the needs of our present day.

In analyzing the teaching practices of these journalists, I strive to carefully acknowledge how Black, Mossell, and La Flesche negotiated gender ideologies of various kinds from different intersectional positions in order to establish persuasive ethe and foreground a range of diverse voices through their journalism. Black, for instance, drew on a model of white middle-class motherhood to help license her rhetorical activities—adopting a conventional gendered identity premised on the role of the "wise mother" whose "female sympathy" propelled her public rhetorical practices (Johnson 113). Although reinforcing normative beliefs about femininity, this construct also opened up a rhetorical space in which children could engage in activist-oriented public writing.[25] La Flesche meanwhile fashioned a complex ethos as "Bright Eyes." This English translation of her Omaha name, Inshta Theamba, was publicly inscribed within both sentimental notions of the "Indian princess" and recognizable conventions of white middle-class femininity, even as it helped La Flesche refute the "rhetorical imperialism" driving commercial press misrepresentations of Indigenous peoples (Lyons, "Rhetorical Sovereignty" 452). Turning to Mossell's columns, one finds the phrase "Edited by Mrs. N. F. Mossell" at the top of each. Logan has observed of this choice that "rather than diluting her independence," this editorial strategy "helped to avoid the appearance of impropriety and to demonstrate that marital respectability could serve as a source of ethical appeal" (*Liberating Language* 117). Attending to nuances such as these reminds us that the pedagogical practices of Black, Mossell, and La Flesche operated within gendered contexts that they navigated in different ways from their various intersectional positions.

Consistent with Royster and Kirsch's advice to feminist rhetorical scholars to "notice what is there and what is missing" (146), I moreover acknowledge gaps in my understanding of reader responses to the newspaper writing of Black and Mossell. While published letters offer a crucial index for how these journalists fostered rhetorical education and literacy learning, they likely do not represent all the letters received by the journalists. This is particularly clear for Black, who at one point comments, "[n]ot a day passes now but what at least sixty children write" (*SFE* Dec. 9, 1894). (This count exceeds the number of letters published in the *Examiner.*) Presumably, Mossell also selected from among the letters she received. If we perceive the *Examiner* and *Freeman* to be archives of sorts for children's and African American women's letters, we are thus reminded that "any single archive of . . . letters is partial in its recording" (VanHaitsma "Archival Framework" 36). This fact raises questions about how unpublished letters would reinforce, complicate, or otherwise affect the arguments I make in chapters 1 and 2. At the same time, the likelihood that unpublished letters existed attests to the breadth of Black's and Mossell's influence on readers' extracurricular literacy endeavors.

While engaged in this study, I moreover tried to remain mindful about ways in which "my personal and professional experiences shape the questions I ask" and the writers I have chosen to research (McKee and Porter 65). As a rhetoric and composition teacher, I am fascinated by the compelling and inspiring teacherly work of Black, Mossell, and La Flesche. Black's ability to inspire in young people meaningful discursive public participation is a type of pedagogy I strive for. Mossell's work underscores the profound importance of inviting students to define questions important to them; of working collaboratively with students; and of extending to students opportunities to help shape syllabus construction. Finally, La Flesche's work highlights the need to promote (and provide diverse contexts for) writing practices that value listening, meaningful relationship building, and relational understanding—"[u]nlike the power-over of traditional argument" (Glenn, *Rhetorical Feminism* 75).

As a white female teacher and feminist rhetorical researcher in the twenty-first century, I endeavored to attend carefully to these writers' particular contexts and complexities by practicing "[a]n ethics of hope and care" involving "looking and looking again, reading and returning to texts, learning about the contexts of those who use rhetorical strategies under conditions that may be very different from our own" (Royster and Kirsch 145–46). "[L]ooking again" frequently led me back to microfilm and to print and digital archives—again and again—not merely to consult more surrounding context but also to explore additional texts published by these writers. I am also grateful for conversations I had with those who offered new perspectives on these writers' contexts—especially Nathan Nakoma, a speaker and activist of Chippewa-Cree heritage, who was adopted by an Oglala Lakota family from Pine Ridge and who is knowledgeable about the Wounded Knee Massacre. I ultimately tried to maintain a stance of continuous critical listening, learning, and reflection throughout this project, which—as Malea Powell has noted of her work on Sarah Winnemucca Hopkins and Charles Alexander Eastman—offers only some among many "*possible* hearings and tellings" of these journalistic texts by Black, Mossell, and La Flesche ("Rhetorics of Survivance" 399). Their scope and richness leave much opportunity for further research. Finally, I keep in view these important words recounted by Shawn Wilson, relayed to him by a friend: "If research doesn't change you as a person, then you aren't doing it right"

(83). This process of change unfolded over the course of the project and is unfolding still.

Overall, *Rhetorical Education in Turn-of-the-Century U.S. Women's Journalism* enlarges our understanding of women's wide-ranging contributions to rhetorical education and public discourses through extracurricular literacy sites in the late nineteenth century. Broadly, this project builds on seminal work by Cheryl Glenn, Andrea Lunsford, Jacqueline Jones Royster, Shirley Wilson Logan, Nan Johnson, Catherine Hobbs, Cristina Ramírez, Jessica Enoch, and many others who have illuminated "ways that women throughout history have made their voices heard or their silences felt" (Enoch, *Refiguring* 12). More specifically, this study enriches scholarship on women using literacy for rhetorical education in extracurricular sites. In selecting Black, Mossell, and La Flesche as subjects for this study, I have aimed to provide both a "nuanced look at [the] rhetorical acts" of women undertreated in our scholarship as well as persuasive support for turn-of-the-century U.S. women's journalism as a dynamic pedagogical site with unique possibilities for dialogic teaching and learning (Ramírez 18).

In pursuing this project, I respond to several calls. First, Enoch has observed that histories of writing instruction in the United States often concentrate on the Northeast; she thus maintains that "our field's historiographic understandings have the potential to be enriched" by research beyond this region ("Changing Research Methods" 56). In this study, I have tried to be geographically diverse in my examinations—exploring newspapers from both coasts as well as the Midwest in order to demonstrate that women journalists across the country were using mass-circulating papers as a venue for literacy development and rhetorical education.

Second, this study responds to Jacqueline Jones Royster and Gesa E. Kirsch's call to "look at people at whom we have not looked before . . . in places at which we have not looked seriously or methodically before . . . at practices and conditions at which we have not looked closely enough . . . and at genres that we have not considered carefully enough" (72). In expanding attention to journalism as a robust pedagogical site, I have also tried to select writers who are currently underexplored within rhetoric and composition. La Flesche, particularly, is largely absent from rhetorical scholarship (although several biographies have been penned and selections of her work have been reprinted in numerous anthologies of

Indigenous writers).[26] In focusing on La Flesche's journalism during the winter of 1890–1891, chapter 3 helps illuminate how Indigenous writers utilized mass-circulating newspapers for activist teaching and as a practice of survivance. This chapter thereby responds to Casey Ryan Kelly and Jason Edward Black's call for rhetoric and public address scholarship to more fully "addres[s] American Indian contributions to American public culture" (6).

For some time, Mossell was "noticeably absent from contemporary discourse" (Wray 435). Within rhetoric and composition, she was then included in *Liberating Language* (after first appearing in Logan's previous book *"We Are Coming": The Persuasive Discourse of Nineteenth-Century Black Women*); she also briefly appeared in Henrietta Rix Wood's *Praising Girls: The Rhetoric of Young Women, 1895–1930* (2016). Overall, however, there remain opportunities for more extensive scholarship on Mossell in rhetoric and composition, particularly as focused on the extracurriculum. My work in this area builds on important scholarship by Nazera Sadiq Wright, a scholar of African American literature and Africana studies whose book *Black Girlhood in the Nineteenth Century* (2016) analyzes nineteenth- and early twentieth-century writings on black girlhood to chart ways in which "black writers used black girls as tools to put forward their social and political agendas" (2). Wright argues in a chapter focused on "Our Woman's Department" that Mossell "promote[d] models of public citizenship that widened the boundaries of black female purposefulness in the postbellum period" (94). Notably, Wright acknowledges readers' central role within this "intimate, communal, gendered space," but there remains much more to say about the intricate pedagogical operations of this reader-driven column (100). I therefore supplement Wright's valuable exploration of Mossell's advice about a range of topics (including spouse selection, frugality and financial protection, and black girls' employment) with a focused, extensive analysis of the dialogic extracurricular literacy learning fostered by "Our Woman's Department."

Black has also been largely neglected by scholars until recently. Until 2015, there had been very little secondary scholarship aside from Lutes's *Front-Page Girls: Women Journalists in American Culture and Fiction, 1880–1930* (2006), which primarily treats Black's coverage of highly publicized crimes and murder trials. Katherine H. Adams and Michael L. Keene's *Winifred Black/Annie Laurie and the Making of Modern Nonfiction* (2015), however, offers a wide exploration of Black's career including the women's special edition newspaper published in conjunction with the "Little Jim" campaign. I build on this book by focusing on Black's involvement with children writers during this campaign—a valuable addition given the limited amount of rhetorical analysis that exists of children's writing to periodicals (especially mass-circulating newspapers) during this period. My treatment of children's contributions to the *San Francisco Examiner* therefore builds on Schultz's important work on children's letters and school newspapers to further expand "our stories about the nineteenth century's young composers" (8).

Overall, *Rhetorical Education in Turn-of-the-Century U.S. Women's Journalism* illuminates ways that women journalists shaped and participated in robust communities of learning. Turn-of-the-century newspapers indeed constitute a crucial piece of both women's rhetorical histories and extracurricular histories of writing instruction in the United States. The newspaper writings of Black, Mossell, and La Flesche expand our "sense of the roles women have played in rhetorical enterprises of the past" by revealing how diverse audiences and communities found opportunities to both learn from and teach alongside these three women journalists (Johnson 9). The following chapters reveal in greater detail how women's journalism of this period functioned as an influential extracurricular literacy site and dynamic venue for rhetorical education.

CHAPTER ONE

Winifred Black Bonfils's "Little Jim" Campaign: Children's Extracurricular Writing for Social Action

Whenever anyone asks me, as people sometimes do ask me, what is the great reward of the hard work and nervous strain of the newspaper life, I remember Little Jim and his friends—and I smile.
—Winifred Black, *San Francisco Examiner* (August 9, 1924)

"Did you ever hear the story of Little Jim," Annie Laurie asks, "and how he and the children of San Francisco went to work and built up a great hospital for poor children? I'll tell you about it" (*SFE* Aug. 9, 1924). In this retrospective *San Francisco Examiner* article, reporter Annie Laurie— pen name of Martha Winifred Sweet Black Bonfils[1]—recounts the social action efforts inspired by her 1894 story about a lower-class boy with a disability whom the San Francisco Children's Hospital turned away due to insufficient space. "There was no room for him," Black wrote, "not even an inch of room":

> No place for a cot where he could lie and as for a wheel chair—it was useless even to think of it, so Little Jim and his mother who had left their dark little room that morning with such light and hopeful hearts crept back again into the dark and cold and hunger—alone. And there was nothing to do about it, not a thing—and Little Jim's back hurt him so when he got home that he cried all night, though he did his best to cry quietly so that his mother wouldn't hear it. And there was no hope for Poor Little Jim—not a hope in the world. (*SFE* Aug. 9, 1924)

When Black related these events to her managing editor in 1894, he told her, "Write the story of Little Jim, and see what will happen" (*SFE* Aug. 9, 1924).

Winifred Black wrote the story. The original article appeared in the Sunday morning *Examiner* on November 25, 1894. On Monday, Black arrived at work to find "a pile of letters"—all of them "had something to say about Little Jim" (*SFE* Aug. 9, 1924). The *Examiner* responded by printing such letters in the newspaper that week alongside praise for both the children's

35

writing and their social conscience. The combined power of the children's and Black's words inspired still others to write the *Examiner*—now loaded with letters and coverage of "Little Jim." "[W]e went to work," Black remembered, "the children of San Francisco and a plain, everyday newspaper" (*SFE* Aug. 9, 1924). Significantly, their collaborative efforts propelled a vigorous, statewide campaign to fund a hospital ward for children such as "Little Jim and others like him, homeless and friendless" (*SFE* Nov. 29, 1894; *SFE* Dec. 6, 1894). Scores of previously politically inactive California children wrote letters, formed fund-raising clubs, and held public performances to benefit "Little Jim." Ultimately, this movement succeeded not merely in establishing the new hospital ward but also an eye and ear center facilitated by the efforts of California schoolchildren who composed a special Christmas edition of the *Examiner*.

This campaign is significant because it illustrates both the rhetorical efficacy of Black's newspaper writing and a particular "public" that her writing created—one in which children learned and practiced the skills of discursive public participation and activism grounded in their engagement in "mass" yet personal relationships. In this chapter, I demonstrate how Winifred Black constructs a persuasive ethos capable of inspiring the writing and social action efforts of children from various socioeconomic classes. Specifically, Black revises the rhetorical tradition of the "stunt girl reporter" in order to craft a teacherly ethos anchored in a "symbolic motherhood"—a term I borrow from Mari Tonn to understand how Black forged an effective rhetorical strategy grounded in close cultural links between teaching and mothering (Tonn 2).[2] Combined with aspects of what Karlyn Kohrs Campbell terms a "feminine style," this teacherly ethos allows Black to promote not merely social change but also a particular kind of rhetorical education that (1) privileges moral principles over prescriptive grammatical and mechanical standards and (2) blurs gender and class lines. Black's persuasive ethos moreover paved the way for children's public writing and activism to continue far beyond the boundaries of the initial campaign through a children's "Christmas Examiner"—a collective literacy project that provided children an opportunity to write, edit, manage, and publish their own newspaper. Overall, then, this chapter illustrates how a "subaltern counterpublic" of children found channels into public participation with the intimate support of Black, whose teacherly ethos initiated their extracurricular writing and social activism (Fraser 67). It also contributes to our broader understanding of children's writing "produced at the edges of school or outside of school." As Lucille Schultz has argued—and as the "Little Jim" campaign affirms—it is within the extracurriculum that young people "were most likely to write outside the lines" (109).

Given that Black has received too little scholarly attention, I begin with a brief biography that situates her entry into journalism within the rhetorical tradition of the "stunt girl." I then discuss alternative characterizations of Black as a "sob sister" and argue that both of these commonly referenced categories insufficiently encapsulate the complexities of her persuasive ethos as reflected in the "Little Jim" campaign and a preceding charitable project, "The Orphans' Santa Claus." The second section, to this end, analyzes how Black constructed a teacherly ethos anchored in a "symbolic motherhood," while the third section demonstrates how she mobilized this ethos to inspire children's discursive public participation and social action efforts. I conclude by exploring the 1895 "Public School Children's Christmas Examiner"—a special edition that not only sustained children's civic action and public writing through experiential training in journalism but that also supplied a venue for subversive writing aimed at challenging unjust social structures. This case study of Black illuminates the important role of the newspaperwoman in initiating children's public writing and the need for more complex notions of ethe in understanding how female journalists stimulated such writing by using mass-circulating daily newspapers as extracurricular spaces for writing instruction during the late nineteenth century.

Stunt Girls, Sob Sisters, and Winifred Black's Teacherly Ethos

Winifred Black was born on October 14, 1863, to Gen. Benjamin Jeffrey Sweet and Lovisa Denslow Sweet in the remote northeastern woods of Wisconsin (Zuckerman 13). Her family then relocated "to a little farm of 160 acres just twenty miles west of the raw, boisterous, ambitious, surging city of Chicago." In her "good-sized, comfortable" home surrounded by "space and leisure and moonlight," Winifred Sweet enjoyed a serene childhood and received visits from "spectacular friends" of her father including James Garfield and Ulysses S. Grant (*GH* Jan. 1936 151). Her father's death in 1874 unsettled the eleven-year-old Black, who esteemed him as "life itself. He was day and night and sunrise and sunset" (*GH* Jan. 1936 152). When

Black afterward lost her mother in 1878, she remained in the care of her older sister, Ada Celeste, until an emerging career in acting, following her completion of school, initiated her travel "throughout Canada, New York State, and the South" (Zuckerman 13). At the age of twenty-three, and while still acting, Black lodged with children's magazine editor and author Mary Mapes Dodge and shared the company of other writers such as William Dean Howells, Mary Wilkins Freeman, and Samuel Clemens (13).

Acting ultimately discouraged Black, yet it paved the way to her career in journalism thanks to a series of letters she wrote to her sister about her profession that were published in the *Chicago Tribune* (13). Black describes the origin and outcome of the initial letter in a 1936 *Good Housekeeping* special article "Rambles through My Memories." "I was on the road playing Henriette in 'The Two Orphans,' and I found some of the experiences in a Number Two Road Company rather amusing," she began.

> Sister Ada took my homesick letter with her when she went to a dinner given by the editor of the Chicago *Tribune*. After dinner, by way of diversion, she took out my ridiculous letter and read it aloud to the company. Something in her way of reading or in her voice made the unimportant letter quite dramatic, and the editor asked if he might publish it in the Sunday paper and if I would please write one or two more letters about the experiences of a young girl on the road. The editor said something about these letters being a lesson to stage-struck girls. Anyhow I wrote some more letters, and they were all published—I don't see why, but they were. And from that minute on I thought it would be very nice to be a newspaper-man. There weren't any newspaper-women to speak of in those far-off and deluded days." (*GH* Feb. 1936 37).

In 1889, Black found her chance to enter the field of journalism after settling in San Francisco following a visit to her brother-in-law. There, she convinced *Examiner* managing editor Sam Chamberlain to hire her (Zuckerman 14). Chamberlain soon dispensed "a practical lesson in popular journalism" that shaped her career development: "There's a gripman on the Powell Street line—he takes his car out at three o'clock in the morning, and while he's waiting for the signals he opens the morning paper. It's still wet from the press and by the light of his grip he reads it. Think of him when you're writing a story. Don't write a single word he can't understand and wouldn't read" (qtd. in Marzolf 34). Black accepted the advice and soon mastered a vivid and straightforward style, which she deployed in one of her first major pieces. Titled "A City's Disgrace," Black's article exposed through her undercover disguise and stunt performance the insufficient and at times abusive treatment of indigent patients at San Francisco Receiving Hospital.

"A City's Disgrace" situated Black within the rhetorical tradition of the "stunt girl" reporter—a persona designed for white female journalists that was popularized by the rise of "new journalism" and fierce competition between newspaper magnates such as Joseph Pulitzer and William Randolph Hearst.[3] Commonly associated with *New York World* reporter Nellie Bly, stunt reporting also attracted other young white female journalists such as Nell Nelson and Ada Patterson—both of whom similarly adopted disguises to expose social injustices or broadcast sensational stories. This form of reporting highlighted the exposure of women's bodies. Jean Lutes has argued in *Front-Page Girls: Women Journalists in American Culture and Fiction, 1880–1930* that stunt girls "used their bodies not just as a means of acquiring the news but as the very source of it" (14). To this end, Lutes notes that "A City's Disgrace" foregrounds the central role of Black's body as it was subjected to institutional mistreatment (33). This is especially evident when Black describes being "dragged . . . across the sidewalk" after pretending to faint, enduring a "tumbling, rumbling, jerking, jolting old rattle-trap" of a prison van, and suffering abusive medical treatment:

> The doctor took two strides and was beside me. He gripped my neck with both hands, digging his thumbs into the hollows below my ears. I screamed with pain and rage and managed to push him aside . . . He grabbed me by the shoulder with so fierce a grip that my shoulder is lame yet. It took the skin right off. (*SFE* Jan. 19, 1890)

While the article inspired change and the praise of a respected physician, Dr. McQuesten (who publicly thanked the "plucky Annie Laurie for making known what lies beneath the surface of this one of our public institutions"), this change was predicated upon publicity centered on Black's maltreated body (*SFE* Jan. 22, 1890).

Aside from a stunt girl, Black has also been frequently identified as a "sob sister." Originally pertaining to white middle-class women's detailed coverage of highly publicized crimes and murder trials, this early twentieth-century newspaper personality emerged when journalist Irvin Cobb applied the derogatory term to the writings of Winifred Black,

Dorothy Dix, Ada Patterson, and Nixola Greeley Smith in the wake of the Thaw murder trial.[4] "Denoting a female journalist who specialized in sentimental or human interest stories, or, more generally, a woman writer 'who could wring tears,' the term was in common usage by 1910, thanks in part to the voluminous newspaper coverage of the Thaw case between 1906 and 1908," explains Lutes (*Front-Page Girls* 65). As the twentieth-century continued, journalism histories often categorized Black as a sob sister: "it was not the public service aspects of her stories which brought Winifred Black minor notice in journalism histories," Madelon Golden Schilpp and Sharon M. Murphy maintain. "As Annie Laurie, she is most often acknowledged as a 'sob sister'" (151). More recently, Lutes's *Front-Page Girls* has usefully "revisit[ed] sob-sisterhood" and Black's Thaw trial reporting in ways that complicate the categorization—showing that "[a]lthough the sob sisters were identified with the overdrawn emotional content of the most aggressive, self-promoting papers, their displays of feeling drew on conventions operating in both the highbrow and lowbrow press" (65–68).

Yet neither the stunt girl nor the sob sister persona (not even more complex conceptualizations of the latter) adequately captures the nuances of Black's role in initiating public discourse and social activism in children. Black constructed a more pedagogically oriented ethos through "The Orphans' Santa Claus" and "Little Jim" campaigns than either of these models accounts for—even as this ethos drew on both "feminine style" as well as two common roles employed by late nineteenth-century white women to authorize their public voices: the "wise mother" and the female teacher. First, Black's writing reflects components of what Campbell terms "feminine style." That is, as a female journalist with "little conferred authority," she adopts discursive practices that helped grant her influence during a period when the large majority of newspaper reporters were male (Campbell, "Consciousness-Raising" 60). These practices include employing personal experience and "address[ing] audiences as peers or supplicants" (Campbell, "Feminist Rhetoric" 263). Black uses the former strategy to build credibility through "the single area of expertise acknowledged for women"; the latter is skillfully used to build close ties with readers and invest them in social action—inspiring their active civic participation ("Consciousness-Raising" 51). Importantly, she supplements this feminine style with two common roles functioning to further justify her public influence.

Nan Johnson has identified the "wise" or "eloquent mother" as a common prescribed role for nineteenth-century women rhetors (113, 119). This role helped authorize the public work of white women speakers such as Mary A. Livermore and the "militant" Mary Harris "Mother" Jones, who reinvented this maternal persona to emphasize both confrontational and nurturing aspects within the context of industrial labor movement agitation (Johnson 116–17; Tonn 2–3). A model of motherhood also helped license Black's public work, as eulogies after her death in 1936 suggested. "You mothered our fire and police departments, our South of Market Boys, our own Ninety-first Division and other veterans groups," declared San Francisco Mayor Angelo Rossi (*SFE* May 28, 1936). An anonymous appraisal in *Editor & Publisher* on May 30, 1936, similarly proclaimed, "[h]er whole career in journalism was a triumph of the mother spirit through the processes of printer's ink." These testimonials indicate that Black's career—as perceived by her contemporaries—was defined not by her public body but rather her symbolic motherhood.[5] This shift is perceptible during two major campaigns of the 1890s, when Black retained her commitment to social action but jettisoned the stunt publicity of "A City's Disgrace" to promote change in a different way. Specifically, Black constructed a teacherly ethos bolstered by associations between mothering and teaching—the second major role that authorized Black's public work.

Nineteenth-century ideals "representing the teacher as a public benefactor" helped many women "cultivate a civic identity and a rhetorically powerful voice" during this period (Rothermel 37). Symbolic motherhood played an important role in this process, as "understandings of the female teacher as a nurturer . . . ran alongside ideas of the teacher as an intellectual and a public leader," according to Beth Ann Rothermel (40). Jessica Enoch has similarly identified "motherliness" as a quality "continually equate[d] . . . with the teacher" in nineteenth-century educational discourse (*Refiguring* 2). As early as 1829, Catharine Beecher affirmed, "[i]t is to mothers, and to teachers, that the world is to look for the character which is to be enstamped on each succeeding generation" (qtd. in Enoch, *Refiguring* 1). When Black joined the *Examiner* staff sixty years later, this ideology had changed very little—there were increased opportunities for the turn-of-the-century female teacher, but "her job description did not shift much from that described by Beecher" (Enoch, *Refiguring* 2). This close correlation among mothering, teaching, and civic leadership enabled Black to craft a teacherly ethos uniquely positioned to stimulate public discourse in children. Yet in many ways, Black did not sustain "those preexisting norms, language practices, and behaviors already firmly entrenched in dominant

American society" (as nineteenth-century classroom teachers were often tasked to do) (Enoch, *Refiguring* 3). Rather, Black promoted a more inclusive range of language practices while also facilitating young people's subversive writing in the "Public School Children's Christmas Examiner."

Children's public sphere discourse has lately attracted the attention of scholars—yet the role of mass-circulating newspapers in stimulating nineteenth- and turn-of-the-century children's writing is ripe for increased exploration. Relevant to the subject are Paige Gray's "Join the Club: African American Children's Literature, Social Change, and the Chicago Defender Junior" (a chapter in *Cub Reporters: American Children's Literature and Journalism in the Golden Age*) and Sara Lindey's "Boys Write Back: Self-Education and Periodical Authorship in Late-Nineteenth-Century Story Papers." Gray's book chapter (attending to a time just after the turn of the century) shows how the *Chicago Defender*, an influential early twentieth-century African American newspaper, "established a youth section built entirely on children's contributions." Its Defender Junior "not only gave voice to the black youth of Chicago" but "also helped create a sense of identity for African American children across the country" (70–72). Lindey's "Boys Write Back" addresses children's self-education through story papers. "[C]ontaining fiction and miscellany," story papers such as *Boys of New York* and *Happy Days* "created space for boys to interact with editors and each other, allowing youth to help direct and produce the print entertainment they consumed" (72–73).[6]

Much other scholarship on children's writing initiated by periodicals focuses on their written interactions with magazines—especially children's entertainment magazines such as *St. Nicholas*. Angela Sorby and Anna M. Redcay both address this popular publication, launched in the late nineteenth-century. While Sorby considers the playfully unpredictable dimensions of children's published writing and sketches (64–72), Redcay argues that young magazine contributors were paradoxically both "'natural' creatures engaged in the ostensibly liberating 'pleasure-ground' of the periodical, and self-conscious, schooled representatives of that existence" (59). Turning to children's missionary periodicals, Karen Li Miller has further shown how children's magazines and papers "created a public space and worldwide audience for Chinese girls' writings" around the turn of the century (20).

These studies offer important explorations of how periodicals have variously stimulated children's writing. At the same time, little attention has been paid to the role of newspaperwomen in ushering children into public sphere discourse and social reform. This chapter therefore explores the medium of the large commercial daily newspaper through a focus on how Black used this type of periodical to stimulate children's reform-oriented writing. By examining "The Orphans' Santa Claus" and "Little Jim" campaigns and the related "Public School Children's Christmas Examiner," I illustrate how Black developed and mobilized a teacherly ethos anchored in a "symbolic motherhood" to initiate and guide a wide readership of children into using writing for social action (Tonn 2).

"The Orphans' Santa Claus":
Developing a Symbolic Motherhood

On Sunday morning, November 23, 1890, the *San Francisco Examiner* printed a "Plea for Christmas Gifts for the Poor Children of This City." Titling the campaign "The Orphans' Santa Claus," the *Examiner* urged readers to provide presents to children who had no one to "give them a happy remembrance hereafter of their childhood's Christmas." Winifred Black served as key spokeswoman for this campaign and reported from public orphanages and shelters where she interacted closely with children.

In one article, "Lads Who Know No Mothers," Black depicts the Youths' Directory—a shelter for boys "from the Police Station and from the streets" (*SFE* Dec. 20, 1890). There, she sits in a chair surrounded by children. Her focus rests on one—a "dear little fellow" who "knotted his hands nervously" while Black waits to hear his Christmas wish. With a "smile dimpling in his cheeks," the child places "his arms around [her] neck" to whisper it, prompting Black to confess that he "looked so shy and pretty that it was all I could do to keep from snatching him up and kissing him."

This scene represents a distinct shift in how Black's body functions in her news reporting. Whereas "A City's Disgrace" focused readers' attention on Black's body as it was carted away and mistreated, "Lads Who Know No Mothers" incorporates the female body in its capacity to love and nurture children. Black longs to "snatc[h] . . . up and kis[s]" the boy, whose bodily attributes are more meticulously characterized than her own. Emphasis on the boy's dimples, knotted hands, and arms entwined around Black's neck serves two functions. First, the details generate sympathy from readers— drawing them into the charitable campaign. Second, they mark a transition from stunt girl to symbolic motherhood in Black's career. This transition is accompanied by a stark juxtaposition in tone. Once Black has elicited reader sympathy for the child, she reminds us: "He has a mother who left him to starve in a cold room while she drank herself insensible, and a father who says boys are in the way." Black's bluntness underscores the child's lack and opens a space in which to assert her symbolic motherhood. Indeed, by longing to "snatc[h] . . . up and kis[s]" the boy, Black assumes the role of surrogate mother. This strategy is similarly deployed in "An Hour with the Orphans," where Black describes "three rosy, dark-eyed sisters" residing at the Maria Kip Home. "Their father is a private solider," Black explains. "Their mother is dead, and they have been at the Home a long time. Their father is in the city, but he never comes to see them, and does not seem to care what becomes of them. Yet they are bright, beautiful girls that would fill a mother's heart with pride" (SFE Nov. 26, 1890). Positioning herself antithetically to the girls' absent father, Black recognizes their worth to a mother and again casts herself in a maternal role.

The accentuated pathos of these "Orphans' Santa Claus" articles might lead some to characterize Black's writing as an example of sob sister journalism. Yet even if this term were anachronistically applied to these 1890 pieces, it still does not encompass the innovative teacherly aspects of Black's ethos during "The Orphans' Santa Claus" campaign. Indeed, through her symbolic motherhood, Black foregrounds more than the children's need for physical and emotional nurturing. She also foregrounds the corresponding development of their minds.

On November 27, 1890, for instance, Black recalls reading Thanksgiving cards written by orphaned children—all expressing gratitude of various kinds. She notes that

> [t]he little cards were carefully written, the letters were very plain and good, but most of them gave rather conventional answers. Three of them, however, were very interesting. One little fellow said he was thankful for the sunshine and for his eyes. This is little Bennie . . . A dear little blue-eyed fellow wrote on his thankful card that he was grateful for the birds and for his brother. There was another card next to his that was written almost exactly like it and that said the same thing.
>
> "Where is your brother?" I asked the first one.
>
> He looked astonished. "Here," he said throwing his arm around his neighbor's neck. Sure enough! Twins, and as like as two peas.

For readers, these cards function not only as a writing lesson but also as a character lesson and impetus to contribute to the charitable campaign. First, Black's analysis of the cards promotes "interesting" writing and unique detail—evident in her contrast between "conventional" answers and responses such as Bennie's, which gives thanks "for the sunshine and for his eyes." Her praise of Bennie's originality and gentle charm notably anticipates the *Examiner*'s own commendation of children's writing ("a great number of the kindest letters ever penned have been received from those who have sent in something for the orphans' Christmas") and later printing of "kindly and interesting" contributions such as the following children's poem (*SFE* Dec. 3, 1890):

> The Examiner's a daisy
> To get the orphans toys
> Here's a box of tops and marbles
> From a couple of Oakland boys (*SFE* Dec. 19, 1890)

This poem—"pasted on the lid of a chest full of tops and marbles"—demonstrates an originality similar to that of the three "interesting" orphans' cards, while also indicating a collaborative writing effort ("a couple of Oakland boys") in response to a public need. Such writing compelled the *Examiner* to declare "how strong is the spirit of Christmas charity that has been roused by the appeal in behalf of the fatherless, motherless, sick and destitute children of San Francisco" (*SFE* Dec. 19, 1890).

This "spirit of Christmas charity" points to the second function of the orphaned children's thankful cards: teaching a character lesson to *Examiner* readers. This lesson is accentuated by the twin's loving gesture ("throwing his arm around his neighbor's neck"), which invites readers to practice generosity. Such a strategy effectively draws readers into the charitable campaign—particularly when Black spotlights the twins' Christmas wish in conjunction with their writing and similarly remarks that Bennie desires only "a box of tools." This strategy is again deployed when Black prints letters from "two boys at the Protestant Asylum" requesting "a book about the civil war" and "a little Newfoundland dog." She thereafter asks: "Is there any one who would like to disappoint that 'hoping'?" (*SFE* Nov. 28, 1890). Here, Black invites readers to demonstrate that they have learned from their character lesson. Such lessons in both character and writing initiate Black's teacherly ethos and bolster the success of "The Orphans' Santa Claus."

The "Little Jim" Campaign:
Children's Writing for Social Action

By 1892, "the name Annie Laurie"—Black's pen name derived from a childhood song sung to her by her mother—"had become a regular feature among the pages of the *Examiner*" (Zuckerman 14, 16). Her influence and rhetorical savvy were also widely recognized at this time. A December 1892 *Examiner* article asserted, "there is not a better all-around journalist in San Francisco than this lady" (*SFE* Dec. 18, 1892). Managing *Examiner* editor Arthur McEwen then remarked in 1894 that Black "possesses that journalistic deftness which enables her to estimate instantly the relative value of her subject and to choose the most appropriate method of treating it" (qtd. in *SFE* May 27, 1936). His praise anticipated a similar posthumous appraisal that lauded Black's "wonderful gift for understanding a public need or a civic dereliction, and phrasing its story in such a way as to appeal . . . to the conscience of the people" (*SFE* Aug. 8, 1948). The "Little Jim" campaign was one such cause—a robust extracurricular literacy project that stimulated children's writing for social action and the construction of a new hospital ward for children in need of care.

On November 25, 1894, Black initiated this campaign by describing her visit to the Children's Hospital in the vividly illustrated article "Annie Laurie's Appeal." Its centerpiece is the story of "Little Jim"—a "little bit of a fellow" seeking admittance to the hospital. Black tells his story as recounted to her by resident physician Dr. Overacker:

> Dr. Overacker has just told me a little story. Dr. Overacker is the resident physician at the Children's Hospital out near the Park. She is so used to the sight of misery and suffering that it takes a good deal to make her unhappy, but she was looking pretty serious as she told me this story. "It is a common thing enough," she said, "for me to turn children away from here, but somehow I never can get used to it. Now, this morning, for instance.
>
> "A woman came to see me this morning. She was a pale little thing with a pinched face, and she looked as if she hadn't laughed in years . . . She had a little boy with her; he looked to me about ten years old. He was dreadfully ill, and his face was as white as a sheet, but his eyes were bright and he looked excited and almost happy. 'This is my little boy,' she said."

After a medical examination suggested "the case was hopeless," Jim's mother "began to beg that I would take him in and keep him for a while, only for a little while, she said":

> "'Maybe,' she said, 'if he had good things to eat and a nice big room with the sun coming in it where he could sleep he would begin to get better right away. I know he would, doctor: he is naturally strong; we all are in my family. If he only had a little chance, just half a chance, he would get well, and anyway, you could keep him from suffering so. If he can't get well and play around like other boys, can't you keep him here where it is warm and pleasant and where he can have some sort of a good time?'
>
> "I explained to her that the hospital was crowded. She asked me if I couldn't move some of the children up a little, whatever she meant by that, and make room for little Jim. 'There must be a place somewhere in this great big building,' she said, 'for my poor little boy. He is real good; he won't make you a bit of trouble, and I can come out to see him Sundays, and he won't be a bit homesick.' I explained to her that we were poor, and that we only had just money enough to take care of the children who could be helped . . . I wish I could forget the look on that boy's face when his mother said, 'Come Jim, we will go back again. Nobody wants us.'"

The "sick and lonely" child then returned to his "dark" cellar—compelling Black to issue this plea:

> The orphan asylums cannot take him, the Home for Incurables cannot take him because he is a child. He hasn't a penny in the world, or a friend, except his mother, and his mother is a poor woman who does not earn over $4 a week. The Boys and Girls' Aid Society cannot take him and there is no room for him at the Almshouse, or even at the City and County Hospital. What is going to become of little Jim? (*SFE* Nov. 25, 1894)

Overall, this article's vivid descriptions, its credibility established by personal experience, and its rhetorical question punctuating the concluding paragraph demonstrate that "Annie Laurie's Appeal" is grounded in two important components of feminine style: (1) addressing readers "as peers or supplicants" and (2) "structur[ing] . . . discourse inductively to draw on personal experience" (Campbell, "Feminist Rhetoric" 263). First,

"NOBODY WANTS US."

1.1. "Nobody Wants Us." *San Francisco Examiner,* 25 Nov. 1894.

Black addresses readers as peers or supplicants by posing the urgent question "What is going to become of little Jim?"—a question that ultimately compels children to respond to her in writing. Having accentuated the problem through a catalog of impossibilities ("The orphan asylums cannot take him, the Home for Incurables cannot take him . . . "), Black turns to readers for a possible solution. Second, she foregrounds personal experience in the article—a means of building "expertise" and expanding her "sphere of influence" (Campbell, "Consciousness-Raising" 51, 60). To this end, Black vividly locates herself within the Children's Hospital and describes the setting with sensory detail. She writes that

[w]e were sitting in the reception-room of the big hospital. A white-capped nurse opened the door a moment to speak to the doctor. I heard a shrill cry which died away in a smothered groan.

"It is nothing," said the doctor, smiling a little at my nervous start. "One of the little boys is getting a bad burn dressed." (*SFE* Nov. 25, 1984)

Descriptions of personal experiences like this one, vivid in its visual and auditory details, suggest Black's efforts to establish "sympathetic connection" with her readers (Engbers 308). By asking readers "to *look* at various scenes and *feel* appropriately," Black follows in the tradition of nineteenth-century orators such as Elizabeth Cady Stanton, who "wish[ed] to express truly felt emotions that would resonate with auditors' feelings" (309–10). *Examiner* readers are similarly prompted to engage in "sympathetic connection." Notably, Black achieves this outcome through a layering effect. By obtaining Dr. Overacker's testimony through "conversational interaction" and amplifying its impact with descriptions of her own interactions with young patients, Black builds credibility with readers, conveys a sense of immediacy, and evokes sympathetic feelings (Campbell, "Consciousness-Raising" 58, 60). Readers see the vivid image of "Little Jim"—his face "white as a sheet"—and hear the "shrill cry" of the injured boy, who later asks Black, "Is oo dot burned?" (*SFE* Nov. 25, 1894). These sensory descriptions and pieces of personal narrative help spark a commitment to social action among the newspaper's readership.

At the same time, representations of "Little Jim" clearly involve a sentimental rhetoric of disability. The *Examiner* image "Nobody Wants Us," for instance, "produces the sentimental victim or helpless sufferer needing protection or succor" by depicting "Little Jim" sitting beside his crutches with a forlorn face and posture (Garland-Thomson 63). Written representations, too, present "Little Jim" as an "object of pity" and as "rhetorically expedient but never rhetorical in [his] own right" (Dolmage 35; Cedillo, "What Does It Mean"). Thus, while such representations "appeal . . . to the conscience of" *Examiner* readers—sparking types of social action that ultimately result in the provision of medical care to lower-income children—they simultaneously sustain limiting and "easily consumed" stereotypes of disability (Dolmage 31).

Considered within the context of the perceived ideological incompatibility of public rhetorical activities and true womanhood for white middle-class women during this period, a sentimental rhetoric of disability appears to be linked to Black's use of feminine style and projection of symbolic motherhood (seen particularly through her desire to protect "Little Jim"). Black, that is, incorporates into her writing "stylistic elements that projected femininity" while adopting a conventional gendered identity premised on the role of the "wise mother" whose "female sympathy impels her to speak out for the helpless and the weak" (Campbell, "Consciousness-Raising" 51; Johnson 113). Through this strategy, Black circumvented lingering constraints on white middle-class women journalists by a way of writing that navigated the ideological tension between true womanhood and public rhetorical practices.

This tension was evident in late nineteenth and early twentieth-century women's rhetorical education, which was often channeled into encouraging their "healthy moral influence over domestic life" (Johnson 118). Public lectures, conduct manuals, and letter-writing guides encouraged women to acquire elocutionary and persuasive writing skills but to do so only in the service of being better wives and mothers. "For eloquence," Johnson explains, "no one could match the devoted mother instructing her children or the wise and loving wife counseling her husband. The ideological force of this assumption exerted its influence before and after the Civil War and well into the turn of the century" (118). Even visibly public figures such as Frances E. Willard were reinscribed in turn-of-the-century compilations of American orators as ideologically at home in front of a crowd. In Willard's case, her oratorical skill was attributed to and "energized by mother-love" (Johnson 146). By foregrounding a motherly persona entailing protection of "the helpless and the weak" and by employing components of feminine style, Black thus draws on prescribed roles and styles for female rhetoricians during this period in order to usher previously politically inactive children into public discourse (Johnson 113).

This process began when children offered initial answers to her question "What is going to become of little Jim?" As Black later related, "[t]he article appeared on Sunday. On Monday morning I found eight letters on my desk. The letters were all about the sick boy who had been turned away. They all offered to help the boy, and every single one of them was from a child" (*SFE* Dec. 9, 1894). As more letters arrived in the days following "Annie Laurie's Appeal," the *Examiner* began printing this correspondence from children. One representative letter from "Saturday's Cash Boy" begins: "I have been reading this morning about little Jim . . . I feel so sorry for those poor little children. Will you please except 20c toward the children's hospital" (*SFE* Nov. 28, 1894). This letter points to a body of children who both read and responded in writing to Black's rhetorical appeal.

Importantly, their correspondence reflects a much broader trend of nineteenth- and turn-of-the-century children writing to the mass media. Children's magazines such as *Robert Merry's Museum* and *St. Nicholas*, for instance, routinely invited and published children's letters. *Robert Merry's Museum*—founded in 1841 and one of the first of such U.S. periodicals to "regularly prin[t] letters from its young readers" beginning in 1842— published "several thousand" over the magazine's thirty-two-year span (Pflieger v, xv). *St. Nicholas* followed this trend by carving out "a space for letters and reader contributions" under the editorship of Mary Mapes Dodge. The periodical introduced "The Letter-Box" in 1874 and later the "St. Nicholas League" in 1899 (Van Horn 124; Erisman 380). Meanwhile, missionary periodicals such as *Children's Work for Children, The Children's Missionary Friend*, and *Everyland: A Magazine of World Friendship for Girls and Boys* "often included letters and narratives written by American and Chinese mission girls" (Miller 20). Some newspapers also invited written correspondence from children. These included large commercial dailies like the *San Francisco Examiner* (its children's page was launched and briefly directed by Black in 1895 prior to her New York relocation to assist with Hearst's newly acquired *Morning Journal*) and an array of additional newspapers such as the Cincinnati *Sabbath Visitor* (Adams and Keene 41–42; Klapper 113).[7] Overall, publications such as these offered important, wide-ranging opportunities for children to enter public discourse by way of nineteenth- and turn-of-the-century periodicals.

Compared with much other newspaper and magazine correspondence written by young people during this period, children's "Little Jim" letters are rather distinctive. First, children's literacy practices during this campaign centered on social activism as opposed to entertainment or the development of professional literacies. The *Examiner* in this way departed from the philosophy of popular children's magazines such as *St. Nicholas*, which under the editorship of Mary Mapes Dodge declared that youth periodicals should be a "pleasure-ground" where children can "tur[n] their backs without ceremony on what does not concern them" (qtd. in Sorby 59). Winifred Black instead illuminated social problems and urged children to respond proactively—even if these problems did "not concern them" directly. Nor did the *Examiner* function as a venue for children's professional identity development (via their letters), as did late nineteenth-century story papers such as *Boys of New York* (Lindey 72–73). This is not to argue that children's periodical writing rarely addressed socially or culturally serious topics during this period. For example, the forum that missionary periodicals provided for Chinese and American girls' writing enabled important cross-cultural understandings and exchanges of ideas (Miller 30, 33). Later, the early twentieth-century *Chicago Defender* "familiarized black youth with critical issues affecting their communities" and "gave them a space to write, reinvent, and legitimize their identities through its Defender Junior section" (Gray 76). Amidst this periodical landscape, children's literacy practices during the "Little Jim" campaign remain a distinct phenomenon because few children's magazines or instances of children's newspaper discourse reflect as sustained a conversation about a single social issue as that which occurred during the "Little Jim" campaign. Over one year later, "still the work of Little Jim was not done," and young writers continued to use extracurricular literacy to help construct another new ward for children whose needs had not been fully met by the "Little Jim" campaign (*SFE* Aug. 9, 1924).

Black played a crucial part in instigating and shaping San Francisco children's activist extracurricular literacy. Specifically, through her "Little Jim" campaign journalism, she participated in a form of rhetorical educa-tion that privileged moral principles over prescriptive grammatical and mechanical standards. This unique form of rhetorical education is initially evident in the *Examiner*'s response to "Saturday's Cash Boy" on November 28, 1894. "'Saturday's Cash Boy' may not spell like a college professor," the newspaper writes, "but he has something that is worth more to him and to the world than if he were a Webster's Unabridged Dictionary" (*SFE* Nov. 28, 1894). This statement posits features of his writing as useful for civic par-ticipation, while creating an evaluation scale that values the letter writer's social conscience over his adherence to prevailing spelling conventions.

This principle is reinforced several days later by a letter from Mabel Poole. "My mama read me about poor little Jim," Mabel writes. "I will send you my Christmas money for a ward for Jim. I am seven years old and a very poor writer, so please excuse mistakes" (*SFE* Dec. 1, 1894). The *Examiner*'s response? "Mabel Poole may not compose like a professor of languages at seven years, but she will not be able to write a letter with better grace and in a better cause if she lived to be a hundred." Reminiscent of its evaluation of "Saturday's Cash Boy," the *Examiner* here suggests that not all rhetorical situations require conformity to prevailing conceptions of correctness and eloquence; the newspaper extols the young girl's endearing style and moral rectitude.

Such a stance was notably at odds with *St. Nicholas League* editor Albert Bigelow Paine, who believed young contributors should "mee[t] normative standards of spelling and grammar" (Redcay 61). Similarly, late nineteenth-century story papers offered (at their readers' requests) writing instruction along primarily conventional lines by "help[ing] [young readers] improve their professional literacy" (Lindey 73). For Black and the *Examiner*, however, "correctness" was less important than values such as sincerity, style, and rhetorical awareness. Throughout the "Little Jim" campaign, Black instructed readers in these values through direct analysis of children's letters and critique of the businesslike nature of dominant discourse.

First, Black teaches readers strategies of effective written correspondence by analyzing model children's letters such as Joey's (*SFE* Dec. 9, 1894):

> Dear Examiner:
> It's my birthday and I give 10 cents for the sick children. I aint not sick. If I get some more I will give it to.
>
> > Good-by,
> > JOEY

Black's printed response does not attempt to relay prescriptive standards of grammar, spelling, and punctuation but rather dwells on the endearing image of a civically concerned child: "I can't look at that letter without fairly seeing a chubby face all wrinkled up with the very serious task of writing a little letter to a big newspaper," she writes. This response notably recalls the same symbolic motherhood that incited her desire to "snatc[h] . . . up and kis[s]" the "dear little" orphan during the "The Orphans' Santa Claus" campaign (*SFE* Dec. 20, 1890). Black's goal here is not to enhance (along conventional lines) the professional literacy of those who "struggled with their own preparedness" but instead to commend those who demonstrate social conscience and attention to audience and purpose (Lindey 73).

To emphasize this point, Black analyzes a letter by a four-year-old. She writes:

> It was all in printed letters and was done with a lead pencil by Ralph Hyde. It was his first letter and told what he could do for the little sufferers. By-and-by, when he grows to be a man, he will think it a funny

letter, and then, perhaps, some one will say to him, "It's funny, but the people who read that letter first must have felt like hugging you" . . . He is a credit to the whole city. (*SFE* Dec. 6, 1894)

Ralph's letter provides Black the occasion to teach readers about rhetorical context. Although turn-of-the-century rhetorical instruction often subordinated effective written communication to mechanical correctness—a culturally constructed indicator of class membership and professional status—Black chooses to promote the rhetorical situation. She does not issue an acontextual and prescriptive critique of his style but instead highlights how Ralph appeals flawlessly to his intended audience (Black, the *Examiner*, and newspaper readers) and achieves his purpose. As Black concludes, "[a] few such boys as these to start the ball rolling, and we'll have every friendless, ailing child in California taken care of in no time."

A third letter, prefaced by Black's introduction, reveals her commitment to an alternative form of citizenship building:

Here is a letter from a little boy who lives in Oakland. He says his father is not a rich man. He may be a rich man himself one day, though, and I don't believe the biggest check he will ever sign will do half the good that this little letter of his does:

ALAMEDA, Cal. December 7, 1894.

My Dear Examiner:

I am a little boy living in Alameda, and I want to be a Little Samaritan. I have read of the good you are doing and I want to add my mite. Do not think that I can give gifts like dear Baby Sunshine for my father is not a rich man like hers most likely is. Could you let me in, too? I can help some, because there is some trouble even here in this little city. If there is a pledge to sign let me know and I will sign it.

Hoping you have room for me, I am your friend,

ALEXANDER G. BOOTH

Alexander G. Booth writes that he cannot "give gifts . . . for my father is not a rich man." Nonetheless, he resolves to "help some" by proposing to sign a pledge (*SFE* Dec. 9, 1894). Black responds by commending this young boy's character. "He may be a rich man himself one day," she writes, "and I don't believe the biggest check he will ever sign will do half the good that this little letter of his does." Here, Black accentuates the role of humanity in both writing and public citizenship. Specifically, she inverts the hierarchy of status markers by heralding the "little letter" over a check signature—asserting that while both discursive acts respond to an exigence, the former carries more cultural power. Its moral principles are more meaningful than the less personal ethos of a check writer and invite others to imitate such acts of humanity.[8]

Black further highlights the importance of humanity in writing through a second instructional tactic: critiquing the businesslike nature of prevailing professional discourses. In "The Bear with a Scarlet Cross," Black describes being confronted by a man with a "brisk, self-confident air which may have been business-like, but it was certainly not alluring." He offers to enlist a secret society to support the campaign but then immediately declares, "I am a man of business, my time's worth money. How big of a commission will you give me?" (*SFE* Dec. 9, 1894). Stunned by impersonal encounters such as this one, Black seeks relief in "a pile of letters" and draws a strong contrast between two in particular: "[t]he top letter was addressed in a business-like hand—a hand that would have been business-like if there had not been so many flourishes about it," she describes. "It was exactly the kind of a hand the secret society man would have written. I put it aside." In sharp contrast, Black describes "a funny, little crumply thing" that "looked as if it had been carried in somebody's pocket. It was addressed in purple ink, and I could tell that the person who wrote the superscription of that envelope spent at least half an hour on it. And then I knew that the bright spot in the day had come" (*SFE* Dec. 9, 1894).

Black juxtaposes here the self-serving and embellished businesslike discourse of adults with the sincerity and painstaking effort of this child's letter.[9] The contrast indicates important ways that Black reinvents the letter-writing lessons of those nineteenth-century composition textbooks that "stress[ed] that the appearance of the letter is a sign of the writer's character" (Carr et al. 187). In this case, rather, it is the purple ink, effortful "superscription," and "crumply" (versus "business-like") appearance that signals character. Children's letters such as this one reflect authenticity and civic engagement grounded in intimate caring; they are thus for Black rhetorically powerful (*SFE* Dec. 9, 1894).

Ultimately, Black proposes to bind the "Little Jim" letters "into a big book, mistakes, blots and all" and to "put that book in some prominent place, so that every one who visits that ward may see who the children were who helped to build it" (*SFE* Dec. 7, 1894). Yet Black has, in part, already accomplished this feat by printing children's letters in the *Examiner*—a prominent venue for public discourse at this time. These letters thus contribute to the public's rhetorical education by promoting specific values and rhetorical principles. Most notably, these children's letters often depart from normative conceptions of correctness upheld by both magazine spaces such as Paine's *St. Nicholas League* and much composition instruction during this period. Many nineteenth-century school readers, for instance, stressed correctness and presented "[t]he power of the upper class . . . as a 'manner' or 'grace' of speaking, behaving, writing, and living—a grace that can be learned and that will conceal the 'natural awkwardness' of the unlearned" (Carr et al. 143). Black and the *Examiner*, however, largely eschew such normative teaching; more so, the *Examiner* redefines "grace" as synonymous with social conscience (as in the case of Mabel Poole). Thus, even while Black's reference to "mistakes" to some degree reifies prevailing conceptions of correctness, her overall teaching practices and the "Little Jim" campaign as a whole work not to endorse "the promise of social success, of rising to positions of power and financial benefit" through diligence in mastering conventionally polished communication; rather, the campaign promotes authentic expression and social activism along with the importance of rhetorical context (143).

One might therefore align Black with those nineteenth-century scholars and teachers who resisted prevailing pressures to prioritize the teaching of prescriptive grammar and standardized mechanics. As early as 1839, for instance, educator and textbook author John Frost advised teachers against scrutinizing "trifling mistake[s]"—encouraging students instead to "say whatever comes into [their] head[s] in a natural though inaccurate manner." Black similarly frees children from the "stiffness and constraint" of an overly regulated prose style, while moreover promoting rhetorical awareness (Frost 58–59). In doing so she anticipates John Dewey's early twentieth-century position that language instruction should "gro[w] out of the real desire to communicate vital impressions and convictions" (50). Here, Dewey suggests that students must have an exigence (or "real desire") that motivates communication and an audience to whom they can communicate. Students, in other words, require a social context for writing: "when the language instinct is appealed to in a social way," Dewey claims, "there is a continual contact with reality. The result is that the child always has something in his mind to talk about, he has something to say" (50).

Black's extracurricular pedagogy appeals to children's language instinct "in a social way" by providing them an exigence, an invitation into public discourse, and an audience to whom they can communicate meaningfully. Through these priorities, Black and the *Examiner* help children like Ralph, Alexander, and Mabel "to feel somewhat *at home* in the use of [their] pen[s]" (Frost 79–80).

Examiner illustrations accompanying the prose further promote these pedagogical values and rhetorical principles. Consider, for instance, "From the Generous Children to Little Jim"—part of Black's article "The Bear with a Scarlet Cross."

1.2. "From the Generous Children to Little Jim." *San Francisco Examiner,* 9 Dec. 1894.

This illustration posts several "Little Jim" letters from children in an outdoor public setting. These letters jettison concern for a flawless appearance or depart from prescriptive conventions of grammar, mechanics, and spelling. The letter at top center, for instance, has replaced the crossed-out word "mooney" with "money." The letter at top right begins, "Here is one dollar for the sick children I don't like to be sick," while the bottom left letter reads, "I am a Little girl in the Country and give you all I got. I may be hurt by a Hors some Time—all Children in the Country may get Hurt—I hope Not dont you. 20 cents," signed "Katie KaVagnagh" (*SFE* Dec. 9, 1894). By printing letters such as these, Black and the *Examiner* uphold the expressive power of these children's writing and teach that public writing need not adhere to prescriptive grammar, spelling, punctuation, or capitalization to carry rhetorical sway, establish moral character, or spur social change.

By valuing children's civically oriented letters as rhetorically powerful, Black thus advocates rhetorical awareness at a time when individualism, economic competition, and professionalization had—according to William N. Denman—diluted "the relationship between education, rhetoric, and civic life" (3–4). Black and the *Examiner* reaffirm this relationship, commend unique and endearing style (rather than "the flat voice of mechanical correctness"), and promote "the sense of a large social purpose for writing" (Denman 10).[10] Their support of young writers led more and more children into public discourse, promoting excitement about literacy development—even for those of a very young age. As "Little Ffarington" boasts, "I am most two years old, and when someone holds the pencil I can write my name" (*SFE* Dec. 9, 1894).

Notably, Black and the *Examiner*'s deemphasis of dominant usage standards and promotion of a shared "social purpose for writing" helps blur both gender and class lines within the "Little Jim" peer community (Denman 10). Consider this letter (followed by the *Examiner*'s commentary):

Dear Examiner:

I thought that I would save up for Christmas but when I heard about little Jim it made me think of all the dayes that I used to be praying for somebody to send a present no matter how little it was. I send only ten cents now but wait till you see the next one.

Your Truly
LITTLE FRANKIE

The Christmas dime little Frankie gave up represents more to him than a fortune does to a great many men in San Francisco. If the spirit of the gift and of the season strikes them only a fraction as hard as it struck him there will be no lack of funds with which to build and equip the new ward. (*SFE* Nov. 28, 1894)

By donating his Christmas money, Little Frankie demonstrates selfless generosity that the *Examiner* encourages grown men to emulate. His letter also reflects important ways in which boys, through the "Little Jim" campaign, engaged in a form of literacy typically reserved for females at the close of the nineteenth century. During this period, female literacy was often channeled into daily correspondence as "the woman of the house." This correspondence involved charitable solicitation and letters regarding other "good works typically associated with enterprises outside the home that women were expected to view as their concern"—including orphanages, hospitals, and children's missions (Johnson 97). It is thus notable given this gendered context that at least two out of the three children's letters published on November 28 were written by boys, indicating that early on in the "Little Jim" campaign, Black and the *Examiner* were ushering young males into the traditionally female genre of charity letter writing.[11]

The rhetorical efficacy of "Annie Laurie's Appeal" helps account for this outcome. In the article, Black collapses the distance between males and charitable activity by establishing literacy-related common ground with her young male readers. She achieves this by describing "[a] tall, slim boy about thirteen years old," a patient at the Children's Hospital, engaged in reading:

The bright morning sunshine made a little glimmer of gold around his close-cropped flaxen hair, and his pale skin looked almost transparent in the strong light. An open book lay on his lap. It was worn and thumb-marked and every page bore the evidence of close and loving study. The name of the book was "Robinson Crusoe." The pale boy smiled when I asked him how he liked the book. He would not speak at first and I saw he was painfully shy. "Have you read it before?" I said. The boy nodded.

"How many times?"

"Eight," said the boy.

"Which part do you like the best?"

"The part where Friday comes to be company for poor Robinson Crusoe," said the boy, brightening up and forgetting all about his shyness, "he must have been awful lonesome on the desert island before Friday came, I guess, and I keep feeling so sorry for him for being lonesome that it makes me feel bad. After Friday comes I feel better . . . I think bein' lonesome is the worst thing there is in the world," he said, "even worse than having your back ache."

Black confides to readers that

[t]here is not money enough at the Children's Hospital to keep any one who cannot be cured, and the boy will probably go back to the squalid room where he learned what loneliness was and die there.

It is pitiful to see how all these boys, who are sick and suffering, love to read stories of outdoor life . . . [T]hey like heroes that can run and jump and have wild adventures, and their wan faces kindle at any story of bravery or daring. (*SFE* Nov. 25, 1894)

This portrait of the young book reader serves two key functions. First, Black's opening description reasserts her symbolic motherhood. Lingering on the boy's features, Black paints an angelic "glimmer of gold" about his head. Her metaphor (similar to her description of Joey's "chubby face") reminds readers that she carries the doting affection of a mother. Second, the book reader is described as enjoying "stor[ies] of bravery or daring"— qualities stereotypically assigned to boys in contemporary schoolbooks and children's magazines and depicted in boys' adventure novels like *Robinson Crusoe*. The "worn and thumb-marked" copy of *Robinson Crusoe*— reflecting "evidence of close and loving study"—to this end creates literacy-related common ground as young male readers are invited to identity with the book reader and moreover to take up their pens on his behalf. This motivation is encouraged by the boy's description of Crusoe's loneliness and Black's parallel statement that limited hospital funds will soon send the boy "back to the squalid room where he learned what loneliness was." Through such strategies, Black draws young male readers into the genre of charity letter writing. Ultimately, the publication of boys' letters in the *Examiner* promulgates an understanding that boys, too, could exhibit sympathy and support public interests symbolically associated with "the maintenance of home and family" (Johnson 97).

The "Little Jim" campaign blurs class as well as gender lines. For instance, the December 1 *Examiner* article "The Money Coming In" features a series of letters from children of various classes—all written to fund the new hospital ward. Displaying a presumably middle-class child's donation of a "lately received . . . present of a dollar bill" and another child's gift of "25 cents" from the "10 cents a week [my mama pays me] for counting when I practice," the newspaper also includes this letter:

> Dear Annie Laurie:
>
> I inclose 10 cents to the benefit of the poor little Children Hospital. I am poor and so is mama. I would like to send you more. Accept this with my good wishes.
>
> Yours truly, Little Rosey.
>
> P.S.—Mama read it to me out of your paper—we take your paper—about little Jimie. (*SFE* Dec. 1, 1894)

In her letter, Rosey identifies as "poor" but is categorized by the *Examiner* as part of a broader group of children "Conveying Sympathy and Contributions to the Fund." Children's periodicals such as *St. Nicholas* notably enabled children to identify themselves as members of "a distinct group" (Sorby 64). For the *Examiner*, this group is defined less by class than by the desire to help "Little Jim." Occasionally, adult letters are incorporated to reinforce and expand this collective sense of community. The *Examiner* published, for instance, a letter to Annie Laurie from "A Lover Of Poor Children." It states that while "I am myself little less than a beggar . . . I beg the privilege of contributing my mite to your noble work in behalf of the poor, sick children" (*SFE* Dec. 1, 1894). By uniting young people (and even adults) of all classes "in behalf of" children like "Little Jim," Black and the *Examiner* foster the formation of a unique counterpublic defined less by class difference than by a shared commitment to a social cause.[12]

Importantly, Black's influence on children's writing and public involvement was not limited to their letter writing. In her 1924 reflective article, "How Little Jim Helped the Children," she remembers how "we went to work—the children of San Francisco and a plain, everyday newspaper—and we had fairs and we had baseball games and we had benefit performances." Throughout the campaign, Black continues, "every one of those children was getting up a fair or having a party or starting a raffle or forming a committee to do something about Little Jim" (*SFE* Aug. 9, 1924). These various forms of public involvement are significant. While letters forged children's initial bond around a common project, these young writers proceeded to network among themselves by planning community events and forming statewide public organizations for "Little Jim." Through these varied activities, children developed entrepreneurial and elocutionary skills while raising funds for the hospital ward. The *Examiner* notes, for instance, "a number of children's entertainments in different parts of the city" including that of Ruby Dawson, who—along with "nine other little girls"—performed in an amateur operetta (*SFE* Dec. 8 and 13, 1894). Dawson describes the event in a letter to Black:

> My Dear Annie Laurie:
>
> This letter is from the little girl who gave the operetta for the benefit of the Children's Hospital . . . I worked so hard for weeks to get my little troupe perfect. Mama says I was talking all night in my sleep while we were having rehearsals. I have a miniature stage and scenery painted by Mr. Bell, former painter at the Tivoli. We charged 5 cents admission and gave three performances in a neighbor's basement. We took nothing out for the expense of costumes . . . but gave all we made to the hospital. Mamma says I may give another operetta if papa will only get our basement fixed suitable for the occasion, as it will not accommodate a large enough audience now. (*SFE* Dec. 13, 1894)

The "Little Jim" campaign provided Dawson the opportunity to undertake public leadership, singing, fund-raising, and event planning. Through the operetta, Dawson and her friends also developed elocutionary skills. Turn-of-the-century elocution notably included performances such as "singing, dancing, and acting for church benefits, concerts, vaudeville, the theater, and other venues"—all of which "empowered" female participants in important ways (Whitburn et al. 391, 403). Efforts to "evok[e] desired audience responses and praise," for instance, helped girls and women acquire "communication abilities and confidence" (403). The "Little Jim" campaign is notable for rousing children not only to perform but subsequently to write about their performances.

Aside from children's entertainments, the *Examiner* also inspired "a little school paper" written and edited by the "children of the Clement School" on behalf of "Little Jim" (*SFE* Dec. 12, 1894). Deeming it "quite a feature," Black boasts that the children will "have it printed in regular type just like the grown-up newspapers" and "sell it next Saturday night at their fair at Armory Hall" (*SFE* Dec. 12 and 13, 1894). Entrepreneurial activities again merge with public writing—in this case, however, children did not merely contribute to a late nineteenth-century newspaper. They created their own. Black in this way initiates a ripple effect of journalistic activity by modeling socially driven professional writing and inspiring children to follow suit. The Clement School paper may have even inspired a second and much larger children's special edition newspaper: the "Public School Children's Christmas Examiner" of 1895.

The "Public School Children's Christmas Examiner": Ongoing Extracurricular Literacy

After the campaign initiated by "Annie Laurie's Appeal" had fully funded the "Little Jim" Ward, the building soon followed. The completed ward—a circular structure described as a "beautiful home"—contained spacious accommodations, a full nursing staff, and a "glor[ious]" sunroom. The *Examiner* further described the building as "even more commodious than the hospital from which [Little Jim was] turned [away], much more permanent," and "much more cheerful" (*SFE* Dec. 20, 1895). At the ward dedication ceremony on December 21, 1895, Mr. Henry E. Highton "paid a glowing tribute to Mrs. Orrin Black (Annie Laurie), to whose sympathetic nature and able pen and untiring exertions he attributed most of the success of the campaign." Mrs. Willard B. Harrington, speaking on behalf of the board of managers of the Hospital for Children and Training School for Nurses, similarly proclaimed: "especially are we indebted to the loving heart and sympathetic pen of her whose recital of the story of 'Little Jim' . . . was the first step in the work whose completion we are here to celebrate" (*SFE* Dec. 22, 1895).

Yet children's public involvement did not end here. As Black recalled in a retrospective essay, "still the work of Little Jim was not done" (*SFE* Aug. 9, 1924). While the ward offered treatment and comfort to many children, it could not sufficiently cater to those who were blind or deaf. This compelled the *Examiner* to launch a new collective literacy project: "A Christmas 'Examiner' written and edited by the boys and girls of the Pacific Coast" (*SFE* Nov. 10, 1895).

Titled the "Public School Children's Christmas Examiner," this special-edition newspaper offered almost three hundred primary, grammar, and high school children from an array of California public schools the opportunity to write, edit, manage, and publish their own issue. Notably, proceeds from this edition would contribute to funding the construction of an Eye and Ear Ward at the San Francisco Children's Hospital to serve children—including those with "no money to pay for treatment" (*SFE* Dec. 8, 1895).

The project—which appears to be one of the first of its kind—was enthusiastically introduced by the *Examiner*. "What a glorious chance it

1.3. "Public School Children's Christmas Examiner."
San Francisco Examiner, 25 Dec. 1895.

will be for every one who takes part!" the newspaper declared. "The boys and girls will gather the news, write it up, send and receive the telegrams, illustrate the articles and attend to everything in the editorial rooms and the business department of the paper. They will have full charge of the paper" (*SFE* Nov. 10, 1895). Notably, the paper also applauded the opportunity for children to "be real live newspapermen and women for one day, just as much as Arthur McEwen and Annie Laurie" (*SFE* Nov. 10, 1895). An exploration of this literacy project demonstrates how Black's persuasive ethos enabled children's public writing and activism to surpass, remarkably, the success of the initial social action campaign.

The resulting "Public School Children's Christmas Examiner" provided both civic involvement and experiential training in journalism. "What an opportunity to learn the newspaper business!" the *Examiner* exclaimed. "The workers will learn more about practical newspaper work in that one day than they would in a whole year's reading on the subject" (*SFE* Nov. 10, 1895). Here, the *Examiner* adopts a newfound emphasis on professional preparation—one absent from its responses to children's letters a year earlier. The "Christmas Examiner" aligns in this respect with late nineteenth-century story papers that generated "real dialogue about professional authorship" and with *St. Nicholas League* editor Albert Bigelow Paine's "desire to professionalize the child" (Lindey 80; Redcay 72). Yet the special edition also innovates on what these children's periodicals were doing in three important ways. First, the "Christmas Examiner" invites children to assume leadership roles within the adult profession of journalism. Second, the *Examiner* desires to "professionalize the child" in response to a civic exigence and for the purposes of social action (construction of the Eye and Ear Ward). Third—and perhaps most notably—this special edition would provide a venue for subversive writing by young people that observes, questions, and challenges structural reasons for poverty.

The "Public School Children's Christmas Examiner" thus functions as an activist-oriented literacy site and extracurricular internship for children—offering young people a unique form of writing experience that many schools did not provide. Lucille Schultz confirms that "training in journalism was very much outside the high school curriculum for most of the nineteenth century" (137). Only some high schools offered students apprenticeships with printers, while others provided the peripheral experience of school newspapers. Textbooks, meanwhile, included few directives on writing for such papers, which were mostly "seen as a form of enrichment, not as professional training" (Schultz 137–38). Interestingly, however, evidence suggests that experience in journalism helped prepare students for college and professional writing. For instance, a late nineteenth-century Harvard entrance exam test-taker reported that while school provided "no instruction" for the test, newspaper experience and "editing of the school paper" built preparatory writing skills (qtd. in Brereton 80). Many student editors relatedly believed that "writing for the school newspaper would help prepare students for their writing in college" (Schultz 140–41).

Dr. Charles Lewis Tisdale, president of the board of education of Alameda, advanced a similar claim regarding this unique newspaper writing opportunity provided by the *Examiner*. He asserted:

> I believe that it is the duty of every Board of Education in the State of California to endorse "The Examiner's" action . . . I have heard it said that the children's minds will be diverted from their studies and that it may be the means of retarding their advancement. Such talk is nonsense. There is one view I take of this glorious proposition which has not been advanced. I regard the work which the children will do for "The Examiner" as a study. It will prove part of their education. (*SFE* Nov. 21, 1895)

By characterizing journalism as a valuable "study," Tisdale attempts to collapse the distance between journalism and high school curriculums. His critique of those who oppose the project similarly situates journalism as "part of"—not tangential to or a distraction from—students' education.

Almost 300 schoolchildren ultimately contributed to this collective literacy project by writing stories, running editorial rooms and business offices, and acting as city and town correspondents. Importantly, these dynamic extracurricular writing opportunities offered more than mere experiential training in journalism and the opportunity to help fund an Eye and Ear Ward. The "Christmas Examiner" also provided a space in which young people used journalism to question the capitalist underpinnings of the *Examiner* and industrial capitalism at large during this period. Examples of this writing, unlike many children's letters previously discussed in this chapter, generally adhere to prevailing conceptions of correctness—possibly due to these writers' older age (and related application of normative school-based conventions), their desired alignment with usage standards in adult journalism, or the *Examiner*'s oversight of the edition. Their writing nonetheless indicates ways in which California children resisted "values that reinforce[d] the lifestyles and belief systems of those in power" through examination of structural reasons for late nineteenth-century poverty (Enoch, *Refiguring* 24).

At the time the "Public School Children's Christmas Examiner" was published, late nineteenth-century capitalistic competition largely defined urban life and heavily influenced mass journalism. While Pulitzer and Hearst competed for the largest national circulation, for instance, Hearst also scuffled with San Francisco papers such as the *Chronicle* for local supremacy. "Journalism to-day is a business," summarized J. Lincoln Steffens in 1897 (447). Another critic in 1893 claimed, "[t]he fundamental principle of metropolitan journalism to-day is to buy white paper at three cents a pound and sell it at ten cents a pound" (Keller 691).

The "Public School Children's Christmas Examiner" was enmeshed in this context. It was both a conduit for social action and children's alternative discourses and yet also a means of advancing *Examiner* circulation and influence. The capitalist logic underlying the *Examiner*'s emphasis on circulation and profit is evident in the newspaper's call for a child "Business Manager" who

> has got to be a wide-awake, energetic, hustling lad with an eye not only to see every dollar in sight, but with a head to devise a way of capturing it. He will almost be expected to march into the business office . . . punch various buttons that turn the wheels in the office for the day, turn to the speaking tubes and say:
> "Smith, how are the day's ads coming in?"
> "Sixty-seven squares at 10 per cent advance."
> "Good, shake up the boys and try and make it 100 before the noon gun." (*SFE* Nov. 10, 1895)

This characterization alludes to the race for financial success that prompted many late nineteenth-century commercial newspapers to adopt principles of "new journalism." The *Examiner*, for instance, succeeded in rapidly increasing circulation through dramatic stories and a visually striking format. "[E]asy to glance through and with ads large enough to catch the buyer's eye," the turn-of-the-century *Examiner* used approximately 39–40 percent of its space for advertising in summer and winter issues (Quinn 19–21).[13] In such ways, the mass-circulating newspaper "emerged as a serious commercial enterprise" in the competitive context of late nineteenth-century industrial capitalism (Edelstein 116).

Many articles in the "Public School Children's Christmas Examiner" notably critique economic inequalities and commercialism present during this period. The issue as a whole spans a range of topics including local and global events, economics, sports, literary culture, and drama. Yet a pronounced focus concerns the ramifications of capitalistic competition and class hierarchies. The article "Society as We Find It," for example, condemns U.S. money culture that renders "talented" men useless without wealth (*SFE* Dec. 25, 1895). "Ah, what a farce society is!" the article asserts:

> If a searchlight were thrown upon the members that constitute the so-called high society, we wonder how many could creditably stand it. Reputation is a great deal, but character is greater. One may be the proud possessor of a good reputation and be literally a wolf in sheep's clothing. The men who are ornaments in society are those whose time is occupied in amassing large fortunes, who tread ordinary beings under their heels. They are so taken up with their own greatness that they have no sympathy for the masses. (*SFE* Dec. 25, 1895)

Here, the authors draw a key distinction between reputation and character. This distinction is soon extended to implicate contributors to the new Children's Hospital ward who donated primarily for the sake of public recognition and self-promotion. The article specifically critiques a business owner who—after signing a check—was rewarded with his name "in large black letters in the paper, together with his generous contribution." "Doubtless he felt very proud when he gazed on this," the authors state, even though he "ride[s] in a private carriage," "occupies a beautiful mansion," and "paid $80,000 for some property" (*SFE* Dec. 25, 1895). This critique questions not only the character of the contributor but simultaneously the motivations of other contributing firms, whose checks and special-edition advertising contracts had been printed in the *Examiner*. Ultimately, the article challenges the *Examiner* itself for advertising practices that sell "good reputation" so readily. Furthermore, it rebukes newspaper preoccupations with "the receptions, weddings, parties, etc., given by the society people. Day after day they gaze on their names in the public print, the regal appearance presented and the social success they scored" (*SFE* Dec. 25, 1895). This passage implicates commercial newspapers for encouraging upper-class preoccupations with status and appearance, thereby reinforcing the dangers of reputation without character.

Several other "Christmas Examiner" articles extend the "counterdiscourses" present in "Society as We Find It" (Fraser 67). Two that address child labor are Ernest J. Cross's "By the Sweat of the Brow" and Frank English's "The Newsboy and the Rat Boy." In the former article—featured on the front page—Cross visits the Labor Bureau and learns there is insufficient work for boys who seek it. This is especially evident in an interview with an itinerant working boy: "I haven't had a steady job for about three months," the boy tells Cross. "I came from Los Angeles, where my brother lives. I came to look for work . . . I have found odd jobs here and there, but nothing steady." Testimony such as this compels Cross to conclude, "[i]t seems a pity that so many boys want and need work and are forced to be idle through lack of it" (*SFE* Dec. 25, 1895). This comment implicitly critiques industrial capitalism's volatile economic patterns. Yet Cross also offers a solution. He proposes to "interest some philanthropic capitalist in establishing an industry that shall furnish employment for all poor worthy youths who ask nothing of the world but a chance to do the work that shall give them support" (*SFE* Dec. 25, 1895). This proposal challenges wealthy capitalists to do more than simply sign a check. Cross argues that they must instead "establish an industry"—reflecting his use of literacy for active public citizenship grounded in a growing awareness of the systemic roots of poverty.

Frank English of Lowell High School also explores labor-related inequalities. Donning newsboy apparel, English goes undercover to "find out for myself just how newsboys fare" (*SFE* Dec. 25, 1895). His use of a disguise here reflects the popularity of stunt journalism at this time. English adopts this approach to illuminate the harsh labor conditions endured by newsboys, who, as Brian Fehler observes, "embod[ied] the poverty of the Gilded Age" (157). After struggling to sell papers in a competitive terrain, he seeks lodging only to learn that "[t]here is no newsboys' home in San Francisco." English proceeds then to the Salvation Army "Life Boat," where he meets "men out of work and struggling for an existence." The frigid conditions of the "Life Boat" shock English: "[i]t was so cold for the first part of the night," he recounts, "that sleep was out of the question" (*SFE* Dec. 25, 1895). English introduces *Examiner* readers to life in a late nineteenth-century shelter, one of many such lodging types that proliferated industrial-era U.S. cities with severe unemployment and wherein workers without steady wages attempted to stay afloat (DePastino 74). English presents just the tip of these severe social problems but nonetheless works to direct public attention toward inequitable labor conditions and homelessness in California.

Overall, these children use writing to grapple with and expand public awareness of the economic inequalities facing working-class adults and children—even when it means implicating the *Examiner* itself. This is significant insofar as many other venues for children's periodical discourse during this period do not appear to reflect such pronounced political commentary or opportunities for social activism. Many children's magazines, for instance, "facilitated genteel consumer roles for American children" according to Paul B. Ringel (15). As Ringel explains, "[f]rom its emergence in the 1820s until the onset of its declining cultural influence in the 1910s, the American children's magazine industry . . . defin[ed] and legitimiz[ed] young readers' expanding roles as consumers" (4–5). In comparison, the "Christmas Examiner" article "Society as We Find It" issues a potent critique of consumerism and the commercial press. And while late nineteenth-century children's periodicals such as *Youth's Companion* did "occasionally addres[s] the challenges of impoverished urban children," the *Examiner* articles by Cross and English stand apart as examples of children's firsthand learning and public writing about economic inequalities facing working-class adults and children (Ringel 169).

Additional "Christmas Examiner" articles provide further evidence of these unique counterdiscourses at work. In an article titled "She Tramped to Biggs," for instance, a teenage girl describes her father's abandonment of the home and her subsequent travels to find work. "My home was sold to strangers," she narrates, "my mother getting weaker and weaker; slowly dying by inches." To support her sick working mother and siblings, Minnie St. Clair leaves home to secure a job and ultimately finds one with a family acquaintance—yet the story as a whole depicts the thin line between security and poverty, as well as the "hard and unprofitable nature" of industries such as steam laundry (*SFE* Dec. 25, 1895). Ultimately, St. Clair's narrative—like the three articles previously discussed—spotlights working-class suffering during an era of rigid class stratification.

In closing, these "Christmas Examiner" articles demonstrate how children participating in this literacy project used writing to investigate, and enhance public awareness of, social and economic inequalities of the late nineteenth century. Their writing in fact points to ways that extracurricular involvement with newspapers—at least in this case—fostered moral and ethical thinking and development. Recognition by the *Examiner* alludes to this point in praising the children's maturity and insight: "In many respects [the editorial page] was a model," commented the *Examiner*. "It touched upon subjects that maturer minds might have neglected" (*SFE* Dec. 26, 1895). Reception of this special-edition newspaper also indicates that the schoolchildren executed their purpose with rhetorical effectiveness. "The children took a serious view of life," the *Examiner* asserted, "but presented their views in the most apt and winning way" (*SFE* Dec. 26, 1895). This assessment suggests that the maturity of the "Christmas Examiner" was conveyed with rhetorical savvy. In characterizing the special edition as "serious," this assessment also resembles the children's own understanding of their purpose. They state:

> Several weeks ago "The Examiner" turned over its plant to us public school children, with orders to take charge of the Christmas edition and raise all the money possible to build a ward for the blind and deaf of the Children's Hospital. We were told to take full charge of the paper and to do just as we pleased. We have tried to carry out the instructions.
> If you don't believe it,
> Read
> This
> Paper.
> P.S.—We specially want to impress on the public that we were told to speak right out and say what we thought as boys and girls. We have tried to speak right out. If in any instance it seems as if we have said too much, remember, we spoke as managers and editors of a big paper "for one day only." To-morrow the older folks can have all the say, as usual, and we will take our places as plain boys and girls again, as usual. (*SFE* Dec. 25, 1895)

This statement on one hand reinforces how the "Public School Children's Christmas Examiner" empowered children to "speak right out" in their efforts to think critically about social problems and use writing to enter public conversations about them. Yet there is also a disclaimer present. As the children state, "If in any instance it seems as if we have said too much, remember, we spoke as managers and editors of a big paper 'for one day only.'" This statement—possibly a rhetorical concession—reminds us of the limitations of this unique children's public, which would soon cede to "older folks" who "can have all the say, as usual" (*SFE* Dec. 25, 1895). Whether the children who contributed to this special edition were inspired to pursue future periodical writing is largely unknown. Nonetheless, these children authors and their serious articles do invite our more thorough search for the presence of subversive children's writing in other newspapers and magazines during this period. More rhetorical analysis of such writing would enhance our understanding of the powerful forms of "counterdiscourses" by young people that circulated in the nineteenth century (Fraser 67).

Ultimately, the "Public School Children's Christmas Examiner" compelled a range of California children to think critically, compose public writing in pursuit of social action, and, in a striking number of instances, practice a form of extracurricular literacy oriented toward questioning rather than "sustaining the social order" (Enoch, *Refiguring* 3). These outcomes trace back to Black, whose original 1894 article, "Annie Laurie's Appeal," launched the formation of a distinct children's public—one that eventually gave rise to the powerful writing present in the "Public School Children's Christmas Examiner."

Overall, Black is the type of rhetorician who "successfully addressed a large community of people, united them, organized them, and moved them to action" (Mattingly 2). The impressive scope of her "Little Jim" campaign lends credence to the words of Mayor Rossi, who avowed that "no one newspaper man or woman did more for San Francisco than did the beloved writer" Annie Laurie (*SFE* Dec. 11, 1938). A *Visalia Times-Delta* article from December 27, 1894, similarly lauded Black, declaring, "[t]hat the pen is powerful is forcibly shown by what the writer, 'Annie Laurie,' has done for the incurable children of San Francisco." Black's rhetorical competence drove the construction of a needed hospital ward and inspired the influential literacy practices of a wide range of California children for whom literacy was much more than a charity tool or fund-raising instrument. It enabled these young writers to address public issues, forge civic identities, and question prevailing cultural values. These feats are attributable to Black, whose "Little Jim" campaign journalism stimulated the formation of a distinct public—one in which children learned and practiced the skills of discursive public participation and activism. She is a rhetorician whose journalistic work dynamically influenced children's extracurricular literacy development and social action.

CHAPTER TWO

Gertrude Bustill Mossell's "Helpful Sisterhood": Racial Uplift, Raising Girls, and Reader-Centered Pedagogy

> Every letter expressing a felt want is helpful and suggestive, and I feel I am no longer working in the dark. Send letters, join friend to friend, and bind us in a helpful sisterhood.
> —Gertrude Bustill Mossell, *New York Freeman* (July 10, 1886)

On July 10, 1886, a letter appeared in the "Our Woman's Department" column of the *New York Freeman*. Signed "M. H. W.," this letter lamented "the immorality of our young girls" and pleaded for a solution to white male aggression:

ATHENS ON-THE-HUDSON, June 24, '86.

DEAR MRS. MOSSELL:—

As I am a reader of THE FREEMAN, I have taken great pleasure in reading our "Women's Department," and there is one subject that I have thought about a great deal, and that is the immorality of our young girls. Oh, it grieves me to see so many falling away from purity. And who is it bringing them down? The white men of our land. Oh, how I despise these men! Can nothing be done to stop it? Who will do it? There is a great work of this kind to be done. You will see that these few words are from no scholar, only the words of a poor tried woman who has not fallen herself, but who has many dear ones who have. Hoping I have not intruded upon your time. I am yours, most humbly,

M. H. W.

Column editor Gertrude Bustill Mossell offered some initial advice: "Look after your little ones and see that the minds of their associates are pure. Teach them to enjoy innocent pleasures. Keep them out [of] the streets. Let their clothing teach modesty." After also encouraging mothers to promote frugality, secure a daughter's "confidence," and "listen to her conversation," Mossell advised: "Teach her the value of virtue. Don't be afraid to speak to your daughter about such matters as are possibly discussed by her daily with her schoolmates. Get good books, written especially for girls" (*NYF* July 10, 1886). Several readers offered similar recommendations in the coming weeks. While M. E. L. asserted that mothers must model "the value of virtuous and upright living," E. V. M. urged them to teach children "the beauty of morality" (*NYF* July 24, 1886, and Aug. 14, 1886). An anonymous reader meanwhile wrote, in a letter dated August 23, 1886, that "[i]n regard to bringing up children, and girls in particular, mothers cannot be too careful. They should talk to them and show them what course to take and set an example themselves" (*NYF* Oct. 16, 1886).

This dialogue points to both the role of moral reform in late nineteenth-century racial uplift and the centrality of literate practices to uplift efforts. Driven by emphases on respectability and on "the belief that through education, economic independence, and sanitary living conditions, black people could thrive," such uplift efforts assumed many forms during this period (Logan, *"We Are Coming"* 153). The role that education played in uplift is particularly evident in a wide range of leadership expressions—many of which foregrounded links between literacy and social change. Black women activists used "speaking and writing" as "a form of doing, of social action"; social scientists such as W. E. B. Du Bois pursued empirical research aimed at improving African American lives; national Black organizations like the Bethel Literary and Historical Association fought discrimination through reading, research, discussion, and debate; and a multitude of periodicals provided literacy forums while celebrating African American educational and professional achievements and rallying for change (Peterson 3; F. Wilson 13, 17; McHenry, *Forgotten Readers* 141–43).

Gertrude Bustill Mossell was one such activist who led educational efforts by orchestrating dialogic literacy instruction among African American women. Her "Our Woman's Department" column for the *New York Freeman* functioned as an extracurricular learning space committed to African American women's literacy development and "true womanhood"—and by extension, to that of their daughters (*NYF* Dec. 26, 1885). The column in this sense fostered literacy activities intended to both edify readers and promote "the value of virtue" (*NYF* July 10, 1886). This was a significant topic of concern for many African American reformers at this time. As

Michele Mitchell explains, "[s]ince slavery had purportedly engendered wanton sexual behavior[,] . . . striving race members of the postemancipation period considered it critical that women radiate inviolable modesty" (11–12). Elite educated race leaders assumed considerable responsibility for this and related forms of uplift work. "During the post-Reconstruction period," Logan confirms, "those who had acquired education and prosperity felt a duty to educate those less fortunate. This education extended to morality and economy as well as reading and writing" (*We Are Coming* 21). Mossell contributed to these goals in innovative ways through the vibrant extracurricular space of "Our Woman's Department."

Importantly, the extracurriculum played a vital role in education and racial uplift at this time. The African American church was "an important site of literacy and language learning"; college debate teams "publicly performed" the "enterprise of racial uplift"; and African American clubwomen used literacy and "raised [their] voices" in their "roles as critical sources of support for the educational, cultural, social, political, and economic development of the African American community" (Moss 5; Gold 43; Royster 217). The press was also a crucial extracurricular space during this period. According to Jane Rhodes, nineteenth-century Black newspapers facilitated community building and functioned as "an influential forum for the assertion and dissemination of African Americans' ideas" (xii).[1] Logan has also observed that "[t]he black press offered multiple opportunities for [the] rhetorical education" of both journalists and their readers. Drawing on Hugh Blair, she argues that nineteenth-century African American newspapers disseminated knowledge, encouraged literacy activities, emphasized "diligent effort," and promoted "moral and mental improvement" among readers (*Liberating Language* 97–98).

Many women assumed leadership roles in the educational work of the Black press. As Royster argues, "[t]he periodical press was established right from the beginning as a primary mechanism whereby African American women participated in public discourse, demonstrated their desires to be agents of change, and were enabled by this forum to act on these desires" (220). One primary example is Josephine St. Pierre Ruffin's *Woman's Era*— "the first journal owned, managed, and edited by an African American woman to be dedicated to issues related to the lives and progress of African American women" (Royster, "Long Nineteenth Century" 328). A national newspaper that became the official publication of the National Federation of Afro-American Women, this 1890s periodical notably featured a column by

Mossell titled "The Open Court" (Streitmatter 69, 65). Mossell's column and *Woman's Era* as a whole constituted a powerful extracurricular space "that brought black women together, especially around the importance of literary activity"; indeed, the newspaper "fashioned itself as a primary source of both literary discussion and the printed texts that would allow readers to congregate and learn from each other" (McHenry, "Reading" 499). To this end, Mossell herself accentuated the importance of collaborative learning in stating her column's purpose. "The Open Court," she writes,

> is a department open to all, a letter box into which may be slipped the note that suggests the text, and even the sermon itself. It is intended to "fill a long felt want"; it is a department in which the people "are going to be heard" . . . We desire to impress upon the readers of this column they are expected to help "run it" by subscriptions, by literary contributions, by commenting upon the matter found within its limits, or upon that which they think the column should contain. (*WE* Apr. 1895).

The link between such literate activities and racial uplift is indicated by Mossell's thankfulness toward readers in the July 1895 issue: "I can but express my heartfelt gratitude to those who have shown and are still showing by every means in their power the interest they take in the uplifting of the womanhood of the race by their labors on behalf of the WOMAN'S ERA" (*WE* July 1895). In ways such as this, the Black press provided a crucial space for promoting public literacy in support of uplift.

This chapter addresses how Gertrude Bustill Mossell contributed to these efforts well before the emergence of "The Open Court" in 1895. By analyzing her column "Our Woman's Department" (1885–1887) for the *New York Freeman*, I show how Mossell encouraged public conversation about issues important to readers while teaching and modeling the type of studious civic engagement many believed would cultivate morality in young girls. I use the term *studious civic engagement* to refer to Mossell's promotion of "a communal and civic identity" for African American women and their daughters oriented around racial uplift and anchored in a dedication to literacy learning and virtuous behavior (Enoch, *Refiguring* 7). To promote such studious civic engagement, Mossell adopted a set of extracurricular teaching practices premised on interchanges with and among readers, who contributed in various ways to her research and writing process. Specifically, African American women who used the *Freeman* for literacy instruction often wrote to Mossell, who published and answered many of their letters. Mossell, in turn, relied on readers to supply raw materials for her column—asking "our friends who read this column to send us clippings or communications" on subjects ranging from "the Negro problem" to "some household experience" (*NYF* Aug. 28, 1886; *NYF* Dec. 25, 1886). By publishing readers' letters and inviting African American women into her writing process, Mossell inspired informed and collective conversations about vital public issues such as education, woman's suffrage, and sexuality.

"Our Woman's Department" is therefore a powerful extracurricular site situated within Black women's rich history of discursive public participation. As Royster asserts, "[t]hey have written for and spoken to many audiences within various social and professional networks, as well as to many general (that is, cross-community) audiences, including national and international groups" (104). In this chapter, I show how Mossell forged a public voice and invited robust discursive contributions from column readers through the pages of the *Freeman*, a nationally circulating newspaper that helped shape public attitudes and policy decisions within African American communities and across the larger United States.

The *Freeman* thus operates as part of "the ethnic public sphere—a set of broader institutions designed to provide intellectual and political leadership to the African-American population as a whole. Although these institutions were located primarily in the North," Carla Peterson explains, "they were conceived as national since they were dedicated to the national interest of all African Americans" (10). And while Peterson posits the elite leaning of the ethnic public sphere—observing that African American urban elites "separate[d] [themselves] out to some degree, working, speaking, and writing from within the ethnic public sphere"—Black newspapers nonetheless "addressed concerns across social class" while "educat[ing], unit[ing], and mobiliz[ing]" a wide variety of people (Peterson 10; Conaway 216). Mossell's "Our Woman's Department" occupies an influential and particularly inclusive part of the ethnic public sphere because it strongly values collaboration across class lines. The column operates in this inclusive, democratic capacity by way of ongoing dialogue between Mossell and her "diverse readership" (N. Wright 101). Through their contributions, readers constitute an active public committed to using this newspaper forum to address problems collectively, exchange ideas and resources, and work toward positive change. Importantly, this public transcends the boundaries of an imagined community. Mossell and her readers not only share a community identity and interest in racial uplift—they also energetically engage in dialogue with one another and interact through writing.

This chapter therefore argues that Mossell practices a reader-centered pedagogy to encourage extracurricular literacy and public participation among "Our Woman's Department" readers. I define the term *reader-centered pedagogy* in relation to current understandings of student-centered classrooms within composition studies. In her extracurricular teaching site, that is, Mossell foregrounds content drawn from readers' own lives, thoughts, knowledge, and experiences; she does not (solely) control the column's discourse. Her role is to co-investigate, facilitate, guide, and collaboratively pursue change alongside her readership. As a pedagogue, her work to this end echoes words by Harriet Jacobs, who wrote that Black teachers could "inspir[e]" African Americans "with confidence to help each other" (qtd. in Masur 82).

In this collaborative capacity, "Our Woman's Department" contributes to the writing instruction and rhetorical education of African American women by way of collective conversations that emphasize the central role of literacy and education in child-rearing. Positing idleness as a source of immorality and intelligent, moral mothers as the model through which daughters can flourish, "Our Woman's Department" aims to cultivate in mothers a studious civic engagement. Mossell to this end orchestrates continuous dialogic exchanges with readers while extending to mothers and their daughters various reading lists, proposed writing tasks, and research assignments. This pedagogical strategy allows Mossell to (1) prepare mothers to serve as moral and intellectual guides for their daughters (and African American women, broadly, to serve as role models for young girls in their communities) and (2) contribute to the larger project of racial uplift.

In advancing this argument, I build on important work by Nazera Sadiq Wright, who has recently argued in *Black Girlhood in the Nineteenth Century* that Mossell's "columns showed a wide readership how to educate their daughters so they could participate in civic life, become efficient household managers, and engage safely in work outside the home" (100). In surveying the editor's advice on a range of topics (including frugality and financial protection, spouse selection, and employment), Wright focuses especially on Black female employment and "navigat[ing] the public sphere safely"—arguing overall that Mossell "promote[d] models of public citizenship that widened the boundaries of black female purposefulness in the postbellum period" (100, 94). I further Wright's recovery of Mossell's "rarely studied columns" by analyzing their educational function through a different lens (100). By attending to the reader-driven roots of the column's conversation about female purity, I analyze the dynamics of Mossell's reader-centered pedagogy—presenting a detailed examination of the dialogic extracurricular literacy development fostered by "Our Woman's Department."

In the following pages, I first provide a biography that contextualizes Mossell's writing within African American journalism of this period—particularly the *New York Freeman*. Second, I discuss why "Our Woman's Department" may have highlighted African American mothers' role in ensuring moral purity (and proper literate practices) in young girls. In doing so, I compare Mossell's column to work by Ida B. Wells and the White Rose Mission founded by clubwoman and journalist Victoria Earle Matthews. Third, I analyze the dynamic ways in which "Our Woman's Department" offers extracurricular instruction to mothers in reading, writing, and research. I conclude with a treatment of Mossell's "Women and Journalism" series, which promotes specific reading and writing strategies designed to prepare aspiring women writers to shape public opinion through professional writing.

This chapter builds on my earlier discussion of Winifred Black Bonfils, whose teacherly ethos provided the occasion for children's civic involvement, public writing, and professional training in journalism. Whereas Black and the *Examiner* defined the issue that prompted such activities, Mossell from the start establishes a reader-centered space—one that invites African American women to identify the concerns around which their civic literacy will develop. A collaborative ethos thus drives Mossell's extracurricular pedagogy, which prepares readers to name, shape, and pursue solutions to important social problems. In doing so, "Our Woman's Department" not only blurs class boundaries but also furthers the democratic potential of newspapers as extracurricular literacy sites.

Gertrude Bustill Mossell and the Nineteenth-Century Black Press

Gertrude Bustill Mossell was born into the prominent Bustill family on July 3, 1855. "[A] Philadelphia family that had been politically active community builders for decades," the Bustills claimed a long-standing and "'continuous record' of achievement" (N. Wright 95; qtd. in Gatewood 100). Mossell's great-grandfather Cyrus Bustill founded a Philadelphia school for African American children and was a member of the first Black mutual aid society in the country (N. Wright 96). Cousin Sarah Mapps Douglass and her mother, Grace Bustill Douglass, were members of "and helped found" the Philadelphia Female Anti-Slavery Society and were both prominent abolitionists (Robbins and Gates 38; Guy-Sheftall 55). Mossell's father, Charles Hicks Bustill, and her uncle Joseph Bustill meanwhile assisted in the Underground Railroad (N. Wright 96). Tonya Bolden writes of Mossell that she "was a typical Bustill, a striver, a doer, an achiever." Growing up, Mossell and her sister were "encouraged" by their father "to immerse themselves in the Bible and such literary classics as *Paradise Lost*, as well as such contemporary reading material as the *Atlantic Monthly*" (Streitmatter 39). Mossell became absorbed in this reading—and indeed "any books available to her, and when there were no more books to read, she read the encyclopedia" (Price-Groff 79). As a pupil of the Institute for Colored Youth, Mossell secured "the best education available to black students in Philadelphia" (N. Wright 96).

Her journalistic involvement took shape with contributions of essays and poetry to the *Christian Recorder*, a "nationally distributed church newspaper"; Mossell then began writing for two Philadelphia-based African American papers—the *Echo* and *Independent*—while simultaneously teaching school in Philadelphia and Trenton during the 1870s (Streitmatter 39; N. Wright 97).[2] In 1881, she married Nathan Frances Mossell—a member of "a prominent family from upstate New York" and a student of the University of Pennsylvania Medical School who went on to become an influential Philadelphia physician and the founder of the Frederick Douglass Memorial Hospital, "the first hospital in the North to be staffed entirely by blacks" (N. Wright 99, 97; Streitmatter 47). Mossell began publishing under the byline Mrs. N. F. Mossell and commenced editing "Our Woman's Department" in 1885. Her journalistic work also included contributions to the *AME Church Review*, the *Philadelphia Times*, the *Press Republican*, and the *Indianapolis World* (N. Wright 98). Beyond her journalism, Mossell assisted in organizing Philadelphia's branches of the National Afro-American Council (forerunner to the National Association for the Advancement of Colored People) and the Young Woman's Christian Association, for which she also served on the board of directors (Streitmatter 47–48). Overall, as a teacher, writer, and social activist, Mossell strove to advance African American civil rights and literacy practices—her "eloquence and social stature ma[king] her an important figure around whom many women could rally" (Robbins and Gates 526). They did so enthusiastically throughout her editorship of "Our Woman's Department" for the *New York Freeman*, the leading African American newspaper in the United States at the time.

The *Freeman*—established in 1884 after publisher T. Thomas Fortune fully acquired the *New York Globe*—held its name for only three years before becoming the *New York Age* (N. Wright 98). In the period when the *Freeman* emerged, the African American press was vigorous and vastly influential. Publications like the *Freedom's Journal, Colored American*, and Frederick Douglass's *North Star* had played prominent roles in the fight for abolition, and Black newspapers proceeded to "gr[o]w at an astonishing rate following the Civil War," according to Teresa Zackodnik.[3] "This explosion facilitated the work of black women in journalism, both North and South" (204). Publications like the *Freeman* were among those "important outlets for women journalists," which simultaneously served as "valuable forum[s] for political discourse within the black community" (Harris xxxi; Conaway 216). As a national Black newspaper circulating throughout the North and West, the *Freeman* promoted the circulation of political ideas, educated and joined together readers, and rallied for change (N. Wright 98; Conaway 216).

At its helm was editor and publisher T. Thomas Fortune, "the dean of black journalism," who was also "supportive of women journalists" (Streitmatter 148; Zackodnik 133). Headlines such as "A System of Slavery" reflected the editor's belief that it was the responsibility of the Black press to oppose "outrages" and social injustices (Rhodes 204). Condemning exploitive Arkansas employment systems that prevented Black laborers from "ris[ing] above the most abject and miserable poverty," this particular article joined a multitude of others in addressing urgent political issues and racial injustices (*NYF* Aug. 7, 1886). These issues and injustices included the oppressive southern prison system, obstructions to Black voting rights, "The Race Question in Education," and lynching. "The Southern Lynch Law: Bloody Murder Rampant," for instance, recounted the mob lynching of a Louisiana laborer while also critiquing "[t]he white press" for failing to "publish half the crimes committed upon colored people by their white brothers" (*NYF* May 15, 1886). Also present in the *Freeman* during this period were headlines such as "Influence of the Saloon" and "Sketch of

Shaw University: Growth of a North Carolina Institution," indicating the newspaper's investment in promoting racial uplift (*NYF* Dec. 25, 1886, and Jan. 15, 1887).

Much like "Our Woman's Department," the *Freeman* reflects dialogic exchange with its readers. One example involves its sketch of Prudence Crandall, a white Quaker schoolteacher whose education of African American female students in Connecticut resulted in her 1830s arrest and subsequent poverty (*NYF* Jan. 30, 1886). In a later issue, the *Freeman* featured a letter from First Sergeant John M. Harper, which read:

> I see in your paper of Jan. 30, 1886, a piece headed "Miss Prudence Crandall—the Heroic Woman living in Poverty." I have a copy of a magazine with a short sketch of her history in 1833, and her trials with her school for colored girls. At that time there were very few of her mind among the white people, and it seems none brave enough to take the stand she did, when in answer to a clergyman's wife, who said, "If you continue that colored girl in school it will not be sustained." Her reply was that it might sink, "for I shall not turn her out."
>
> It is well to say "Heroic Woman," but must we stop there? Is that all which is to be done or said, while our race is continually making up money for monuments for dead heroes and friends, and yet overlook our living heroine who alone, away back in the dark days, dared to try and elevate the race?
>
> Now, Mr. Editor, can you not receive or name some one who will take contributions toward helping this poor woman? (*NYF* Feb. 27, 1886)

In response to this entreaty, Fortune offered to take contributions for Crandall—deeming her "eminently worthy of any assistance we could give her" (*NYF* Feb. 27, 1886). Harper's assertion that "I think if you would speak through your paper something can be done . . . " affirms the role of newspapers in facilitating charitable work and civic participation during the late nineteenth century while also revealing a parallel between this fund-raising effort and those of the *San Francisco Examiner.*

The "Our Woman's Department" audience likely read (or at least noticed) this dialogic exchange concerning Crandall. Indeed, the February 27, 1886, "Our Woman's Department" column appeared adjacent to Harper's letter and nearby articles on the "Status of the Irish Question," "Hereditary Influence," and Thomas McCants Stewart's book *Liberia: the Americo-Africa Republic*—in addition to another letter from African

American Sergeant Charles B. Turner rearticulating Fortune's call for increased support of the Black press, a vehicle for securing "rights as citizens" (*NYF* Feb. 27, 1886). N. Wright has observed that this "cross-pollination layout strategy suggests that domestic activities, the politics of the nation, and current events of the world would not have been viewed as mutually exclusive"; to this end, "Mossell's advice column would have been an invaluable resource for African American women well versed in world events, politics, financial matters, and social matters" (99).

Importantly, the *Freeman* and *Woman's Era* were not the only newspapers for which Mossell penned a column. She also became the woman's editor of the *Indianapolis World* for a period and launched its own "Our Woman's Department." In its first appearance on June 11, 1892, Mossell references her past work for the *Freeman* (now the *New York Age*):

> As it is the custom upon assuming the charge of any special of a paper or magazine to make some sort of salute to the hoped for audience, I shall esteem it both as a privilege and a duty to do likewise. Some five years ago, I edited a Woman's Department in the *New York Age* and at the present I have charge of an editorial column in a local journal. This week I assume the new duty. There is always a feeling that each week has its quota of good work to be done where one is part of the great power contained [*sic*] in the press, of a race or nation. And on starting forth once more on this mission to Our Women and Children, I feel that I have my garden plot to be planted and watered to the bringing forth of fruit that I hope may prove worthy of gathering. May its fragrance pervade many homes lingering as a sweet memory. (*IW* June 11, 1892)

Consistent with her *Freeman* column, Mossell also invites "those interested" to "send communication to my address stating what interests them most and giving helpful suggestions."

Statements such as this in the *Indianapolis World*, *New York Freeman*, and *Woman's Era* suggest that reader-centered writing was a cornerstone of her journalism. A dialogic stance even surfaces in *The Work of the Afro-American Woman* (1894).[4] After listing publications in the chapter "A Sketch of Afro-American Literature," Mossell writes: "[w]e should be glad if authors would send us the names of omitted volumes to be used in a possible future edition" (66). This example demonstrates that even beyond journalism, Mossell valued reader input.

During her career, Mossell also contributed to magazines such as *the Colored American Magazine, Our Women and Children*, the *African Methodist Episcopal Church Review, Ladies' Home Journal*, and *Ringwood's Afro-American Journal of Fashion* (Streitmatter 40). She then diverted from journalism in 1902 to produce a different type of text—a children's book titled *Little Dansie's One Day at Sabbath School*. Around this time, her newspaper writing waned as Mossell adopted a growing focus on involvement with civic organizations and the Frederick Douglass Memorial Hospital until her death on January 21, 1948, at ninety-two years old (47–48).

Contemporary critics deemed Mossell an exemplary journalist. An Ohio newspaper asserted in 1887 that "Mrs. Mossell is a ready writer, a good gatherer of news, has literary judgment and is altogether a clever woman." *The Journalist* echoed this praise in 1889 when proclaiming, "[o]n matters pertaining to women and the race, there is no better author among our female writers. Her style is clear, compact and convincing" (qtd. in Streitmatter 46). The *Indianapolis Freeman* called Mossell "one of the most gifted, as well as versatile women writers of the country," while I. Garland Penn deemed her "a telling writer, her thoughts being clear and clean-cut" in the first published history of African American journalism (qtd. in Lutes, *Front-Page* 47; qtd. in Streitmatter 46). The remainder of the chapter explores the powerful means by which Mossell appealed to readers of "Our Woman's Department" for the purposes of collaborative extracurricular literacy learning and activism.

Refuting Stereotypes and Mitigating Threats to Black Females

In the decades following emancipation, emphasis on moral purity was an integral part of racial uplift—a means of working to oppose vicious stereotypes and curb white crimes. Michele Mitchell explains that during this period, "black women were considered sexually available to any man," and "mainstream discourse generally portrayed black women as indiscriminate and insatiable, black men as oversexed and bestial, and black children as so sexually precocious as to preclude innocence" (11). Of the unjust defamation of African American women, Ida B. Wells in 1887 commented that of all "accusations . . . none sting so deeply and keenly as the taunt of immorality; the jest and sneer with which our women are spoken of, and the utter incapacity or refusal to believe there are among us mothers, wives and maidens who have attained a true, noble, and refining womanhood" (qtd. in Robbins and Gates 564). It is not surprising, then, that much literature and periodical writings "featuring black girls advised parents on how to cultivate upright conduct in black girls" during this period (N. Wright 19). Among Black women reformers, particular efforts were made "to counter the prevalent stereotype of black female immorality and to combat the sexual exploitation of black women at the hands of white men that had been a central feature of slavery and continued as a form of racial domination after the Civil War" (Odem 27).

The impetus for discussions of female purity in "Our Woman's Department" was a letter that highlighted such sexual exploitation of black females by white men. When M. H. W. bemoaned "the immorality of our young girls" on July 10, 1886, she also asked: "And who is it bringing them down? The white men of our land. Oh, how I despise these men! Can nothing be done to stop it? Who will do it? There is a great work of this kind to be done" (*NYF* July 10, 1886). In response, a second reader's letter on the subject appeared two weeks later, on July 24, 1886, in the column:

ITHACA, July 12, '86.

DEAR MRS. MOSSELL:—

Being an earnest admirer of THE FREEMAN, I take great pleasure in perusing its various columns, especially the one devoted to women. In reading your last edition I saw a letter from "M. H. W." which impelled me to write this in reply. I have seen the effect that the immorality of our women and girls has had upon the society in which they move, and I am inclined to think that the white men have less to do with this evil than some of the mothers and the women of maturer years, who, by their own examples teach their daughters and friends lessons of immorality, and I think the sin should be laid at their door. When mothers who are jealous of their daughters' good name will exclude from their homes all young people who are likely to lead them astray, and shun themselves the appearance of evil, then, and not until then, will they be able to teach their daughters the value of virtuous and upright living.

M. E. L.

This letter highlights the dialogic nature of "Our Woman's Department." Similar to Black's *Examiner* articles, the column prompts readers' public writing about issues they care about.

Unlike the "Little Jim" campaign, however, this conversation in "Our Woman's Department" was instigated by a reader (M. H. W.) who in turn drives the public writing of others. M. E. L. opens with reference to the previous reader's letter: "Being an earnest admirer of THE FREEMAN, I take great pleasure in perusing its various columns, especially the one devoted to women. In reading your last edition I saw a letter from 'M. H. W.' which impelled me to write this in reply." Notably, however, her letter adopts a different emphasis in foregrounding the responsibility of mothers, "who, by their own examples teach their daughters and friends lessons of immorality" (*NYF* July 24, 1886).

Other readers such as E. V. M. agreed:

ITHACA, July 27, 1886.

DEAR MRS. MOSSSEL:—

I am a devoted reader of THE FREEMAN, and especially "Our Woman's Department." I perused with unusual interest the communications of last week. I agree with "M. E. L." in her statement that white men had less to do with the immorality of our girls than the mothers. Immorality is an inherited disease, just as much so as consumption or scrofula is inherited physically. We must take into calculation the hereditary tendency. There is such a thing as good blood and there is such a thing as bad blood. There are families that have had a moral twist in them for a hundred years back. They have not been careful to keep the family record in that regard. There have been escapades, and maraudings, and scoundrelisms, and moral deficiences all the way back. Our girls are not only being ruined by white men, but by colored men as well. There is nothing said about the immorality of our boys. Mothers should teach their sons and daughters alike the beauty of morality. Who has the mind or character in hand while it is yet so flexible and ductile that it can be turned in any direction, or formed in any shape? It is the mother. From her own nature and the nature of her child, it results that its first impressions must be taken from her. And she has every advantage for discharging the duty. She is always with her child—if she is where she ought to be—sees continually the workings of its faculties; when they need be retrained, and when led and attracted. Early as she may begin her task, let her be assured that her labor will not be lost, because undertaken too soon. Mind, from the first hour of its existence, is ever acting. Let mothers watch, and they will be surprised to find the elements of character already fixed when she has least expected it. It behooves us as a class, as a race, as mothers, daughters and sisters, to be up and doing if we would counteract the debasing influence and evils of immorality. The sooner we commence, the sooner will success crown our efforts. As this is my first attempt and fearing I am trespassing upon your valuable time, I will close. Wishing you success, I am yours truly,

E. V. M.

"I agree with 'M. E. L.' in her statement that white men had less to do with the immorality of our girls than the mothers," writes E. V. M. in this letter (*NYF* Aug. 14, 1886). Characterizing herself as "a devoted reader of THE FREEMAN, and especially 'Our Woman's Department,'" E. V. M. questions, "Who has the mind or character in hand while it is yet so flexible and ductile that it can be turned in any direction, or formed in any shape? It is the mother" (*NYF* Aug. 14, 1886).

Although such statements may appear conservative from a modern perspective, these letters did not articulate atypical positions for the time period. As Mary E. Odem argues, late nineteenth-century African American women "did not focus solely on the sexual aggression of white men. They also sought to reform the moral behavior and attitudes of the young men and women of their race through education and voluntary efforts within the black community" (27). Many reformers looked to mothers—in conjunction with teachers and community leaders—to provide education in moral character. Lecturer and novelist Frances E. W. Harper called for an "enlightened motherhood" in a speech delivered before the Brooklyn Literary Society in 1892, for example: "We need mothers who are capable of being character builders," she proclaimed. "This is one of the greatest needs of the hour" (qtd. in Robbins and Gates 284, 292). During the same period, African American clubwomen held "Mothers' Meetings" centered on the welfare of children that "direct[ed] attention to women's needs as they reflected and revealed the needs of children and families" (Royster 215). The 1897 resolutions of the second annual Atlanta University Conference deemed the home "the great school for the molding of character," while endowing Black mothers with moral responsibility for their families (qtd. in F. Wilson 99).

E. V. M. articulates a similar vision in her estimation of mothers:

> From her own nature and the nature of her child, it results that its first impressions must be taken from her. And she has every advantage for discharging the duty. She is always with her child . . . sees continually the workings of its faculties; when they need to be restrained, and when led and attracted. Early as she may begin her task, let her be assured that her labor will not be lost, because undertaken too soon. (*NYF* Aug. 14, 1886)

This individualized, mother-oriented response may have possibly appealed to Mossell and such readers because it created empowerment within Black female communities—particularly for those women who may have often felt politically powerless to change systemic inequalities—through its focus on preventive action. As Mossell writes in response to M. H. W.'s letter, "help is needed. Who shall give it, and how? In the first place, 'an ounce of prevention is worth a pound of cure.'" (*NYF* July 10, 1886). Proceeding to catalog advice for mothers on raising virtuous daughters, Mossell, along with readers M. E. L. and E. V. M., foreground Black women's agency more strongly than white men's responsibility in advocating a preventive form of education—one that noticeably resonates with Victoria Earle Matthews's White Rose Mission.

Matthews, a leader in the Black women's club movement and "one of the major figures in social welfare on the East Coast," founded the White Rose Mission in 1897 and White Rose Travelers' Aid Society subsequently in 1905 as responses to sexual threats facing Black female migrants to New York and other cities (Logan, *We Are Coming* 172–73; F. Wilson 94). Her efforts prioritized preventive education. As Logan notes, "Matthews recognized that it was not worth the time and money to ferret out the culprits. It was better, she claimed, to enlighten the women to the dangers that awaited them and to teach them how to search for jobs intelligently. Most, she pleaded, should stay at home" (*We Are Coming* 173). Matthews's social welfare organizations and "Our Woman's Department" share a commitment to protective care of African American communities. And while, overall, Mossell's column promoted both "push[ing] to remove structural obstacles" and "advis[ing] young people how best to cope with" such obstacles, the topic of female purity as it unfolded in "Our Woman's Department" gravitated toward the latter response (N. Wright 95).

This approach is somewhat distinguished from that of Ida B. Wells, whose anti-lynching journalism spotlights the atrocities of white crimes against African Americans—including white men's sexual assault of Black girls. While "Our Woman's Department" shifts away from this focus, Wells confronts it in detail. This is highlighted by a passage from *Southern Horrors* that describes a white man

> who outraged a little Afro-American girl, and, from the physical injuries received, she has been ruined for life. He was jailed for six months, discharged, and is now a detective in that city. In the same city, last May, a white man outraged an Afro-American girl in a drug store. He was arrested, and released on bail at the trial. It was rumored that five hundred Afro-Americans had organized to lynch him. Two hundred and fifty white citizens armed themselves with Winchesters and guarded him. A cannon was placed in front of his home, and the Buchanan Rifles (State Militia) ordered to the scene for his protection. The Afro-American mob did not materialize. Only two weeks before Eph. Grizzard, who had only been *charged* with rape upon a white woman, had been taken from the jail, with Governor Buchanan and the police and militia standing by, dragged through the streets in broad daylight, knives plunged into him at every step . . . A naked, bloody example of the blood-thirstiness of the nineteenth-century civilization of the Athens of the South! No cannon or military was called out in his defense. He dared to visit a white woman. (Wells-Barnett 26–27)

Wells foregrounds the brutal hypocrisy of white communities governing the excusal of Black female assault by documenting two examples of sexual assault and the murder of a Black man who "dared to visit a white woman." And while Wells at times throughout her career adopts strategies that more closely resemble those of "Our Woman's Department" (she writes in 1887 that "[o]ur race is no exception to the rest of humanity, in its susceptibility to weakness . . . We only wish to be given the same credit for our virtues that others receive, and once the idea gains ground that worth is respected, from whatever source it may originate, a great incentive to good morals will have been given"), her anti-lynching journalism strongly exposes violent systemic racism (qtd. in Robbins and Gates 564–65).

The front page of the *Indianapolis World* on July 2, 1892, in fact encapsulates the different rhetorical strategies of Wells and Mossell. This issue contains work by Mossell and Wells published on the same page—Mossell's "Our Woman's Department" and Wells's "How the Constitution Is Being Trampled under Foot by the South." In the latter article, Wells reprints the *Memphis Free Speech* leader that was the impetus for her exile ("If southern men are not careful they will over-reach themselves and public sentiment will have a reaction . . ."). She then quotes a violent threat printed in the *Evening Scimitar* in response to her article, reporting that "whites had declared that they would bleed my face and hang me in front of the court house." On this same front page, Mossell meanwhile cautions young Black men against the perils of "unbecoming" behavior:

> This is the season when numbers of the young men of the race come into this city enroute for the adjacent watering places. Their behavior in many instances is very rude and unbecoming, gratuitous insults are often offered to the quiet and sedate equally . . . with the rude women of their own race. This is the rule and not the exception the very conduct shown toward a white woman in their own section which would have been met with threats of lynching . . . It would be well for our home makers, our pastors, and teachers to dwell on this point to the young men for in many instances they are sowing the wind of insult to their own women that will force them to reap the whirlwind of lynching if continued as a habit until it reaches the women of a race whose fathers, husbands and brothers have determined to protect them from such conduct at all hazards. (*IW* July 2, 1892)

Both Wells and Mossell address lynching in their respective articles, yet each does so using different rhetorical strategies aimed at distinct goals.[5] While Wells spotlights brutal threats of racist violence, Mossell draws attention to what "our home makers, our pastors, and teachers" can do to prevent such violence. Specifically, she advises their rhetorical intervention in types of young men's behaviors that could be used by whites as an excuse for lynching. Both writers ultimately value education. Yet while Wells broadcasts resonant facts about lynching (writing in *Southern Horrors* that "[t]he people must know before they can act, and there is no educator to compare with the press" [Wells-Barnett 42]), Mossell tasks mothers and community leaders with assuming a pedagogical and preventive role for young Black men. Put differently, she calls on readers to become teachers themselves.

The cultural power of the African American teacher may in fact further explain why the conversation in "Our Woman's Department" about female purity shifted to emphasize an individualized mother-oriented response. For within Black communities at this time, "teachers were the figures most often presented as role models for girls and young women." Recognized for their "intellectual attainment and assistance to the race," teachers were considered indispensable to both local education efforts and the broader "'up lift' of the entire black community" (Carlson 65).[6] Mossell promotes mothers' role in this project by preparing them to act as effective teachers. She even explicitly argues that home training must complement formal schooling. "Parents and teachers should co-operate in an attempt to keep the minds of the little ones filled with pure thoughts," she wrote in her first *Freeman* column (*NYF* Dec. 26, 1885). Later, the column reaffirmed that "a large amount of instruction given to the girls in the public schools is lost, from the fact that it is not preceded or supplemented by the home or family training" (*NYF* Aug. 28, 1886). In response, "Our Woman's Department" privileged and enthusiastically promoted mothers' extracurricular literacy practices, "true womanhood," and corresponding education of children (*NYF* Dec. 26, 1885).

"Our Woman's Department": A Reader-Centered Extracurricular Space

The "Our Woman's Department" column of the *New York Freeman* first appeared on the second page of the December 26, 1885, issue. Mossell's column announced the following "aim":

> This column will be devoted to the interests of women and will aim to promote true womanhood, especially that of the African race. Suggestions as to how this department may be improved and its usefulness increased will be gladly received. All success, progress or needs of our women will be given prompt mention. We shall be glad also to receive for exchange or for our book table such publications as may be deemed helpful.

All communications or contributions for this department should be addressed to Mrs. N. F. Mossell, 924 Lombard street, Philadelphia. (*NYF* Dec. 26, 1885)

Mossell's reference to "true womanhood" here recalls the nineteenth-century social image of the pure, pious, domestic, and submissive white middle-class wife and mother for whom child-rearing and family devotion were the "apex of womanly fulfillment" (Welter 21; Theriot 17). Yet the "cult of true womanhood" differed significantly from its "counterpart" expression, "[t]he ideology of black female moral leadership" (Waters 373–74). While this latter ideology "may have modeled itself consciously on the white cult as a way of gaining credibility in a racist society," Kristin Waters asserts that the two ideologies were far from interchangeable (374).

First of all, emphasis on passivity and domesticity in the cult of true womanhood inadequately captures the "proactive[ness]" of African American women "engaged in every part of public life" (375).[7] In cities like New York, for instance, African American women "assumed prominent roles within the black community." "Not only were they not dependent on black men," explains Jane E. Dabel, "but they were able to negotiate with whites and shape the city in ways that black men could not. As a result, they forged autonomous identities, created family stability, became activists, resisted racial attacks, shaped the geography of the black community, and provided financial security for themselves and their families" (4).

Second, while the cult of true womanhood was constructed to (comparatively) restrain white middle-class women, African American women generated the ideology of Black female moral leadership for the explicit purposes of empowerment and uplift (Waters 374).[8] "[S]truggle against oppression" characterized the ideology of Black female moral leadership, which aimed "to help bring women to consciousness about social conditions in modern society and about the kinds of activities, education, and organizing required to bring about change" (375). Alternatively termed "Black Victoria" by Shirley J. Carlson, the African American female moral leader was assertive, vocal, and "highly esteemed by her community which frequently applauded her as a 'race woman' and role model for young people" (62).

Through her "Our Woman's Department" column and influential civic engagement, Mossell contributed to the period's wave of Black female moral leadership by orchestrating extracurricular education, promoting morality, and presenting herself as "the embodiment of [her] message"—much like many other Black female rhetors during the nineteenth century (Logan, *"We Are Coming"* 22). She both embodied and fostered studious civic engagement—sharing reading lists, proposing writing assignments, and encouraging discussion and debate in a column that aspired to cultivate habits of self-enrichment, respectability, and community concern among African American women and girls. This process notably relied on assistance from readers in the form of letters, research initiatives, and dialogue (among other literacy activities). Moreover, by involving readers of various socioeconomic backgrounds in the column's operations, Mossell blurs class boundaries in ways that resemble Black's "Little Jim" campaign. The conclusion to M. H. W.'s letter crystallizes this boundary blurring: "[y]ou will see that these few words are from no scholar, only the words of a poor tried woman." The impetus for the column's conversation about female purity, this letter points to ways in which the work of Black female moral leadership involved inclusive, collaborative efforts.

The second part of the mission statement for "Our Woman's Department" furthers this collaborative emphasis: "Suggestions as to how this department may be improved and its usefulness increased will be gladly received" (*NYF* Dec. 26, 1885). One of the first women's columns edited by a Black female journalist published in an African American newspaper, "Our Woman's Department" notably depended on dialogue between Mossell and her readers.[9] This practice was somewhat common among female editors of the period, whose "editorial role allowed them to create a sense of communication—or 'conversations'—with and among readers" (Harris xxvii). Readers of "Our Woman's Department" participated in column dialogue by writing to Mossell, who invited their "communications" and "contributions" and published and responded to many of their letters (*NYF* Dec. 26, 1885). These letters influenced subjects discussed in the column and helped shape the direction of conversation about them. When M. H. W. introduced the issue of female impurity, for instance, Mossell credited her reader's influence, writing, "[w]e have never spoken in this column of this evil, but believe from the receipt of this letter that the time has come to say what we can to help these erring ones" (*NYF* June 10, 1886).

Mossell not only credits reader input—she actively solicits it. On December 25, 1886, for example, readers are encouraged to send Mossell "some household experience, some remedy for trifling injuries, a description of some department of industrial work, a record of good accomplished by some invalid woman, and so on." Similarly, Mossell requests that readers "[s]end us clippings, receipts, suggestions" and "write us letters"—"[n]ot do our work, but help us to do our own in the best possible manner" (*NYF* July 17, 1886). Mossell hence situates reader input as central to the column's success. Both statements indicate that she seeks a wide range of resources to bolster "Our Woman's Department" and collectively benefit African American women. These entreaties create a sense of interconnectedness among contributors who cannot see one another face-to-face but whose shared responsibility in this project intimately links them together.

The collective nature of "Our Woman's Department" is again indicated by Mossell's expressed "desire to draw near my readers": "women of the race with which we are allied. Their hopes and fears and interests are to be here looked after" (*NYF* Dec. 25, 1886). Importantly, Mossell shares this charge with a broad audience. She addresses women across a range of occupations—"[w]e invite the domestic women, the intellectual, the temperance reformer, the White Cross workers, the suffragist, the missionary worker, and the mothers generally to draw near and by suggestion or comment tell us how they desire to have the work go forward"—as well as those in particularly marginalized positions. "If you feel cross, if you are homely, or illiterate, or what not, that prevents you from succeeding in influencing those you come in daily contact with, here is a place where untrammeled by such drawbacks you may wield a power for good" (*NYF* Dec. 25, 1886). This invitation emphasizes inclusivity by characterizing "Our Woman's Department" as an extracurricular space for a diverse audience.

Overall, Mossell promotes a democratic form of civically oriented literacy development. And while it is difficult to identify who, exactly, read the *Freeman* during this period, it is likely that the newspaper reached a wide range of individuals. Martin Dann in *The Black Press, 1827–1890: The Quest for National Identity* explains that "[p]apers passed from hand to hand or, in the time-worn tradition, were posted in a local pub or other common meeting place. In this way, a single paper may have been (and probably often was) read by a hundred people" (7). Patrick S. Washburn adds that income restrictions among many Black families necessitated practices of sharing: since "many could not afford a black paper even if they could read, one copy of a paper was sometimes passed throughout an entire neighborhood" (50). Mossell therefore extends a role to all readers, regardless of socioeconomic status, in the column's collective operations.

"Every letter expressing a felt want is helpful and suggestive," she assures, "and I feel I am no longer working in the dark. Send letters, join friend to friend, and bind us in a helpful sisterhood" (*NYF* July 10, 1886).

The third part of the column's mission statement—"All success, progress or needs of our women will be given prompt mention"—expands this "helpful sisterhood," as Mossell complements her community-oriented ethos with that of other accomplished African American women. She spotlights the success and civic contributions of professionals such as Miss Peterson, whose "energy" resulted in "one more school . . . open to teachers of color in Philadelphia" (*NYF* Feb. 6, 1886). Similarly, Mossell praises ordained minister Sarah A. Hughes of Raleigh, North Carolina, for becoming "it is believed, the first colored woman preacher in the world" (*NYF* Mar. 27, 1886). The editor's short sketches of accomplished Black women also notably link education, literacy, and uplift. This is evident in a column sketch that lauds two female oratory school graduates and encourages readers to follow suit:

> Among the class of ladies graduating at the National School of Oratory in Philadelphia last week were Miss Tillie Herbert of Trenton, a teacher at West Chester, Pa., and Miss Edwina Kruse, a teacher at Wilmington, Del. Both of these ladies acquainted themselves creditably to themselves and the race, and we hope others will emulate their example, that the race may continue to be represented in this school. To read well is an accomplishment that will always be found useful, both for the instruction and amusement of oneself and friends. (*NYF* June 19, 1886)

These tributes promote the importance of education while upholding such women as models of professional attainment and civic contribution—in this way promoting "an orientation toward achievement" among readers and their daughters (Shaw 1).

Mossell's sketches resonate with those published by other late nineteenth-century African American periodicals that "praised individual and joint achievements, victories, and accomplishments to promote shared values and shared communal identities" (Fleckenstein 250). These periodicals included *Woman's Era*, which, like Mossell's "Our Woman's Department," emphasized education and uplift. A May 1894 profile of Victoria Earle Matthews, for instance, was accompanied by this introduction by S. Elizabeth Frazier: "We read daily of the progress women are making for the elevation of their sex and are proud to note noble examples among us, who follow in their train, laboring earnestly, yet modestly for their sex and the upbuilding of the race . . . Surely we cannot know too much of their genius and merits, for the inspiration of our girls" (qtd. in McHenry, "Reading" 499). Sketches such as these in widely read outlets including *Woman's Era* and "Our Woman's Department" underscored "the central contribution of black women to the building of the nation" (499).

The last part of the mission statement for "Our Woman's Department" emphasizes the column's intertextuality: "[w]e shall be glad also to receive for exchange or for our book table such publications as may be deemed helpful." Readers appear to have responded to this invitation by sharing printed material from other publications on a wide variety of topics. Indeed, a rich array of exchange material appears in "Our Woman's Department," addressing parenting, education, political representation for African Americans, and much more. This material was published in the column either verbatim or mixed with Mossell's own writing and commentary (Hutelmyer 10–11). Importantly, this material was actively solicited. Exhortations for exchange publications appear not only in the mission statement but also in the body text of many columns. "We should feel indebted to our readers," Mossell writes, "if they would send us from time to time short sketches of value to the Woman's Department, clippings from papers about the race and sex. Many facts worthy of note escape us" (*NYF* June 19, 1886).

Requests like this one contributed to the wide range of periodicals represented within "Our Woman's Department." Exchange material appeared from African American and mainstream newspapers such as the *Indianapolis World*, *New York World*, *Cleveland Gazette*, *Chicago Inter-Ocean*, *Chicago Herald*, and *Philadelphia Times* as well as from magazines such as *Good Housekeeping*, *Babyhood*, *Demorest's Monthly*, *Faith and Works*, *Fashion Quarterly*, and *Woman's Work*. Their content ranged considerably. A clipping from the *Chicago Inter-Ocean*, for instance, featured statistics reporting that in the United States, "the women largely outnumber the men"—evidence of "the importance of the question of self-support to womankind" (*NYF* Feb. 6, 1886). The *Philadelphia Bulletin* meanwhile advertised classes for working women at the New Century Guild, while myriad clippings on domesticity, child-rearing, and fashion also appeared in "Our Woman's Department." Often derived from white publications such as *Good Housekeeping*, *Babyhood*, and *Christian Union*, these included an excerpt from *Babyhood* offering instructions for making baby slippers (*NYF* Apr. 3, 1886).

Importantly, Mossell did not only reprint but also "select[ed] and invent[ed]" from white cultural materials to express her own aims and interests, along with those of her readership (Pratt 36). Her April 10, 1886, column, for example, adapts a selection from the *Christian Union* denouncing "vulgar" preoccupations with style. "Thus says a writer in the *Christian Union*," Mossell responds, "but we are hopeful of a change for the better. Intelligent women throughout our land must at last come to see that living according to their means is the only right way to build up happy homes" (*NYF* Apr. 10, 1886). Mossell here adopts her topic from a white publication while altering its tone and purpose. Specifically, she reinvents this exchange publication to issue an optimistic appeal to readers to practice frugality and further racial uplift.

On the whole, exchange publications play a major role in "Our Woman's Department," appearing in the majority of the forty-seven total columns (Hutelmyer 4). Their presence affords the column a rich intertextuality, and the sheer number of exchange publications suggests the large number of readers who contributed. Widespread circulation of the *Freeman* enabled this process to operate on a large scale—presumably helping Mossell gather source material from geographically diverse areas. To this end, the editor admits the impossibility of personally subscribing "for all the papers that would be helpful to us in our work" and thereby invests readers with a portion of the responsibility (*NYF* July 17, 1886). Readers were therefore a crucial link to the broad range of writers and periodicals represented in "Our Woman's Department." Ultimately, the column's emphasis on exchange publications furthered readers' extracurricular literacy development by encouraging their regular reading of such periodicals and training them to select appropriate material for a particular audience.

MOTHERS AS TEACHERS: INSTRUCTING DAUGHTERS

The "Our Woman's Department" mission statement set the stage for a variety of pedagogical practices intended to foster the extracurricular education of African American women and, by extension, young girls. This instruction occurs both directly and indirectly over the course of the column's duration. First, "Our Woman's Department" explicitly instructs mothers on what and how they should teach daughters. Second, Mossell further prepares readers for this task through reading lists, writing activities, and research assignments—edifying mothers so that they might better teach their daughters.

Mossell's response to M. H. W. in the July 10, 1886, issue offers one example of her explicit instruction. After advising mothers to "watch and work without ceasing," she highlights the importance of "innocent pleasures," modest dress, frugality, and upright "associates" for young girls. Mossell continues:

> Gain and keep their confidence. Don't frighten them into lying. Find out if they are in the habit of meeting men on the street. Accept the fact that your daughter has become a woman, listen to her conversation, read a letter of hers occasionally. Teach her the value of virtue. Don't be afraid to speak to your daughter about such matters as are possibly discussed by her daily with her schoolmates. Get good books, written especially for girls. They would be a cheap library. Let her read "Chastity," by Dio Lewis. Teach her true, and not false, modesty. (*NYF* July 10, 1886)

Mossell here provides direct instruction for raising daughters. She advises mothers to encourage conversation and (it is implied) confront issues of sexuality, opening channels of communication with daughters. Her emphasis on cultivating "confidence" notably echoes an earlier assertion that "[l]ittle children should be made to feel that mother is their best friend"—a means of urging mothers to project qualities of the friend or "schoolmate" to remain trustworthy in children's eyes. Mothers must "get and retain their confidence as long as possible," Mossell writes, "for the child that begins to have secrets from its mother is getting away from its best safeguard" (*NYF* Jan. 30, 1886).

The editor also proposes recommended reading in the form of Lewis's *Chastity* (1874). Beyond its promotion of purity, this recommendation also points to the central place of reading in nineteenth-century culture. Indeed, the topic of reading "circulated widely" beyond school boundaries in a range of venues including "religious and political circles," periodicals, libraries, and lyceums and literary societies (Carr et al. 87). Within extracurricular sites in African American communities, the importance of instructive reading was often tied to uplift. As Elizabeth McHenry writes of the Black women's club movement, for instance, "[t]hrough their own literacy activities and through the campaigns they initiated to disseminate their literacy and literature in black communities, clubwomen asserted their belief that reading was essential to the development of a racial dignity" ("Reading" 494). By assigning material such as Lewis's *Chastity*, "Our Woman's Department" similarly supports uplift by operating as a forum for the promotion of extracurricular reading. Mossell to this end further suggests that mothers keep a "cheap library"—advice that anticipates race leader Julia Layton Mason's 1902 recommendation that African American parents "no matter how humble [their] home" should "strive to start a good library" (qtd. in Mitchell 178). The library that Mossell proposes here is one containing "good books, written especially for girls." Ultimately, then, Mossell advises mothers to design reading curriculums for daughters that will facilitate both literacy development and moral learning.

A related passage in an earlier issue of "Our Woman's Department" suggests why such an emphasis on wholesome education must be sustained by parents. As Mossell relays: "Most nations teach their girls carefully that which will be required of them. American parents do not seem to realize the necessity for this training as fully as they should. Too often after the routine of school days is at an end that of the ball room begins, and the spare time is spent in gossip, novel reading, or dawdling" (*NYF* Apr. 3, 1886).[10] *Freeman* readers shared this concern. "[O]ur young girls . . . fritter the time away in idle gossip," wrote Henriette Vinton Davis. "As soon as they have finished school they think the time for study is over" (*NYF* July 24, 1886). An anonymous reader meanwhile articulated concern about the "many children that are just coming up in idleness, running the streets and receiving no home training" (*NYF* Oct. 16, 1886).

Throughout the nineteenth century, race leaders often spoke out against idleness and advocated self-enrichment. The *Freedom's Journal* advised African Americans in 1827 to use free time not on "frivolous amusements" but on activities able to "render us more respectable to the world at large" (*FJ* July 20, 1827). In 1840, the *Colored American* urged African American mothers to prevent children from wasting time, and in 1878, the *Christian Recorder* of Philadelphia declared, "Oh! Mothers, to you this nation is crying for those purifying and elevating qualities that will make us equal in every respect to any nation" (*CA* Oct. 24, 1840; *CR* Dec. 5, 1878). Through its promotion of home libraries full of "good books, written especially for girls," "Our Woman's Department" affirmed mothers' moral influence and instructive role for children. Libraries and productive reading, as the column presents them, can not only supplant "dawdling" and "frivolous" novel reading but also productively redirect daughters' time toward beneficial literacy practices. The importance of such practices is further underscored in a selection encouraging mothers to combat children's idleness through the provision of "plenty of good books and papers amusing and interesting to the young" (*NYF* May 22, 1886). Another selection titled "What Mothers Should Do" promotes children's intellectual pursuits and their productive use of time by advocating the study of living systems: "Make your boys and girls study physiology; when they are ill try to make them comprehend why, how the complaint arose, and the remedy so far as you know it" (*NYF* July 3, 1886). In such ways, the column promoted extracurricular reading practices and studies intended to encourage wholesome learning and, in doing so, advance racial uplift.

MOTHERS AS STUDENTS: EXTRACURRICULAR EDUCATION OF COLUMN READERS

To further prepare mothers to effectively raise children—especially daughters—Mossell fosters the extracurricular literacy of her audience through a series of reading lists and recommendations. This was a regular practice of the *Freeman*. The newspaper's column "Magazine Literature" reviewed periodicals, short stories, and serial novels, while other articles expressly promoted certain publications. One titled "The A.M.E. Church Review" endorses this periodical as "wonderful evidence not only of the capacity, but more, of the phenomenal progress of the Africo-American." The article proceeds to review an issue's contents (including an article by Fortune that "must be read . . . if one wants to thoroughly comprehend the question of civil rights") and also provides information on how readers can acquire the magazine (*NYF* Jan. 16, 1886). Suggested reading was also a common practice of other late nineteenth-century periodicals including *Woman's Era*.[11] Journalist Medora Gould's "Literature Notes" column, for example, reviewed and recommended various African American authors' texts—including Mossell's *The Work of the Afro-American Woman*—in addition to texts by white authors James, Lowell, and Longfellow (Gere, *Intimate Practices* 168).

"Our Woman's Department" promotes the assiduous reading practices of mothers to develop their minds—and by extension, their children's. This philosophy is crystallized in a selection titled "Equal Rights at the Fireside" that encourages mothers to read daily:

> One hour a day given to good instructive works will amount to about fifteen days of brain culture in a year, and that certainly is much to the mother whose duty it is to answer the many questions of the bright inquiring minds about her. It is a parental duty that will bring its own blessed reward to store our minds with useful information that can

instruct and delight the hearts of our children, and to accomplish this we must keep abreast with the times by frequent additions to our books, and providing some practical magazine each year. (*NYF* Mar. 12, 1887)[12]

Mothers' routine and enriching reading is presented as a crucial aspect of children's education. Characterizing mothers as teachers, Mossell demonstrates how the "instructive works" mothers absorb will in turn impart wisdom to children. To "keep abreast with the times," mothers are encouraged to regularly augment their library with new books and magazines—a task with which Mossell routinely assists.

"Our Woman's Department" regularly suggests useful books and magazines for readers. Sometimes, Mossell simply issues a reading recommendation with no review commentary. On June 19, 1886, for instance, she writes, "*Harper's Bazar* and *Demorest's Monthly* continue to pay us periodical visits. These two publications, with *Good Housekeeping*, the *Woman's Magazine* and *Babyhood*, should form a part of every mother's reading." At other points, Mossell briefly reviews the works in question. "*Harper's Bazaar* contains excellent engravings, stories by the best writers, valuable editorials, poetry and fashion and cookery notes," she writes (*NYF* Sept. 4, 1886). Notably, this publication—along with *Demorest's Monthly*—is one of the most frequently endorsed periodicals in "Our Woman's Department." Urging readers to "obtain these valuable and pure publications," Mossell emphasizes their role in building edified homes.

And while it is impossible to ascertain how many readers obtained the magazines Mossell suggests, many likely embraced the role of reading in conjunction with child-rearing as evident in this reader's letter:

> Baby Bertha is so young and dear I have been quite a recluse this season, and as a counterbalance we are taking my favorite magazines, the *Century, Brooklyn* and *Good Housekeeping* for 1887. And I find, quite contrary to expectations, my Winter passing more pleasantly than any other in my married life. So very much interested have I become in my daily readings, that when at liberty to take up social duties again, they shall be made secondary to mental improvement for my own good and my child's best development. (*NYF* Mar. 12, 1887)

This reader uses her domestic "reclus[iveness]" for self-instruction and "mental improvement," explicitly correlating her self-improvement with "my child's best development." Consistent with Mossell's pedagogical program, this mother suggests that daily periodical reading will prepare her to raise an enlightened, upright daughter. Mossell applauds women such as this, writing "[c]ertainly under such tutelage that child will grow into noble cultured womanhood" (*NYF* Mar. 12, 1887). Her response champions women's extracurricular literacy in ways that simultaneously make broader cultural arguments about the moral purity, intelligence, and civic responsibility of African American women at this time.

Notably, Mossell's extracurricular reading recommendations also introduced issues of women's rights. In her inaugural column on December 26, 1885, the editor addresses "those who have thought little of the subject of Woman's Suffrage, Woman's Rights, Wrongs, etc." and

> recommend[s] the reading of the following publications: The "History of Woman's Rights"; The *New Ear*, organ of the Woman's Rights Association,; "History of Woman;" "A statement of Woman's position in all parts of the World during the past," and "The Subjection of Woman," by John Stuart Mill. We feel that a perusal of this book of Mr. Mill will lead those who have never thought upon the subject to see in it something worthy of their earnest consideration. Those who have thought, but unfavorably of the matter, will think more favorably; and those who have thought favorably will become enthusiastic in their efforts for the advancement of this cause. (*NYF* Dec. 26, 1885)

This list of texts promotes extracurricular reading that addresses and advocates women's rights. Particularly recommending Mill, Mossell goes on to highlight his "fair statement of the subject at issue"—namely, that "the legal subordination of one sex to the other [is] wrong" (qtd. in *NYF* Dec. 26, 1885). Her pedagogy in this way raises readers' political awareness and, what's more, suggests ways in which young girls, through their mother's knowledge, might learn about and become invested in women's rights.

"Our Woman's Department" supplements assigned reading with various research and writing assignments. In an August 1886 column, Mossell writes:

> It would be of great advantage to us in preparing two articles for the press if we could get our friends who read this column to send us clippings or communications concerning "Colored Inventors," all over the United States. Any one who could send us in any form information on this subject (that can be vouched for), should be doing us a great service.

> We would also like to prepare an article on the Negro Problem, showing by the number of articles written for or against, how great a hold the subject has on the popular mind. If any one who may have chanced to read a number of articles on the subject would drop us a card stating the title of book or magazine containing such, it would also be of value. (*NYF* Aug. 28, 1886)

Mossell invites readers into her writing process by assigning them preliminary research tasks. Her request resembles a student-centered pedagogy in which both teacher and student contribute to the task at hand. Specifically, the editor's willingness to accept information on Black inventors in "any form" invites readers to investigate different genres and deliver information in the form of note cards with book titles, clipped or transcribed material, or some other means. She restricts submissions only by stipulating that all information must "be vouched for," thus emphasizing the importance of source credibility.

"Our Woman's Department" welcomes all readers into this research process regardless of education level. In a corollary, Mossell writes, "[w]e make these requests believing that there are many who do not write themselves who would be glad to assist in any way possible in making known the good accomplished by our people" (*NYF* Aug. 28, 1886). Similar to Black, Mossell encourages the literacy practices of those with less privileged class status and those without formal education by offering them a role in her writing process. The collective spirit that drives "Our Woman's Department" further characterizes this column as an inclusive, reader-centered space.

This collective spirit is reinforced by several other literacy assignments designed as public memory projects. First, Mossell praises the accomplishments of Happy Ferguson, founder of New York City's first Sabbath School. Mossell then encourages readers to inscribe Ferguson's name in public memory and participate in oral history for children: "Now we may not erect costly monuments to the memory of those we love and reverence, but surely we can do something to keep in memory of the coming generations the fragrance of such lives." She makes suggestions: "Name some Sabbath School chapel 'Happy Ferguson Chapel;' put a memorial window in some prominent church; name some band of little Sabbath School workers 'The Happy Ferguson Band;' at some anniversary of the Sabbath School, some

Children's Day, tell the little ones of our race this fact to cheer their loving hearts in all helpful work" (*NYF* July 3, 1886). Sara VanderHaagen has observed, in *Children's Biographies of African American Women: Rhetoric, Public Memory and Agency,* that "[h]istorical understanding is 'passed on' to children through family, museums, commemorative sites, school pageants, textbooks, and teachers" (7). Mossell's "Our Woman's Department" here positions readers to "pass on" such understanding by creating commemorative sites and functioning as teachers who engage "the little ones of our race" in processes of remembering Ferguson and emulating her values. Mossell concludes this selection in a way that implicitly invites readers to extend her practice of documenting Black female accomplishments: "Let us each and all treasure *and record* the good works done by our race that it may bear fruit and that we may no longer remain a reproach in the land" (*NYF* July 3, 1886; italics mine). Her column thus promotes memory-based literate activity, raises and advocates public awareness of Black women's achievements, and works to curb negative stereotypes, while also casting readers as agents in public memory construction.

Mossell plants additional seeds for future research projects oriented around public memory. Reflecting on two articles about Frederick Douglass that she had recently clipped, Mossell notes

> how valuable and interesting would be a scrap book composed of newspaper clippings speaking of this one colored man. How it would show the honor and reverence he had gained through a long life—the changes of public sentiment. A book could be filled with them, and what grand lessons his speeches, the comments upon them, his quiet talks, the influence they had upon others, would teach. What an interesting unwritten history it would be! (*NYF* July 31, 1886)[13]

This suggestion offers the germ of an idea with the potential to promote remembrance, learning, and literacy among parents, children, and their communities, while cultivating racial pride in children. The scrapbook genre is especially significant. At this time, African American scrapbooks helped form important historical records, intended "to fill gaps in mainstream accounts and assert African American importance in the nation's history" (Garvey 131). And although Mossell admits that "it is too late to make anything like a complete collection," she also cautions readers against an unrecorded past in order to promote other historical scrapbooking projects. "Let not idle regrets be all we shall have to show for the future," she urges, "but facts from which some able writer in the future may write a volume of interest and value to us as a people. Everything thought of us as a people has a value" (*NYF* July 31, 1886).

Mossell later proposed a similar project: the formation of a historical association for which "all publications of interest to us as a race, pamphlets, speeches, volumes, etc. be gathered and placed in this collection. How valuable and useful such a collection would be" (*NYF* Aug. 7, 1886). This project echoes both the scrapbooking proposal described above and Mossell's "Colored Inventors" research assignment in promoting compilation of diverse materials. More so, Mossell's suggestion of a historical association housing "all publications of interest to us" emphasizes the importance of preservation to robust historical understanding and memory. As Jessica A. Rose and Lynée Lewis Gaillet have argued, "while memorialization is important for materializing a strong legacy, it is not the same as preservation, which, when accessible, can establish and advocate for more exact cultural memory" (234). Mossell advocates for such preservation and highlights the pedagogical role of preserved materials: "How valuable and useful such a collection would be" (*NYF* Aug. 7, 1886).

"Our Woman's Department" also includes writing assignments adopted from other periodicals. Mossell's December 18, 1886, column promotes journal writing, for instance, as a means of monitoring the progress of babies. "Some months ago *Babyhood* suggested that mothers keep a journal of the mental progress of their little ones," Mossell begins. "It drew our attention to the subject and we have been more careful to note the progress of a little girl who has reached her second year. 'What does baby know?' is often the question. Well, we shall see in this one case."

After cataloging the early development of a baby (including learning to "get out of the crib," "how to kiss, say 'da, da'" and "clap"), Mossell describes the little girl's budding visual literacy and other learning:

> At twenty months old, instead of saying what baby does know I am forced daily to wonder what it is that baby doesn't know. I fasten a door with a button and I see baby press against the door shake it, press against it, until at last the button has turned and baby opens the door triumphantly. All the papers and magazines lie idly by; baby lets them rest. I pick up the *Century* keeping it closed and start to read it, but baby pulls it down. I open it where there are no pictures, but baby knows

that magazine, and no artifice suffices, I must open and show her the pictures—each article she knows the place of. I say I must put the baby to bed, and she starts walking up the steps. Does the baby want to go down stairs? Quick she opens the door. (*NYF* Dec. 18, 1886)

Sharing further developments including "new words learned during the day—one, two, five, six, she counts; A, O, T, mamma, papa, baby, boy, girl, broom," Mossell concludes by writing that "[e]ach day brings new surprises. A friend, the mother of six children, has kept a daily journal of the unfolding intellect of each child. It is a mine of instruction and guidance."

Logan has argued that the journal "was at the height of its popularity" during this period (*Liberating Language* 32).[14] By adapting this suggestion from *Babyhood* and advocating the role of reflective writing in child-rearing, Mossell cultivates women's "facility with language" (32). She moreover foregrounds children's cognitive development—seen, for instance, in her description of the baby's interest in *Century* pictures, proclivity for "know[ing] the place" of each article, and increasing knowledge of words. It also appears that Mossell here actively participates in the writing project she recommends to readers: "[w]e have been more careful to note the progress of a little girl who has reached her second year," she writes—presumably in reference to her own daughter. Shared extracurricular literacy in this way strengthens the democratic underpinnings of the "Our Woman's Department" community, which aligns editor and audience in the collective project of edifying children (particularly young girls).

Mossell continued to promote related extracurricular literacy development over the course of her career. One writing task from "The Open Court" illustrates this continuation. She writes in the May 20, 1895, issue of *Woman's Era*:

Very many suggestions have been made in the various Women's Departments of the journalistic world pointing a way toward the desired result of putting off the hours of the first quarrel between the lately wedded benedict and his charming bride; counting up to one hundred, holding water or beans in one's mouth, and many other bright suggestions have often appeared, but I have just come across "the best yet" and give it at once for the benefit of my readers, many of whom are young and all sweet, who may lapse into matrimony at any time. *Quarrel tomorrow*; now tomorrow never comes, hence a quarrel can never come. N. H. Junior,

> in the Evangelist, acts as sponsor for this new method of avoiding a
> quarrel and vouches for its success. Let some of *The Open Court* readers
> try it and report progress at some future day. (*WE* May 1895)

Mossell frames this marital tip as a task on which readers should "report."
Her promotion of writing is notably accompanied by another unique literacy proposal that appears in the same issue. "Some of our magazines
might also inaugurate a correspondence course in English literature and
history," Mossell suggests. "It would give practice and experience to the
teacher of the department and would help to solve the problem among
many of our girls as to what they shall read, and what course of study or
reading would be the most helpful" (*WE* May 1895). More specific reading
assignments in "The Open Court" include "A Carnival Jangle" by Alice
Ruth Moore and "Dorothy's Soliloquy" by Mrs. Amanda Miller Coleman.
And while such reading and writing assignments appear less frequently
than in "Our Woman's Department," they nonetheless attest to Mossell's
continued influence on extracurricular education.

DISCOURSES ON THE TRAINING OF BOYS

Although "Our Woman's Department" foregrounds mothers' training of
girls, advice did surface regarding the education and training of African
American boys. This emerged in both coeducational pedagogy as well as
some explicit references to boys. First, "Our Woman's Department" included pedagogical assignments that called attention to "our young people
of both sexes" (*NYF* July 31, 1886). This is seen, for instance, on July 31,
1886—the same issue in which Mossell promoted the scrapbook of newspaper articles about Frederick Douglass. She writes:

> The aged ones who bore the burden and heat of slavery and prejudice;
> the ones who were pioneer laborers in the work of opening the school,
> church and railroad facilities to us, are fast passing away. How many
> beautiful lessons, how much valuable information might be gathered
> from them. Another race is gathering the curiosities of their dialect,
> or idiosyncrasies, for its own amusement, but this vast treasure house
> of future life and thought we leave idle, or let drift forever from our
> grasp. Let our young people of both sexes wake up to this fact, sit down
> and take notes of the simple talk of some old soldier of the cross, visit
> the "Old Folks' Home" and talk with the inmates. Keep this unwritten
> history. (*NYF* July 31, 1886)[15]

Mossell here promotes literate and dialogic practices intended once again to preserve and "pas[s] on" a "vast treasure house" of historical understanding (VanderHaagen 7). By explicitly tasking "young people of both sexes" with activities such as "tak[ing] notes" in order to record "unwritten history," Mossell encourages children to act as archivists while striving to advance the extracurricular literacy of boys as well as girls.

Aside from column articles addressing children in general, the most significant references to boys include a critique of fathers, E. V. M.'s critique that "[t]here is nothing said about the immorality of our boys," and an article titled "Training of Boys." First, Mossell writes in a selection titled "Morals" that

> [n]o true mother gives her daughter a lax rule for her guidance, but men constantly give such to their sons both by word and example. We need in all things to give our children right principles for their guidance. Teach them what is true and to speak the truth; what honesty consists in and to be honest from principle and not from policy. Teach them to be pure in thought and deed, sons as well as daughters, and not that it is necessary to wade through the mire of vice to become manly. (*NYF* Jan. 23, 1886)

This emphasis on training boys is also evident in a selection (explicitly titled "Training of Boys") by Miss T. Johnson published later that year. She asks, "Do [boys] not need careful training as well as the girls? ... Why not teach them to help lighten sister's and mother's burdens when they are young, thereby creating in them a sympathetic feeling? The reason there is so much trouble among our girls is because mothers do not take more care with the training of their boys" (*NYF* May 22, 1886). By encouraging boys to undertake "home duties," Johnson blurs the gendered division of labor. Her article also links the training of boys with the issue of female purity, suggesting that male-oriented educational discourse sometimes functioned to uphold the same end—the morality of young girls.

Despite Johnson's call for more conversation "about our boys," the topic gained less traction than did discussions about girls. Only a small number of other scattered references to boys appear in the column. One, for instance, advises mothers to allow their son to "feel that there is some place in the house for him to entertain his company. In the house of another, or in the street, you can have no oversight of his actions. So try to be patient and bear with the dirt and noise" (*NYF* Jan. 30, 1886). While offering explicit suggestions for raising boys, this passage also alludes to the greater independence of boys and corresponding activities that sometimes exceed the scope of a mother's control. Phrases such as "be patient" and "bear with" reinforce the limits of a mother's training. These limits also appear in the article "Morals." "Though having great confidence in a mother's influence," Mossell writes, "we hold that the inherited tendencies received from the father and the practical example he may set by words and deeds go farther to shape the son's cause than a mother's counsel" (*NYF* Jan. 23, 1886).

And while Mossell does extend training advice for fathers in the same piece, the column as a whole places a greater emphasis on girls—likely due to beliefs about the efficacy of mothers' home training for daughters. As Mossell asserts, "[g]irls are much more likely to remain what their mothers train them to be than boys. By the time a boy has reached his sixteenth year the world has begun its work on him, and often to a great extent undoes the primary training of the mother. Not so with a girl. She is always more or less subject to home influences" (*NYF* Feb. 13, 1886). This statement directs women's greatest extracurricular influence toward daughters' home training. At the same time, the column invests readers with significant power to shape public discourse through their literacy practices—a means of cultivating their studious civic engagement and even their potential for journalistic work.

Developing Professional Writers:
The Series "Women and Journalism"

On May 8, 1886, an "Our Woman's Department" selection titled "Women and Journalism" declared: "The colored woman of the present day has many opportunities in varied fields of labor. One new and untried awaits her skilfullness and energy" (*NYF* May 8, 1886). This field was journalism. In this four-part series, Mossell posits journalism as a new means of Black women's professional advancement. This career path offered women an active role in generating public knowledge, proposing actions, and promoting uplift and change within a largely receptive field. As Royster asserts, African American women "were very much involved, if not quite co-equal, in [the Black press's] enterprises" (220). And while Mossell characterizes this field as "new and untried," there existed "dozens of women who, since the 1830s, found the African American periodical press to be a platform from which they could speak and be heard" (Royster 221). One objective of Mossell's "Women and Journalism" series appears to have been to expand this number—bolstering the growing presence and public recognition of Black females in journalism. Through her series, the editor invites readers to help further diversify the field of journalism by seizing this "new opportunity for advancement for themselves and their sex" (*NYF* May 8, 1886).

Mossell also likely intended to endorse the Black press through this series. The first article to this end observes the influence of African American newspapers by quoting the *Daily American*: "The Negro Press has got to be a firmly established fact. It is no longer possible to reckon on any matter affecting the colored race without counting in the influence of the colored press" (*NYF* May 8, 1886). This influence was adamantly reinforced in the *Freeman*. Aside from reprinting the *Daily American* article from which Mossell quoted, the *Freeman* published another exchange publication declaring, "[t]he press is the most powerful and potent factor in molding the future of a race" (*NYF* Mar. 13, 1886). Moreover, a letter from Edward Small offered specific praise for the *Freeman*: "Its influence socially, morally and financially on our people is too great to be estimated." As such, he "suggest[s] that every subscriber of THE FREEMAN make himself responsible for one new subscriber ... during the present year" (*NYF* Apr. 24, 1886). While such endorsements worked to build readerships, Mossell meanwhile both promoted African American women's journalism and reasserted the importance of the Black press through her series.

When the "Women and Journalism" series appeared, women's employment was already a familiar column subject. Mossell frequently proposed female occupations such as weaving, beekeeping, and sewing over the course of the column's run. Consistent with its dialogic underpinnings, "Our Woman's Department" also published employment suggestions from readers. Mrs. W. M. Howard Lane, for example, proposed the occupation of canary raising. After meticulously describing the process by which canaries must be mated, Mrs. Lane claims that "any lady can do her house work and yet find time to raise some birds, and by so doing can get considerable pin money" (*NYF* Apr. 27, 1886). A second reader, Mrs. H. G. Miller, writes, "I would like to see some profitable industry started in Wilkes-Barre ... What I have in mind is some kind of a store that will give the women work at their homes to be sold in the store—sewing, knitting, embroidery work, etc." (*NYF* Mar. 6, 1886). While linked to women's domestic roles, these employment options promote entrepreneurialism among column readers and presumably the opportunity to serve "the black community rather than a white clientele" (Peterson 10).[16]

"Our Woman's Department" also promoted circulating libraries as an employment option for women. This suggestion offered readers a means by which to both develop financial autonomy and promote community literacy. Mossell writes that any "woman could with small capital in these days of cheap literature keep a circulating library" (*NYF* Apr. 3, 1886). To illustrate, she relates the story of a reader who successfully opened one in Lockport, New York. She explains that "Mrs. S." assumed this venture for both "pecuniary profit" and "in the earnest hope of improving the moral character of the young people of Lockport, by placing within their reach healthy, helpful literature" (*NYF* Oct. 16, 1886). This passage recalls the link between extracurricular literacy practices and moral learning. Much like the reading lists "Our Woman's Department" provides for mothers and young girls, this library works to shape its patrons' moral and intellectual development. "The enterprise has proved an entire success," Mossell writes. For the library is financially viable, and every young visitor "appears radiant with the hope of finding something worth reading" from among "the best and purest literature . . . on the shelves" (*NYF* Oct. 16, 1886). This characterization promotes literacy as a conduit for purity by underlining children's own enthusiasm for this literature. Furthermore, it parallels Winifred Black's depiction of young children enlivened by extracurricular reading and writing—a means of cultivating others' excitement about literacy.

The series "Women and Journalism" performs a related function by encouraging budding newspaperwomen to inspire active literacy through this important professional role. To begin, Mossell announces that the series will offer information about "some of the pleasant and unpleasant things in this work, and some of the personal experiences of various contributors." She then addresses the qualifications and preparation necessary to become a journalist—exploring these questions by way of a paper authored by *New York World* journalist Eliza Archard,[17] who delivered it to the Women's Press Association of Illinois (it was then published in the *Chicago Inter-Ocean*).[18] Among other suggestions, Archard advises a newspaperwoman to get "[a] fairly good education" and to develop a "habit of steady industry. She should be a great reader of newspapers . . . absolutely keeping track of current events all over the world" (*NYF* May 8, 1886).

This list calls to mind two aspects of the column's discourses on morality and studious civic engagement: the need for industry (as opposed to idleness) and the importance of extensive reading. First, Archard recommends "the habit of steady industry." Mossell reasserts this point in a later installment, advising the aspiring female journalist to "make up your mind to labor earnestly, in season and out of season" (*NYF* June 5, 1886). Second, Mossell furthers Archard's emphasis on reading in this same installment—stating that "[t]wo valuable papers have appeared in the daily *Inter Ocean*, May 15, on this much-discussed subject of women journalists" and proceeding to briefly summarize these texts by western journalist William Busbee and temperance leader Frances Willard. These recommendations notably direct readers to extracurricular material beyond the scope of what the series provides. Ultimately, Mossell's advice to aspiring women journalists in these ways resembles her advice to mothers—both of whom will assume an important teacherly function.

The "Women and Journalism" series also addresses professional writing in conjunction with reading. In the second installment, Mossell continues to "teach from the experience of others" by publishing an essay by Rose Terry Cooke, a poet and writer of both fiction and nonfiction (*NYF* May 8, 1886). Mossell offers Cooke's essay as evidence of the crucial link between extensive reading and effective writing. Cooke argues that

> a great range of reading is needful, even of desultory reading, not merely to obtain general information, though that is necessary, of course, but to prevent the formation of a style so marked as to be obnoxious: We are all imitative beings, and any writer who confines himself to one class of reading will unconsciously adopt the flavor of that class. (*NYF* May 15, 1886)

According to Cooke, wide reading is not simply a vehicle for amassing knowledge but for developing an original writing style as well. Mossell reinforces the importance of personal voice when she soon after advises readers to "[u]se your own style; imitate no one" (*NYF* June 5, 1886). Notably, the multivocal nature of "Our Woman's Department" also underscores Cooke's advice. By incorporating texts from a range of professional writers and readers, Mossell does not "confine" her audience "to one class of reading" but provides them with a palette of styles. Through this means of style development, Mossell helps train aspiring professional journalists.

The editor dispenses further advice about writing development through a series of recommended exercises:

> Writing of compositions (as we called them in our school days), of dialogues, accounts of visits to interesting places, we found of great benefit. Take a picture that impresses you and write out a story from it. If you have talents for versification write in that style, endeavoring to conform to rules, and yet retain some originality. Write a little every day. (*NYF* June 5, 1886)

These suggested activities demonstrate ways in which Mossell used extracurricular writing assignments not only to enhance mothers' child-rearing but also to prepare women for careers.[19] The range of writing activities is also notable. Mossell recommends both compositions and dialogues and, moreover, promotes public excursions by suggesting that readers describe "visits to interesting places." A similar writing exercise instructs readers to "[t]ake a picture that impresses you and write out a story from it." This activity resembles the popular exercise of picture lessons in composition textbooks of the period. Such exercises "taught students to observe" and "invited them to use their imagination to create stories suggested by a picture" (Carr et al. 191). One 1889 textbook, for instance, asked students to reflect on a picture of an elderly man "rescuing kittens from a pond," offering this prompt: "Write a story from the picture, making it as interesting as you can" (qtd. in Carr et al. 191). Mossell also promotes imaginative writing but prompts readers to exhibit agency in taking their own photograph. This exercise—along with Mossell's recommendation for compositions—demonstrates that nineteenth-century extracurricular literacy sites sometimes shared links with school-based pedagogy but also frequently offered participants greater liberty and personal authority.

Notably, all of these exercises appear in the fourth installment, a reader-driven extension of Mossell's original plan for the "Women and Journalism" series. She explains that

> [w]e have finished the third article, but from the number of communications received we feel that the subject is not yet exhausted, and as more information is desired we have concluded to give one more paper on the subject. This is the "Woman's Department," and if they want a subject discussed at greater length, until it becomes tiresome to the masculine readers, there is nothing to be done but continue ... We are

glad that women are beginning to feel that this column belongs to them and not to us. (*NYF* June 5, 1886)

Here, Mossell crystallizes her commitment to a reader-centered pedagogy. Their "communications" serve as the impetus for the fourth installment and mark the growing role of readers in shaping the direction of the column (M. H. W.'s influential letter about purity appeared one month later).[20] Overall, then, this series and the "Our Woman's Department" conversation about female purity share two important elements: reader-centered pedagogy and a commitment to racial uplift. First, the fourth installment not only underlines the centrality of readers to "Our Woman's Department" but also expresses gratitude for their contributions: "We are pleased to receive the articles sent by the ladies to this column: Will not others continue?" (*NYF* May 22, 1886). Mossell here implies that she has incorporated readers' source contributions into the "Women and Journalism" series. By inviting additional readers to join in the column's collective construction, she reaffirms her commitment to a reader-centered pedagogy.

Second, the "Women and Journalism" series also reflects a commitment to uplift. This is particularly evident in the following passage:

> Says one, "Why do you write only on doings of colored people or women?" There is no nobler work than to make known the good deeds of our ancestors, and to build up a pure womanhood for the race. When a letter comes from some pupil or friend in some distant State, saying "I read your article and it gave me just the information needed," "Your last article was so helpful in my work," "Through the paper is the only way I hear from you," it shows us the nobility of this work. (*NYF* June 5, 1886)

Similar to trades such as "keep[ing] a circulating library," women's journalism is here presented as a conduit for racial uplift (*NYF* Apr. 3, 1886). Specifically, newspaper writing disseminates useful information and supports those working for change. Mossell's call for female journalists to broadcast "the good deeds of our ancestors" moreover echoes the column's own short sketches of accomplished Black women and corresponding efforts to inspire further achievement. Meanwhile, her reference to "a pure womanhood for the race" reinforces links between morality and uplift while underscoring the "nobility" of journalism as a profession.

What is more, this series anticipates other aspects of the column's conversation on raising girls. This is evident when Mossell casts mothers (and here, fathers too) as writing coaches: "Let your parents and teacher be your friends and critics," she writes, for "no truer and more helpful ones will you find" (*NYF* June 5, 1886). Parents and teachers act as co-tutors of aspiring writers. Mossell explains that their love will oblige candor and "keener insight into your needs and more courage to speak them to you than another friend will ever have." In addition to seeking such parental and teacherly guidance, readers are encouraged by Mossell to write consistently, read "the best literature," and "study newspapers" tirelessly: "every article is to be studied, the style of matter, the headings, the departments of the paper. The daily, Sunday and weekly, each represents a different phase of work" (*NYF* June 5, 1886). By occupying readers with these research and writing assignments, Mossell trains professional writers in ways that noticeably resonate with her efforts to edify mothers.

She concludes the "Women and Journalism" series by highlighting the personal satisfaction, civic significance, and financial reward that can result from this career path. Emphasizing the intimate ties that journalism can foster, she writes that "[t]he friendships formed, the kindness shown, will furnish pleasant memories through life." To illustrate, she references a reader's "offer of conveyance to a distant point in gratitude for a helpful article"—"[o]ne of the kindest acts and pleasantest experiences" of her career (*NYF* June 5, 1886). This example underscores ways in which women's journalism far exceeded the boundaries of an "imagined community" to facilitate intimate connections of various kinds. Mossell promotes this enriching career path with confidence:

> we find this work the most congenial of any we have ever attempted. The best means of reaching our people, and even making money. Yes, after five months of professional work, we candidly say, Work, and you can succeed and make money. From three to five hundred dollars yearly can be made with less effort than at teaching. (*NYF* June 5, 1886)

Mossell's praise of journalism is anchored in a comparison with teaching. Yet Mossell never stopped teaching when she began editing "Our Woman's Department." Indeed, it is through journalism that Mossell practiced a wide-reaching and highly collaborative form of extracurricular instruction that promoted the reader-centered education and literacy development of African American women and their corresponding public participation through "Our Woman's Department."

CHAPTER THREE

Susette La Flesche's Relational Journalism and Literacy Teaching: Collaborative Practices of Survivance

In traveling through the country I notice a condition of affairs for which it is not easy to account. Here on the one hand are hundreds of white people leaving their homes because they are afraid of the Sioux. On the other hand there are hundreds of Sioux fleeing to the Bad Lands because they fear the white people, troops having been sent among them. No one has been killed, no blood shed, no assault made by the Indians on the whites and none on the Indians by the whites.

Nothing has been proved which can justify the presence of the troops . . .

—Susette La Flesche, *Omaha Morning World-Herald* (December 11, 1890)

On December 27, 1890, Omaha journalist Susette La Flesche Tibbles (Insh-ta Theamba, or Bright Eyes) urged *Omaha Morning World-Herald* readers to protest the planned disarmament of a group of Lakota Sioux traveling toward refuge at Pine Ridge. Under the direction of the Miniconjou Lakota leader Chief Spotted Elk, this group had left Cheyenne River Reservation following the attempted arrest and shooting of the Hunkpapa Lakota Chief Sitting Bull at Standing Rock in the wake of intensifying U.S. government interference in the Ghost Dance movement, "the religion of renewal" that had been spreading across the Plains tribes (Marshall 131–32; Andersson 294; Treuer 5; Vizenor, *Manifest Manners* 105). Fearing for their lives, they traveled toward the camp of the Oglala Lakota Chief Red Cloud at his invitation as rumors abounded that the U.S. military would disarm them (Lee 132; Treuer 5–6). "I wish some attempt could be made to protest against the taking away from the Indians of their ponies and arms," wrote La Flesche:

This protest should come from the white people as it would be to the interest of the white people themselves of both the states immediately concerned. When an Indian "gives in," as they call it, he does it in earnest . . . If it is done it will fail in its purpose and only create feelings which may last for years. In all this so-called war and with all the arms the Indians are supposed to possess, there has been no white man shot and not a single white man's or woman's life taken.

BRIGHT EYES (*OMWH* Dec. 27, 1890)

Reaffirming her declaration was Thomas Henry Tibbles, La Flesche's white journalist husband, whose article appeared directly below her own:

One battalion of the Seventh cavalry, with two Hotchkiss guns, pack mules and a wagon train left camp and started toward Wounded Knee at 2 P.M. What they went for I do not know, as there is not an Indian within 100 miles of here who wants to fight. I have information through Indian couriers that the hostiles have decided to come in and they are now all on the way. Perhaps fifteen or twenty may slip away, but the matter is settled and within three or four days all the Indians will be at their agencies. But there is still great danger. If an attempt is made to disarm these Indians and take their ponies there will be no peace for years. Already great damage has been done to Nebraska and Dakota by the sensational reports of battles never fought sent by frightened correspondents who could not distinguish between a prairie fire and an Indian signal. (*OMWH* Dec. 27, 1890)

La Flesche's writing—a strong declaration of sovereignty articulated "in the presence of" a vast newspaper-reading public—works in collaboration with Tibbles's article to interlink assertion of Indigenous rights with the need for more accurate reporting by journalists and more astute critical reading among white audiences of commercial newspapers (King, *Legible Sovereignties* 6). Their collaboration moreover situates a call for readers' discursive public participation ("[t]his protest should come from the white people as it would be to the interest of the white people themselves") within a critique of both the U.S. government's planned military intervention at Wounded Knee and the barrage of "sensational" journalism that mischaracterized the Lakota as intent on war.

These December 27, 1890, articles by La Flesche and Tibbles—part of their broader efforts to teach critical literacy, intervene in the "rhetorical imperialism" of "sensational" commercial journalism, and model a more responsible form of news research and reporting—did not prevent the disarmament of the Lakota (Lyons, "Rhetorical Sovereignty" 452). This military action by the Seventh Cavalry occurred two days later on December 29, 1890, precipitating the devastating massacre of more than 150 (and likely 300 or more) Lakota men, women, and children at Wounded Knee (Treuer 6; Lee 130; Hopson 266).[1] As Ojibwe writer David Treuer has underscored, however, this massacre was not "the end of Indian life," despite its representation as such "[i]n the American imagination and, as a result, in the written record" (1). Rather, Treuer continues,

> [l]ooking at what actually was and is, beyond the blinders that the "dead Indian" narrative has imposed, means reckoning with relentless attacks on our sovereignty and the suffering it has created. But it also brings into view the ingenious and resourceful counterattacks we have mounted over the decades, in resistance to the lives the state would have us live. (Treuer 17)

This chapter analyzes the "ingenious and resourceful" *Omaha Morning World-Herald* writing of Susette La Flesche, who in frequent collaboration with Tibbles produced journalism as a practice of "survivance" while stationed at Pine Ridge. Establishing what Gerald Vizenor has described as "an active sense of presence over absence, deracination, and oblivion," La Flesche's news research and writing employed conversation, careful listening, and relationship-building to supply "readers with accurate information" and, in doing so, to spark commitments to critical reading, ethical newswriting, and discursive public participation for justice (Vizenor, *Literary Chance* 13; *OMWH* Dec. 13, 1890). Her claim to "rhetorical sovereignty"—defined by Scott Richard Lyons as "the inherent right and ability of *peoples* to determine their own communicative needs and desires in [the pursuit of self-determination], to decide for themselves the goals, modes, styles, and languages of public discourse"—opposed the "rhetorical imperialism" that drove both misperceptions of Indigenous peoples and corresponding government policies undermining their rights during this period ("Rhetorical Sovereignty" 449–50, 452). La Flesche's journalism in this way intervened in discourses "of dominant powers" that "assert[ed] control of others by setting the terms of debate. These terms are often definitional," Lyons explains, in that "they *identify* the parties discussed by describing them in certain ways" (452).

The rhetorical imperialism of much commercial journalism in 1890 (and during the late nineteenth century more generally) mischaracterized Indigenous peoples in devastating ways—often as "peculiar being[s]" or savages (La Flesche, Introduction [to *Ploughed Under*] 3). Such mischaracterizations carried policy-related consequences. As Lisa King explains, "language and image drive action and policy, and policy has material consequences for Native nations." Emphasizing the role of rhetorical sovereignty in influencing these interrelations, King writes:

> Rhetorical sovereignty directly addresses the language, rhetoric, and representations concerning Native peoples and wishes to place more of the control over that language and rhetoric—and therefore control over the representation and the images derived from them, and therefore the policy and action derived from those—in Native nations' hands. To claim rhetorical sovereignty is to claim the right to determine communicative need and the right to participate in the process of public image making and meaning making. (King, "Sovereignty" 26)

An active participant in this "process of public image making and meaning making," La Flesche claims rhetorical sovereignty through research-based newspaper writing that reshapes white commercial press narratives about Lakota people and seeks to establish more just policies and actions. In doing so, she pens and models a type of journalistic public discourse embedded in relationality.

My understanding of relationality in this chapter is indebted to Opaskwayak Cree scholar Shawn Wilson as well as several additional scholars. First, Wilson's *Research Is Ceremony: Indigenous Research Methods* situates relationality at the heart of an Indigenous research paradigm. Wilson writes in his discussions of ontology and epistemology that "reality *is* relationships or sets of relationships" and that "all knowledge is cultural and based in a relational context" (73, 95). An Indigenous methodology is therefore rooted in "relational accountability"—entailing "[r]espect, reciprocity and responsibility" and interconnected with research ethics also anchored in relational accountability (77, 11). I hear in the research paradigm Wilson describes important resonances with the relationally based news research and reporting of La Flesche, whose journalism relatedly reflects ways in which "studying culture is a relational practice, requiring interaction with and investment in the communities whose practices are being investigated" (Powell et al., "Our Story"). La Flesche's journalism to a significant degree emerges from close interaction with Lakota people and deep investment in Lakota communities, reflecting her commitment to what Malea Powell, Daisy Levy, Andrea Riley-Mukavetz, Marilee

Brooks-Gillies, Maria Novotny, and Jennifer Fisch-Ferguson, drawing on Julie Lindquist, call "a relational practice."

La Flesche carried out this commitment within a complex rhetorical situation. As an Omaha woman writing to a primarily white audience while living and writing in close relation to the Lakota, La Flesche occupies an asymmetrical space of power. She generates from within this space flexible, community-oriented journalism that additionally reflects what Elizabeth A. Flynn, Patricia Sotirin, and Ann Brady term "feminist rhetorical resilience" anchored in "relational webs." These scholars explain that "feminist rhetorical resilience includes actions undertaken by rhetors, usually women, who, with varying degrees of success, discursively interact with others, resulting in improved situations despite contexts of significant adversity" (7, 1). Such practices are highly relational. "[A] feminist rhetoric of resilience," they affirm, "emphasizes relationality, mutuality, and an ethic of connection"—all values embodied by La Flesche (11). By exercising resilience, rhetors like La Flesche, without "taken-for-granted access" to rhetorical resources, find in "relational webs . . . the basis for resilient agency" (7).

Relationality thus constitutes a primary means by which La Flesche, alongside her husband, Tibbles, both understands and carries out her *World-Herald* journalism. Through such a relational framework, La Flesche claims rhetorical sovereignty by working to reshape narratives about Lakota people and teach wise forms of reading and writing intended to encourage more ethical representations of Indigenous peoples and, by extension, more just policies. La Flesche specifically uses three interrelated strategies in her relationally based journalism to advocate for Indigenous rights, promote critical commercial newspaper reading, and model responsible news research and reporting. La Flesche (1) collaborates with her husband, Thomas Henry Tibbles, a *World-Herald* journalist and Native American rights activist; (2) works to "build alliances"[2] with her primarily white audience using a relationally based logic and storytelling (King, *Legible Sovereignties* 7); and (3) employs conversation and relationship building, especially with Lakota people, as a key methodology (S. Wilson 79). Altogether, La Flesche uses these three interrelated strategies for survivance that "resist[s] . . . marginalizing, colonial narratives and policies so indigenous knowledge and lifeways may come into the present with new life and new commitment to that survival" (King et al., "Introduction" 7).

First, La Flesche and Tibbles function as a journalistic team whose collaborative practices lend credibility to their newspaper appeals. Their partnership—anchored in prior activism in support of the Poncas—aims to reconstruct representations of Indigenous peoples in ways that encourage both critical understanding and protest of attacks on Lakota sovereignty. And while Tibbles's status as a long-established journalist and white male surely influenced her audience's perception of her ethos, La Flesche was renowned in her own right. Lecture tours of the eastern United States, England, and Scotland had established La Flesche as a skilled orator beloved by many as a result of her passionate advocacy on behalf of the Poncas. Furthermore, the collaboration of La Flesche and Tibbles embodies a commitment to reciprocal and dialogic activism. Through close conversations with Indigenous peoples as well as white members of proximate communities, and by penning a form of collaborative journalism in which their pieces often appeared side by side, La Flesche and Tibbles resisted the monolithic tendencies of turn-of-the-century commercial newspapers and upheld both cooperation and community knowledge as values central to ethical journalism (Kilcup 4).[3]

Second, La Flesche seeks to "build alliances" with the primarily white readers of the *Omaha Morning World-Herald* (King, *Legible Sovereignties* 7). Foregrounding connections among human beings as a means of asserting Indigenous rights and illuminating Lakota knowledges, cultural practices, and worldviews, La Flesche offers "new frameworks and new language for making sense of multiple histories and voices." She thus encourages the cultivation of more "respectful and reciprocal relationships" and the implementation of more just policies (King, *Legible Sovereignties* 7; Powell, "Down" 41). La Flesche's specific techniques for building alliance include both relationally based logic and storytelling. Through such means of alliance building, La Flesche challenges her readers to rethink crucial issues facing Native peoples including not only the threat of Lakota disarmament but also interrelated injustices such as the ration system and U.S. governmental opposition to the Ghost Dance movement. In reframing such issues, La Flesche demonstrates through a commercial news outlet the limitations of a Eurocentric point of view cut off from relational understandings.

Third, La Flesche engages in close conversation and relationship building, especially with Lakota people, as a key methodology. Indeed, La Flesche's newspaper writing was intimately shaped by dialogue with the Lakota Sioux, her stay at the home of a Lakota host, and further conversation with white members of proximate communities. As an Omaha journalist stationed with Tibbles at Pine Ridge in order to "visit the Sioux" and share learnings with *World-Herald* readers, La Flesche prioritized relational knowledge building in ways that resonate with S. Wilson's description of relationship building as an Indigenous methodology (*OMWH* Dec. 11, 1890). He writes:

> with all of these knots of being/relationships as our reality, we can go one step further and ask, "How can I find out more about this other being, or idea, or whatever you decide to call a particular knot?" The answer, which is our methodology, seems obvious—the more relationships between yourself and the other thing, the more fully you can comprehend its form and the greater your understanding becomes . . . So the methodology is simply the building of more relations. (79)

Through relationship building with Lakota people, deep investment in their communities and understanding of Lakota relationships to land, and presentation of Lakota testimonies and perspectives through her journalism, La Flesche both practices and models a form of news research that situates knowledge "in a relational context" (S. Wilson 95).

The dialogic practices of La Flesche are notably distinguishable from those of Black and Mossell. While the latter two journalists respond directly to readers in print (that is, a dialogic quality is evident in the interactions between the journalists and their readers on the newspaper page itself), dialogue for La Flesche is an intimate form of news research. Extending opportunities for discursive public participation to the Lakota and white members of proximate communities, La Flesche interweaves their expertise (combined with her own) in a lecture-like format for a mass market. This format appears purposeful. Growing from her activism and oratory on behalf of the Poncas, La Flesche builds on prior experiences as a translator and lecturer while utilizing her ethos as "Bright Eyes" (the English translation of her Omaha name) to again make space in white public discourses for the perspectives of Indigenous peoples. This chapter is thereby further differentiated from the previous two by its focus on an Indigenous writer's attempt to educate an enfranchised Euro-American public through an "inter-epistemic" form of mass-circulating newspaper discourse (Mignolo, "Delinking" 453).

Overall, I argue that La Flesche's *Omaha Morning World-Herald* writing sought to function pedagogically both for turn-of-the-century journalists and for readers. First, La Flesche's critique of inaccurate newspaper

discourse and modeling of relationally based news research and reporting
may be seen as a type of extracurricular teaching during a historical moment when press reformers were advocating improved education for journalists (Seidel 68). Such calls often emphasized the importance of accuracy,
moral character, and "ethical principles" in news reporting—values that
make La Flesche's writing a particularly relevant intervention in turn-of-
the-century conversations about journalism education (Pulitzer 667). Second, for *World-Herald* readers, her journalism functioned as a pedagogical
platform for critical literacy teaching and an invitation to pursue social
protest. La Flesche promoted critical reading attuned not to sensational
or surface interpretations but to logical and relational understandings
capable of driving social protest—which she both directly and indirectly
called on her Euro-American audience to pursue.

By mining this piece of the rhetorical histories of Indigenous women's
journalism, I respond to calls by Victor Villanueva and Jason Edward
Black to attend to "American Indian rhetoricians speaking to or with white
folks" (Villanueva qtd. in Powell, "Down" 38)—a means of examining ways
in which Indigenous peoples "'talked back,'" thus "reconstitut[ing] their
own identities, rebuk[ing] governmental policies, and reconfigur[ing] US
identities in the rhetorical process" (Black 6).[4] Malea Powell has meanwhile urged rhetoric and composition scholars to "take American Indians
seriously" in disciplinary conversations; Black furthermore reminds us
that "[f]ocusing on Native-centered interpretations of Native-US history
and affiliations confronts and restructures dominant representations of
colonized dealings within those relationships" (Powell, "Down" 41; Black
11). My work in this chapter aims to extend a growing body of scholarship
concentrated on ways in which Native American rhetors have "resisted,
and continue to resist . . . racist constructions of Indian identity even as
they reassert their rights as sovereign peoples" (Monroe 4).

The following pages begin with a biography of La Flesche's early life and
discuss her influential activism in support of the Poncas. Next, I situate her
World-Herald journalism within the contexts of late nineteenth-century
commercial press depictions of Native Americans and the Ghost Dance
movement as well as professional discourses about journalism education
and ethics. I then analyze La Flesche's relational news research and reporting from Pine Ridge, which often operated collaboratively alongside
writing by Tibbles. To conclude, I discuss La Flesche's continued articulations of rhetorical sovereignty and survivance after the Wounded Knee

Massacre. Overall, I demonstrate how the relational journalism of Susette La Flesche aimed to function as both activism and extracurricular pedagogy for white audiences by teaching the importance of critical literacy and by modeling responsible practices of news research and writing.

Susette La Flesche: Early Life, Advocacy, and Oratory

EARLY LIFE AND TEACHING

Susette La Flesche was born to Joseph (Iron Eyes) La Flesche, principal chief of the Omaha Tribe, and Mary Gale in Bellevue, Nebraska, in 1854. She grew up on the Omaha Reservation with three sisters born to Mary Gale: Marguerite, Rosalie, and soon-to-be-doctor Susan—"the first female American Indian M.D. in the country" (Powell, "Down" 48, 53).[5] Susette and her sisters shared a mixed ancestry of "Omaha, Oto, Iowa, Ponca, French Canadian, and European American," and they gained three additional siblings from their father's second marriage to Ta-in-ne (Elizabeth Esau) (Powell, "Down" 48; Peyer 286). Among them, Francis La Flesche became an ethnologist with the Smithsonian Institution who wrote and lectured on Indigenous traditions. Reflecting on her family in a speech given later in her life, Susette shared:

> You might search the world over and you could not find a better father and mother, intellectually and morally, and I speak this understandingly for I have had the privilege of knowing intimately some of the very highest and best among your people in all parts of the world. No child could have had a happier childhood than I. Family affection among the Indians is peculiarly strong. ("Political Speech")

As they grew up, all of the La Flesche children received Anglo-American-style education, which they believed "was an essential component of a future for Omahas and other Native peoples" (Powell, "Down" 52). Joseph La Flesche had to this end "recognized the need for Omaha people to be educated in the ways of white people" (Stromberg 100). At the same time, Joseph La Flesche immersed Susette in vital aspects of her Indigenous heritage (Thorne 235; Kilcup 169). She participated in "the life-passage and naming ceremony, 'Turning of the Child,' under the watchful gaze of her mother and her grandmother, Nicomi," and also accompanied her family on buffalo hunts during her childhood (Thorne 235). Of the latter tradition, La Flesche later remembered:

Every summer after the crop was put in the whole tribe started for the buffalo hunt to be gone for about three months. The tribe camped at night in one great circle in the order of bands and families. Each band had its place in the great circle, each family its place in the band and each member of a family his or her place in the tent . . . In the summer the fire was built out of doors and the sides of the tent would be turned up halfway to let the wind blow through, and the fresh green grass with buffalo robes or straw mats thrown over it made as soft a lounging place as one could wish. The life we lived while on these hunts seems like one long joy to look back on and we children were happy all day long. There was such a sense of utter freedom. (S. Tibbles)

In 1872, after attending reservation mission schools, La Flesche departed to attend the Elizabeth Institute for Young Ladies in New Jersey where she graduated with honors (Sonneborn 127). During this period, La Flesche also contributed to the *St. Nicholas* magazine letter-box along with her sisters Marguerite, Rosalie, and Susan; their 1877 letters were published in 1880 (Street 516).

Another foray into public writing occurred after Susette was rejected for a teaching position at a reservation school following her graduation from the Elizabeth Institute. Two years later, upon learning of a stipulation requiring that U.S. government-operated schools hire qualified Native Americans, she wrote a letter of protest to the commissioner of Indian affairs: "It is all a farce when you say you are trying to civilize us, then, after we educated ourselves, refuse us positions of responsibility and leave us utterly powerless to help ourselves. Perhaps the only way to make ourselves heard is to appeal to the American public through the press. They might listen" (qtd. in Sonneborn 127). This letter secured her a teaching position.

Although it is possible that some might view such institutional teaching as "negative and assimilationist" from a contemporary perspective, for La Flesche—like her sister Susan La Flesche Picotte—"belief in the importance of European American education [did not] diminish . . . her sense of responsibility to her people" (Powell, "Down" 55, 52). Her newspaper writing in fact reflects a belief in the possibilities of utilizing resources derived from a Euro-American-style education for practices of survivance—evident in La Flesche's adaptation of such resources to protest attacks on Lakota sovereignty and to assert Indigenous self-determination. Her powerful lectures on behalf of the Poncas moreover reflect

La Flesche's employment of Euro-American-style educational resources for activist ends.

THE STANDING BEAR HABEAS CORPUS CASE

In the late 1870s, La Flesche commenced activism on behalf of the forcibly displaced Poncas—activism for which she is most remembered today and the means by which she met Tibbles. This activism took shape after the Bureau of Indian Affairs reassigned the Poncas' ancestral lands to the Lakota. Malea Powell explains that "[w]hen the Great Sioux Reservation was created in 1868, the [Bureau of Indian Affairs] 'mistakenly' included lands previously reserved for the Poncas. The 'fix' for this oversight was to remove the Poncas to Indian Territory (Oklahoma), where land and food were quite scarce" ("Down" 44–45). Prior to the forcible removal, the Ponca Chiefs White Eagle, Standing Buffalo, Standing Bear, Smoke Maker, Frank La Flesche (Susette La Flesche's uncle), Little Chief, Big Elk, and Gahega traveled with a government agent to see newly proposed lands in 1877. Deeming the lands unsuitable, they were thereafter abandoned by the agent and underwent a grueling thirty-day journey back to Nebraska without money or a translator. The Ponca chiefs afterward issued a statement at Susette La Flesche's house "on their return from Indian Territory" that recounted these abuses. It was then "published at their desire" in a Sioux City newspaper (La Flesche, Letter).

La Flesche's advocacy on behalf of the Poncas grew following their removal to the malaria-prevalent Indian Territory, where "[t]here [was] very little food" and where one third of the tribe died within the first year ("Ancestry"; Treuer 123). The 1879 Standing Bear habeas corpus case subsequently took shape. Chief Standing Bear, following the death of his son Bear Shield from malaria and promising his son that he would bury him in the White Chalk Bluffs above the Missouri River, attempted at this time to lead a small group of tribal members back to their homeland ("Ancestry"). Nearly completing this six-hundred-mile journey, Chief Standing Bear and his party were then arrested "for having left the confines of the reservation" ("Ancestry"). These events were soon brought to the attention of *Omaha Morning World-Herald* journalist Thomas H. Tibbles,[6] as La Flesche explained in an 1881 interview:

> I never knew Mr. Tibbles until this Ponca question came up. I was teaching at the time when Standing Bear and his party ran away from the

Indian Territory, to which they had been sent by the government. They stopped on our Omaha Reserve on their way back to their own lands. The Omahas told them that their old homes had been destroyed, and further told them to stay on our reserve and farm so that they could have provisions. This they did, and began to sow some wheat. Our agent telegraphed to the department that thirty runaway Indians were there, and asked what he should do with them. We did not know at that time that he had telegraphed. The Poncas were camped near my house. All of a sudden, one Sunday afternoon, the soldiers came . . . The soldiers carried them off, half of the men and women so sick they could hardly sit up . . . All Standing Bear could say was, "We have committed no crime and done nothing wrong, and why does the government treat us in this way?" As they went off, all felt so sorry for them that we could not even speak or say good-bye. Every one gave up all hope. We all waited for letters from the Indian Territory, expecting to hear that Standing Bear had got back. All of a sudden an article appeared in the Omaha Herald stating that this whole thing was an outrage. We did not know who was the author. Another article appeared, stating that the ministers of the churches in Omaha city had sent a petition to Mr. Schurz [Carl Schurz, secretary of the interior from 1877–1881], asking him to allow Standing Bear and his party to go back to their own lands. This was signed by the ministers . . . The next thing we saw in the Herald was that some one had brought a writ of habeas corpus for the release of Standing Bear and his party. No one knew who was doing all this . . . Then a letter came from Mr. Tibbles, the assistant editor of the Omaha Herald, and we found he was the one who had written all the articles, and who had brought about the writ of habeas corpus, and was the one who had interested the ministers and lawyers in it. (*BDET* Jan. 11, 1881)

La Flesche wrote to Tibbles on April 29, 1879, at the request of Reverend James Owen Dorsey, an Omaha missionary, who asked her to send the journalist "all I knew, as I had an uncle in the Indian Territory, and as I had letters and a telegram that the eight chiefs who had been left to walk back through Kansas and Nebraska . . . had sent to the President, appealing to him for help" (*BDET* Jan. 11, 1881). Thereafter, on May 12, 1879, U.S. district judge for Nebraska Elmer S. Dundy determined in the court case *Standing Bear v. General George Crook* that "Standing Bear is a person, entitled to . . . constitutional rights" who could not be arrested without just cause—thereby mandating "that Native Americans must be treated as human beings under U.S. law" ("Ancestry").

Tibbles then asked La Flesche and her father to visit the remaining Ponca Tribe in Indian Territory and "gather all the information [they] could" (White Eagle, "Statement"; Mathes and Lowitt 27). After her arrival, on May 20, 1879, Susette translated into English a detailed statement by Chief White Eagle that documented the devastation and deaths suffered by the Poncas because of their forced removal, pled for social protest from whites, and called President Rutherford B. Hayes to restore the tribe's homeland: "I now ask the President once again through this message which I send to all the White people of this land, to rectify his mistake," Chief White Eagle concluded. "When a man desires to do what is right, he does not say to himself, 'it does not matter,' when he commits a wrong" (White Eagle, "Statement").

This statement—written by Chief White Eagle for newspaper publication and containing a preface and afterword by La Flesche—anticipates in significant ways the priorities and pedagogical purpose of La Flesche's *World-Herald* journalism. Specifically, it signals La Flesche's role as a conduit for the perspectives of Indigenous peoples in a relational, research-based capacity and by way of intervention in white public discourse. It moreover functions pedagogically while utilizing (and positing the centrality of) newspapers for this end. To begin, La Flesche composes this preface to Chief White Eagle's statement:

> The following statement was made to me by White Eagle, the head-chief of the Ponca Tribe. I translated it into English for him and give it just as he gave it to me. My father and I had been sent by Mr. T.H. Tibbles to the Ponca Reserve to find out the condition of the tribe and gather all the information we could. They told us many things of which we could not tell the half and White Eagle asked me to write this statement for him so that it could be read by all the White people.
>
> Bright Eyes
> Susette La Flesche

Here, La Flesche describes her research-based role ("[we] had been sent by Mr. T.H. Tibbles to the Ponca Reserve to find out . . .")—one guided by relationality. "I feel a deep interest in the subject [of the Poncas] as Frank La Flesche, one of the chiefs . . . is my uncle," she had written in a letter to Tibbles less than one month earlier (La Flesche, Letter). Continuing her activism in support of her uncle Chief Frank La Flesche, Chief White Eagle, and other Poncas, La Flesche situates herself as a conduit between "the White people" and Chief White Eagle's knowledge and point of view. Her preface also suggests the central role of reading in instigating social protest—one that White Eagle explicates: "It may be that you knew nothing of our wrongs and therefore did not help us," he states. "I thank you in the name of our people for what you have done for us through your kindness to Standing Bear; and I ask of you to go still further in your kindness and help us to regain our land and our rights" ("Statement"). Importantly, La Flesche's afterword advances a similar assertion in a declarative, lecture-like style that would come to shape both her oratory and her journalism for the *Omaha Morning World-Herald*: "I now wish to say a few words myself," she writes. "I believe that it has been because the people of the United States were ignorant of the injustice and wrongs committed against my people, by those in authority that they have not helped us" ("Statement").

These statements by La Flesche and Chief White Eagle situate newspaper reading as a vehicle for instructing a white mass public. They notably anticipate Ida B. Wells's 1892 proclamation that "[t]he people must know before they can act, and there is no educator to compare with the press"— as well as her designation of the white press as "the medium through which I hoped to reach the white people of the country" (Wells-Barnett 42; Wells 75). As La Flesche affirmed when speaking of Chief White Eagle's statement in her later U.S. Senate testimony on behalf of the Poncas:

> Q: Did White Eagle make any request that it should be published in the papers?—A. Yes, sir; that was what it was written for. They had heard of Mr. Tibbles, and what he had done for Standing Bear; and they wanted to see whether something could not be done for them, if the white people could be got to understand how they had been treated.
>
> Q. Was any publication of it ever made?—A. Yes, sir; portions of it. I have seen parts of it in print. I do not know whether the whole letter has ever been published or not. (*Removal* 35)

Wells, Chief White Eagle, and La Flesche thus utilized the white press for educational and activist ends—bringing to Euro-American "circuits of print culture" facts and arguments for justice from the perspectives of African American and Indigenous peoples (Pratt 35). La Flesche indicates the need for such interventions in her afterword: "Until this time the Indian has been unable to tell the story of his wrongs," she declares, "while the white people when they have been wronged have spread it abroad throughout the land" (White Eagle, "Statement"). Overall, Chief White Eagle and La Flesche's 1879 collaboration operates pedagogically by disseminating a new story intended to teach, and thereby mobilize, a white newspaper-reading public—anticipating a key function of La Flesche's *Omaha Morning World-Herald* journalism.

LECTURE TOURS

In the fall of 1879, La Flesche joined a lecture tour with Tibbles and Chief Standing Bear, speaking before various reform groups "from Chicago to Boston" (Kilcup 169). This well-organized tour—the first of several that La Flesche would participate in during this period—"generated extensive news coverage" and gained support from Boston and Omaha pastors in addition to politicians and literary authors (Mathes and Lowitt 83).

Through her powerful oratory, La Flesche helped "rais[e] money to support legal suits aimed at restoring the Ponca homeland" and moreover became a widely celebrated lecturer on allotment and Native American

106 TO CLERGYMEN, LECTURE COMMITTEES AND OTHERS.

The Committee in charge of the work of Mr. Tibbles and Miss Bright Eyes, are anxious to secure them engagements to speak in Churches or Halls at once. They both have remarkable power of interesting audiences and have abundant testimonials from Bishop Clarkson, of Omaha. General Crook, and many others. They have won universal sympathy and good will wherever they have spoken.

By sending to the undersigned, arrangements could be made for public meetings in Churches or Halls, as may be found convenient. Collections may be taken up at the meetings, and thus no risk would be incurred by any one. If preferred, lecture committees could make arrangements at a stipulated price, which would be very moderate.

The Churches of New York, Philadelphia, Baltimore, &c., without distinction of denomination, have welcomed Mr. Tibbles and Miss Bright Eyes (daughter of the head Chief of the Omaha tribe) with very large audiences composed of the best people of those cities.

B. W. WILLIAMS,
258 Washington St., Boston.

3.1. An undated solicitation for speaking engagements—likely from one of La Flesche's early lecture circuits (1879–1883). NMAI_AC066/Box_001/Folder_05, Thomas H. Tibbles Papers, National Museum of the American Indian.

citizenship (Mathes and Lowitt 83–84; Sonneborn 128).[7] She gained the fervent support of poet and writer Helen Hunt Jackson, who told La Flesche, "My dear, you have given me a new purpose in life" (qtd. in Coward 217). Massachusetts senator George Frisbie Hoar characterized one of her Boston lectures as "eloquent, sensible, direct, and one of the most moving that ever I heard from human lips" (qtd. in *BDET* Mar. 2, 1881). Henry Wadsworth Longfellow also emerged as an advocate at this time and remarked upon meeting La Flesche: "*This* is Minnehaha" (Mathes and Lowitt 89).

Longfellow's "reference to the wife of his famous poetic character Hiawatha" from *The Song of Hiawatha* points to the "idealized" public image of La Flesche that emerged during this period (Mathes and Lowitt 89; Coward 216). Many commercial newspapers and magazines fueled such sentiments, often ascribing to La Flesche both elements of white, middle-class "true womanhood" and romantic characteristics. While the *New York Times* described La Flesche as "a little woman, about 20 years of age" with "pleasant features" and "a very feminine voice and manner," the *Boston Daily Evening Traveller* reprinted an article from the *Lady's Journal* that stereotypically asserted: "It is a great thing for the Poncas to possess a woman advocate. No such interesting squaw has appeared since Pocahontas as the young woman who rejoices in the above appellation—as pretty a name as was ever devised. 'Bright Eyes' has taken sober Boston captive" (*NYT* Dec. 13, 1879; *BDET* Mar. 2, 1881).

Inscriptions in her signature book also reflect romanticized characterizations of La Flesche. While one deems her "Queen Penelope," another opens, "Yes; bright are the eyes, and regal the grace of Inshta Theamba—true queen of her race" ("La Flesche Family"). While limiting, such testimonies simultaneously offered La Flesche an opportunity to use these types of beliefs to advocate persuasively for Indigenous peoples. To this end she accepted public preference for the name "Bright Eyes" as a useful "tool in her people's cause" and employed certain other prevailing "'beliefs' about Indians in order to imagine a new kind of Indian-ness in which those beliefs are both invoked and destabilized" (Dando-Collins 9; Powell, "Rhetorics of Survivance" 418).[8]

In an 1881 speech delivered in Boston, for example, La Flesche quotes and then refigures a statement by the Board of Indian Commissioners chairman who characterized Native peoples as "children." Her speech begins thus:

> The chairman of the board of Indian Commissioners says: "Reservations are used for Indians very much as nurseries are used for children, as safe inclosures for the weak and defenseless." Does he call them safe inclosures because in them the Indians are powerless to help themselves when robbed? I know that hundreds of horses have been stolen from my tribe, the Omahas, and they cannot do a single thing to recover their property, punish the thieves or stop the robbery. A horse was stolen from my father last spring. He knows who stole the horse, and he knows the white man who has the horse now. He asked the agent to help him get it back. The agent was as powerless as he was, and told me that the best way to do would be for my father to steal it back. (qtd. in "Beauties")

Black has noted that "[o]ften, in rhetorical strategies for imperial conquest European forces and the US government employed the language of fatherhood to rationalize their self-images as colonizers" (4). In the passage above, La Flesche "destabilize[s]" this rationalization and its accompanying characterization of Native Americans as "weak" "children" by critiquing colonial power structures that undermine Indigenous sovereignty. Native Americans are not innately "defenseless," La Flesche shows, but are rather rendered "powerless" by these allegedly "safe inclosures." Importantly, La Flesche uses a personal story to carry the force of this point ("A horse was stolen from my father . . ."). This story—a vehicle for relaying La Flesche's own locally based knowledge—establishes a sense of immediacy while exposing the irony of government policies that would instigate lawbreaking ("[t]he agent . . . told me that the best way to do would be for my father to steal it back").

La Flesche's 1881 Boston speech noticeably builds on another one she gave a year earlier in the same city. In this earlier speech, she similarly "invoke[s] and destabilize[s]" beliefs about Native American "defenselessness" not only to denounce attacks on sovereignty but also to promote Euro-American civic action in support of Indigenous rights (Powell, "Rhetorics of Survivance" 418). "My people have made desperate struggles, year after year, for their homes, for their lives and for their liberty," La Flesche begins. A bit later she continues:

> It has been said that "you cannot compel the government to right a wrong unless the people demand it." I do not know whether it is because

the people do not know enough or care enough to demand justice for
a handful of helpless people in the absolute control of one government
official, who has unlimited authority to kill and butcher if they do
not obey his imperious will, or whether it is because this one government official is greater than the people who elect him, or he is so great
in himself that he can afford to defy public opinion, or he has made
money out of it. It is your place to find out which. ("Lecture Delivered
by Bright Eyes")

In this early section of her speech, La Flesche initially probes the limits
of social protest ("or he is so great in himself that he can afford to defy
public opinion") before ultimately placing civic responsibility in the hands
of her listeners ("It is your place to find out which"). She continues by
narrating the stories of the Nez Perces, Poncas, and Cheyennes—all "forcibly removed from their homes into strange lands, where many had died
in hopeless anguish . . . When the Cheyennes fought to maintain their
rights, they were exterminated; when the Poncas claimed the protection
of the courts, the great Secretary of the Interior tried to kick them out.
Whether he will succeed or not, it is for you to say." Referencing reform
efforts to secure for the Poncas "the full and equal benefit of all laws and
proceedings for the security of persons and property," La Flesche reaffirms
possibilities for civic action and calls listeners to pursue such action by way
of discursive public participation ("it is for you to say") (qtd. in Mathes
and Lowitt 97; "Lecture Delivered by Bright Eyes").

Overall, by collaborating with Chief White Eagle and delivering lectures such as these, La Flesche worked to intervene strategically in white
public discourse through practices of survivance that utilized the press and
podium for educational and activist ends (Vizenor, *Manifest Manners* vii).
Anticipating her later *World-Herald* journalism, this early activist work involving translation and oratory also established her ethos as "Bright Eyes."
La Flesche would continue to use this name in her news reporting from
Pine Ridge as she sought to teach and mobilize *World-Herald* readers while
moreover offering instruction in relational journalistic practices and ethics.

MARRIAGE AND LATER LIFE
La Flesche and Tibbles married on July 23, 1881 ("Marriage"; "Omaha,
Neb."). As described by his journalism colleague Charles Q. DeFrance
in a 1932 memorial article published in the *Nebraska History Magazine*,

Tibbles was "a good-natured, a kindly lion, even when he was launching his invectives against the predatory elements of humanity." Tibbles had in his youth "given gallant aid in the 'underground railway,'" DeFrance also noted, "and what he did for the abused American Indians is a matter of record in the archives of the Nebraska Historical Society; and his marriage and married life with Susette La Flesche, 'Bright Eyes,' the Indian princess, was a happy one, as I have every reason to believe" (DeFrance 239, 241).

From 1882 to 1883, La Flesche and Tibbles continued to lecture in the eastern United States. The couple later conducted a yearlong lecture tour of England and Scotland beginning in May 1886. Tibbles, describing one of La Flesche's lectures in an English church, remembered: "there was as great a crowd pressing around Bright Eyes as I ever saw in America" (Tibbles, "Bright Eyes" 84). In June 1888, Tibbles resumed writing for the *Omaha Morning World-Herald* and began reporting from Pine Ridge with La Flesche in December of 1890 (Mathes and Lowitt 187–88). Notably, the couple's collaborative writing had much earlier roots. La Flesche composed the introduction to Tibbles's *Standing Bear and the Ponca Chiefs* (1880) and argued therein that "the people are the power which move the magistrates who administer the laws" (La Flesche, Introduction [to *Standing Bear*] 3).

Following their news reporting at Pine Ridge, Tibbles founded the populist *Independent* in 1895 and became the populist nominee for vice president of the United States in 1904 (Richardson 363). La Flesche contributed to Tibbles's *Independent* as well as the *American Nonconformist* during this period, when she also lectured on "the money question" while addressing the ineffectual results of severalty and Omaha citizenship ("Political Speech"). Around this time, La Flesche additionally illustrated Fannie Reed Giffen's *Oo-Mah-Ha Ta-Wa-Tha (Omaha City)*—"considered the first book ever illustrated by an American Indian" (Mathes and Lowitt 188). She was inducted into the Nebraska Hall of Fame in 1983–1984 approximately eighty years after her death on May 26, 1903, and six years after the Hall of Fame induction of Chief Standing Bear. It is for her powerful oratory alongside Chief Standing Bear on behalf of the Poncas that La Flesche is best known. The remainder of this chapter will explore La Flesche's less frequently discussed work from Pine Ridge during the winter of 1890–1891, reportage in which she attempted to reconstruct Euro-American perceptions of Indigenous peoples by teaching critical literacy and modeling a strongly relational form of news research and reporting.

Representations of Indigenous Peoples in the
Late Nineteenth-Century Commercial Press

During the late nineteenth century, the commercial press profusely circulated documents "written *about* Native peoples by folks who had something to lose if Indians were seen as fully human"; such documents reflected a "desire to claim knowledge of/over others" (Powell, "Dreaming" 116; Cushman et al. 18). Heather Brook Adams, drawing on Linda Tuhiwai Smith, has identified this desire as "an ongoing violence of colonialism" (Cushman et al. 18). In her introduction to Rev. William Justin Harsha's *Ploughed Under: The Story of an Indian Chief* (1881), La Flesche outlines two primary categories by which Native Americans were classified and by which knowledge over Native peoples was "claim[ed]" at this time. On one hand was the romantic, "peculiar being"; on the other, the "savage."

"With some he is a peculiar being," she begins, "surrounded by a halo of romance, who has to be set apart on a reservation as something sacred, who has to be fed, clothed, and taken care of by a guardian or agent" (Introduction [to *Ploughed Under*] 3). La Flesche here alludes to both sentimentalizing tendencies and the type of gross misperception that led the chairman of the Board of Indian Commissioners to characterize Indigenous peoples as "weak and defenseless." This view was common within Euro-American Indian reform discourses of the period, which similarly characterized Indigenous peoples as powerless; meanwhile, other periodicals contributed to a sentimentalized view (Powell, "Down" 46). A writer for *Harper's Magazine* in the 1880s, for instance, documented "picturesque" Indians on a train trip to Arizona, while *Lady's Journal* compared La Flesche to Pocahontas (qtd. in Bird; reprinted in *BDET* Mar. 2, 1881).

The second category La Flesche points to is the "savage"—described by La Flesche as "a sort of monster without any heart or soul or mind, but whose whole being is full of hatred, ferocity, and blood-thirstiness. They suppose him to have no family affections, no love for his home, none of the sensitive feelings that all other human beings presumably have. This class demand his extermination" (Introduction [to *Ploughed Under*] 3). Many captivity narratives popularized such a depiction during the antebellum period while "[t]he most-often encountered villain of the Western dime novel was the savage Indian" during the century's latter half (Nachbar et al. 283). Constructions of Native Americans as savages also abounded in commercial journalism. Particularly in the second part of the nineteenth century, many newspapers circulated sensational accounts of outbreak and the "mutilating, kidnapping, and killing" of white settlers. "We cannot open a paper from any of our exposed States or Territories, without reading frightful accounts of Indian massacres and Indian maraudings," reported the *New Orleans Picayune* on December 31, 1866 (Coward 5; qtd. in Coward 5). By disseminating images such as the "'treacherous' Seminoles of the Florida swamps" or the "Sioux 'camp of cut throats' along Montana's Little Bighorn River," newspapers promulgated the "racial and cultural inferiority" of Native Americans (qtd. in Coward 5; Batker 15). Such images—"created out of that symbolic Indian 'savage'" of which La Flesche speaks—"were the visual and rhetorical justification for Euro-American manifest destiny" (King, "Sovereignty" 21–22).

Journalistic misrepresentations of Indigenous peoples that circulated during this period bear some resemblance to similar distortions of African Americans. Ellen Gruber Garvey states that "[w]hen the white press wrote about black people at all, especially from the 1880s on, blacks were likely to appear as criminals, or as stereotyped characters in comic dialect stories" (133). Much of the southern and even northern press discourses about lynching were especially appalling in "represent[ing] black men as savage" (Bederman 51). Both Ida B. Wells and Susette La Flesche intervened in types of rhetorical imperialism present within these types of white commercial newspaper discourses that "claim[ed] knowledge of/over" African Americans and Indigenous peoples and sustained various forms of subjugation.

For Indigenous peoples, press rhetorical imperialism contributed to the licensing of stricter governmental control of reservations, increased military interference, and arguments for genocide. "Self preservation demands decisive action," wrote the *Daily Rocky Mountain News* in 1864 when it advised "[a] few months of active extermination" (Aug. 10, 1864). The *Aberdeen Saturday Pioneer* circulated similar words later in the century when L. Frank Baum wrote that "the best safety of the frontier settlements will be secured by the total annihilation of the few remaining Indians" (Dec. 20, 1890). Such portrayals of Indigenous peoples as "necessary villains" in opposition to manifest destiny and the spread of white settlement underscore crucial "interrelationships between writing, violence, and colonization" (Coward 6; Lyons, "Rhetorical Sovereignty" 449). And while critiques of U.S. government policies and actions did appear in the commercial press (for example, the *Washington Post* critiqued "[t]he present system" and forced farming; the *Omaha Bee* relatedly stated on November 25, 1890 that "[t]he Indians are slowly starving to death. That is the real, the way down, deep cause of this war scare"), newspapers overall heavily contributed to colonialist justifications (qtd. in Andersson 209-211). Furthermore, they often diluted "stories of cooperation and mutual respect" during this period (Coward 5).[9] Commercial journalism thereby constituted a central space wherein rhetorical imperialism functioned to "*identify*" and "assert control of" Indigenous peoples with serious "policy" and "material consequences for Native nations" (Lyons, "Rhetorical Sovereignty" 452; King, "Sovereignty" 26).

Commercial press misrepresentations of the Ghost Dance religion that spread across the plains during 1889 and 1890 were especially inaccurate—contributing to the panic that drove a devastating chain of erroneous U.S. governmental responses (Hopson 265). Treuer explains that the Ghost Dance movement "greatly alarmed the U.S. government," which "redoubled its ongoing efforts to break up the Great Sioux Reservation," institute allotment, and relocate Native American children to boarding schools (4). "The Ghost Dance religion was banned," Treuer continues, "and government troop presence on the Pine Ridge Reservation was increased" (4–5). Such attacks on Indigenous sovereignty occurred in the context of severe misunderstandings of the Ghost Dance religion. Through the Ghost Dance, Sicangu Lakota historian and writer Joseph M. Marshall III relays, "our ancestors tried desperately to achieve peaceful change through prayer and dancing." Yet "the US government assumed it would lead to an armed uprising," and commercial newspapers across the United States often characterized it as a vicious prelude to war (22). Headlines such as "Fears of an Ambush" and "Their Orgies Wilder Than Ever" in the *Omaha Bee* generated widespread alarm among many readers (Nov. 20, 1890; Nov. 22, 1890). The *New York Times* meanwhile alleged that the Ghost Dance attracted participants including "those who are filled with race hatred." "Under prospects not more vivid and promises not more grand," it continued, "the Arab Mahdi of the Soudan was able to rally his people to arduous campaigns and bloody battles" (*NYT* Nov. 20, 1890).

Such gross misrepresentations generated rumors of impending war, while incentivizing journalists to embellish or insufficiently verify their reports. As South Dakota senator Richard F. Pettigrew remarked of reporters at this time, "[t]oday he sends three columns of gore to any paper that will buy it and tomorrow he will contradict what he sends today, that his reward may be greater. All he wants is money, and he will write anything to get it" (qtd. in Coleman 58). Commenting on reporters dispatched by the eastern press to the Dakotas, historian William S. E. Coleman has relatedly written: "Some of the dispatches were inaccurate due to the ignorance and ineptitude of the correspondents, but a few were intentionally exaggerated if not blatantly untrue" (56).

The degree to which some newspapers misled readers is particularly apparent in two contradictory reports published on the same day on November 23, 1890. While the smaller *Iowa State Register* announced, "Indian Scare about Over . . . Thought Now That No Further Trouble Will Occur," the *New York World* erroneously declared, "The Bloodshed Begun: Seven White Men Killed by Indians." These types of flagrant distortions and falsehoods (no white men were killed) led Pine Ridge missionary Rev. Thomas L. Riggs to observe that "not one in a hundred of our western Sioux had any thought of making war against the whites. It was in very truth a newspaper war" (qtd. in Coleman 101, 56).[10]

This statement by Rev. Thomas L. Riggs notably anticipates observations about white newspapers made by Ida B. Wells. Following the Memphis murders of Thomas Moss, Calvin McDowell, and Henry Stewart in 1892, Wells wrote that "[t]he [Memphis] daily papers . . . helped to make this trouble by fanning the flames of racial prejudice" (qtd. in Goldsby 44). Jacqueline Goldsby furthermore asserts that "it did not go unnoticed by Wells that the Memphis press did more than sensationalize this lynching. The reporting strategies and publishing tactics of these newspapers functioned to 'create' rather than 'report' the event" (45). Like Wells, La Flesche aimed to mitigate such discursive recklessness through a focus on accuracy. While Wells compiled statistics and factual evidence (often gathered from reputable branches of the white press itself and amplified by Wells's "embodied record-keeping"), La Flesche paired a relationally based logical style with strategies of alliance building to model responsible press discourse as an alternative to journalistic inaccuracy and sensationalism (Libertz 321).

Writing from Pine Ridge during December 1890 and January 1891, La Flesche utilized this form of relational journalism to share Indigenous "histories, knowledges, and meaning-making practices" and to describe contexts surrounding the Ghost Dance during a historical moment defined by severe attacks on the sovereignty of the Plains tribes (García and Baca 32). Following the U.S. government's violation of the second Treaty of Fort Laramie of 1868 and the subsequent defeat of the Seventh Cavalry at the Battle of the Little Bighorn in 1876, the U.S. government "encouraged widespread encroachment by settlers[,] . . . reneged on treaty promises of food and clothing, and funded the wholesale destruction of the once vast buffalo herds of the Plains," without which "the Lakota and other Plains tribes could not hope to survive, at least not as they had been surviving" (Treuer 3). The Lakota were thus forced to depend on deficient reservation annuities of mainly "beef, rice, beans, sugar, and coffee" and "relegated to stand in line once a month to receive them." As Marshall emphasizes, "[t]here was very little or no hope for change and improvement to these tough and humiliating circumstances" (Marshall 130).

The Ghost Dance emerged and grew among the Lakota during 1889 and 1890 in this context of extensive land loss, a severe ration system, and other assimilation measures including forced agriculture on arid land—all of which eroded previous ways of life for the Plains tribes (Hopson 265). Originating among the Paiute in Nevada, the Ghost Dance was inspired by the teachings of Wovoka and spread widely (Andersson 28). The Ghost Dance religion, as Treuer describes, taught that if Native peoples "lived lives of peace and worked hard and danced the Ghost Dance, they would find peace on earth, and they would be reunited with the spirits of their ancestors in the afterlife" (Treuer 4). Sometimes assuming new elements as it spread among various tribes, the Ghost Dance "was done in order that the participants might survive the intense starvation (both physical and spiritual) they were facing" in ways that made it possible "to imagine renewal" (Hopson 265; Lee 132; Krupat 14).

This "nonviolent ceremony of resistance" was nonetheless grossly misrepresented by many late nineteenth-century commercial newspapers (Stromberg 181). As Elmo Scott Watson asserts, it was "the contemporary press" that promulgated false associations between the Ghost Dance and "'war'" (205). Reports of violent outbreak and bloodshed abounded throughout the autumn of 1890, despite the fact that most journalists reporting from Pine Ridge "rarely ventured into the field" according to Coleman. Most instead remained "close to the telegraph office" and "treated anyone coming into the agency as an expert. More than a few of these 'experts' fed gullible reporters stories that were patently untrue. The headlines for one day were often based on events that never happened" (Coleman 58). Offering a corrective to these press misrepresentations was the collaborative news reporting of La Flesche and Tibbles. As the *Omaha Morning World-Herald* characterized it, the writing of these "two absolutely truthful and conscientious persons" stood "[i]n notable contrast to the frantic and contradictory dispatches of the casual correspondents" and supplied "readers with accurate information" (Dec. 13, 1890). Moreover, in promoting the link between journalistic accuracy and justice, their writing contributed in important ways to turn-of-the-century discussions of journalism education and ethics.

Professional Discourses about Journalism Education and Ethics

During the same period in which many mass commercial newspapers circulated severely misrepresentative discourses about Native peoples, related criticisms of journalism emerged that fed professional arguments in favor of more rigorous education for reporters. Chalet K. Seidel explains that widespread critiques of commercial newspaper sensationalism "gained momentum in the last decades of the nineteenth century"—prompting many professionals to "answe[r] this criticism by proposing university training for journalists" (69). In advancing such arguments, the focuses of editors and publishers varied: some advocated pragmatic instruction in vocational skills; others meanwhile aimed "to improve the quality and style of the news texts by improving the minds of the men who edited and commented on the news" (Seidel 69). Despite such differences, present within this body of professional discourse is a discernable concern for improving accuracy in commercial journalism as well as understanding and "ethical principles" among reporters (Pulitzer 667).

Addressing the charge of sensationalism, E. M. Camp, for instance, stated in 1888: "Journalism does not need to be told of its short comings. It does not require the information that it is often sensational. It cannot be surprised with the statement that it is many times inaccurate; that its assertions are, as a rule, hurriedly and crudely made." Camp therefore advocated greater "educational foundations" for reporters, reasoning that "[i]f journalism is to maintain its place as the teacher of the largest class of pupils in Christendom, the future working journalist . . . must be broadened by knowledge, and deepened by research" (Camp 5, 14–15). *Louisville*

Courier-Journal writer Henry Watterson meanwhile proposed that university training in journalism should include "moral training in the obligations of decency and truthfulness, which the individual assumes when he becomes a public writer, or reporter for the press" (qtd. in Camp 11).

Newspaper giant Joseph Pulitzer also assumed a leading voice in this conversation. "One of the chief difficulties in journalism now is to keep the news instinct from running rampant over the restraints of accuracy and conscience," he wrote in 1904 for the *North American Review* (644). He continued:

> Moral courage is developed by experience and by teaching. Every successful exercise of it makes the next easier. The editor is often confronted by an apparent dilemma—either to yield to a popular passion that he feels to be wrong or to risk the consequences of unpopularity. Adherence to convictions can and should be taught by precept *and example* as not only high principle but sound policy. (646; italics mine)

Pulitzer thus adamantly endorsed the role of ethics in journalism education, arguing that "[w]ithout high ethical ideals a newspaper not only is stripped of its splendid possibilities of public service, but may become a positive danger to the community." This threat compelled Pulitzer to propose not merely a single course in ethics for aspiring journalists but rather sustained ethical training "pervad[ing] all the courses" (667). Offering a particularly interesting idea related to this point, Pulitzer suggested that students study "the newspapers of the current day"—learning to distinguish "a brilliant paragraph" from "a bit of sentimental trash" and a "superb 'beat'" from a "scandalous 'fake'" (675).

These comments suggest ways that La Flesche's journalism may be read as an interjection of rhetorical sovereignty and survivance in discourses about journalism education and ethics articulated primarily by white men at the turn of the century. As an Omaha woman reporter writing from Pine Ridge and residing with a Lakota host, La Flesche both directly critiques inaccurate news discourse (promulgated by reporters who "send sensational dispatches when they don't know or are not sure of the truth") and models a socially responsible form of newswriting built on the "relational context" of knowledge (*OMWH* Dec. 16, 1890; S. Wilson 95). La Flesche in this sense teaches by example in producing newswriting that emblematizes commitments to accuracy and relationally based journalistic ethics— values that aspiring and practicing journalists should emulate. In modeling this form of reporting, La Flesche moreover invites her *World-Herald* readers to practice critical literacy themselves by learning to distinguish responsible journalism from "scandalous 'fake[s]'" and "grossly inaccurate and misleading headline[s]" (Pulitzer 675).

La Flesche's *World-Herald* Journalism: Relationality, Collaboration, and Survivance

"WHAT BRIGHT EYES THINKS"

In his 1905 autobiography, Thomas Tibbles recalls arriving at Pine Ridge Agency in December 1890. "We found there an amazing state of affairs," he remembered:

> Though there had been no outbreak of any kind, the place was jammed with "war correspondents" who were expected to produce thrilling "war news." Hanging around the hotel day after day, they constantly dispatched new inflammatory stories made out of whole cloth. Burning arrows were being fired into the agency buildings; the Indians were perpetrating horrors in every direction—according to those writers. (*Buckskin* 301)

La Flesche similarly critiques this type of sensational and erroneous news discourse in an article published on December 16, 1890, titled "What Bright Eyes Says." She reports that, as she prepared for bed one evening, "telegrams began to arrive from Omaha to representatives of the papers here asking them to send full accounts of the battle or go out to where the fight occurred, and send in the fullest details." Yet "[t]here has been no fight and no bloodshed up to date" (*OMWH* Dec. 16, 1890). These firsthand accounts by Tibbles and La Flesche highlight the sharp divide between tabloid-like newspaper writing about the Plains tribes and actual events occurring at this time.

In penning a corrective to "thrilling 'war news'" and "inflammatory stories made out of whole cloth," La Flesche—writing alongside Tibbles—faced a significant rhetorical challenge. As Ernest Stromberg asserts, "Indians who would speak or write on behalf of Native rights and cultures were and often still are addressing an audience that generally assumes its own superiority. It is not a rhetorical situation conducive to mutual dialogue. For many American Indian speakers and writers, establishing a measure of identification with their white audience has been a primary demand" (5).

La Flesche works to create such identification through alliance building involving relationally based logical argument and the compilation and strategic presentation of myriad sources of expertise (including her own, that of the Lakota, and that of white members of proximate communities). The frequent collaboration of La Flesche and Tibbles further contributes to this purpose. Overall, these strategies aim to build "a measure of identification" with *World-Herald* readers through language that does not reify "unutterable and ongoing differences" but rather foregrounds a shared humanity—"one of the most pressing exigencies" for Indigenous peoples (Powell 41, "Down"; Stromberg 5).

La Flesche's first *Omaha Morning World-Herald* article appeared on December 7, 1890. The headline announced, "What Bright Eyes Thinks: The Celebrated Lecturer Writes on the Present Indian Complications: The Government Has No Right to Stop the Ghost Dance—It Should Keep Faith With the Indians and Pay Them." Preceding contributions by Tibbles, *World-Herald* founder Dr. George L. Miller, and Rev. William Justin Harsha (author of *Ploughed Under*), "What Bright Eyes Thinks" reshapes commercial press narratives about Lakota people and the Ghost Dance movement while calling for critical reading by white audiences and policy changes by the U.S. government.

Her article opens by reflecting on the "causes" and contexts for the Ghost Dance movement—"causes" that

> may seem to be very simple if one only stops to think that, first of all, the Sioux are human beings with the same feelings, desires, resentments and aspirations as all other human beings. Taking that as the basis for one's calculations on this particular phenomenon, if one may call it so, and taking into consideration their special environment which has been and is different from that of all the other human beings in these United States, one can directly trace the effect to its causes. (*OMWH* Dec. 7, 1890)

La Flesche opens her article with relationally based logic. First, through phrases such as "the basis for one's calculations" and "trace the effect to its causes," she immediately differentiates her reporting from "thrilling 'war news'" while simultaneously asserting a shared humanity: "first of all, the

Sioux are human beings with the same feelings, desires, resentments and aspirations as all other human beings."

La Flesche goes on to resituate the Ghost Dance within specific local conditions that have contributed to the blending of "traditional Lakota beliefs, Christianity" and interpretations of "Wovoka's teachings" within the Ghost Dance due to a fervent desire for relief and change (Andersson 273). La Flesche writes that the Lakota "have been longing for a deliverer and their minds were ripe for the idea":

> They have begun to realize their loss of nationality through the enforcement of the severalty bill, which makes them citizens, against the will of many of them. In any community there are always some for and some against any proposition or measure. In those tribes where the majority have been educated up to the idea that citizenship is inevitable there will be little trouble in enforcing the law, but in those tribes where the majority still cling to the faith that they can always keep their nationality, the enforcement of the law will bring fright and trouble. All this was inevitable from the very nature of things. To many of them the loss of their nationality is like the cutting off of a limb to save a life. To some of them the loss of their nationality is worse than death. When I was up there a few years ago two or three of the better sort of men there told me they would rather die than give up any more of their land to the government. They said that in some instances when they had sold a piece of land willingly, expecting the government to keep its faith with them in the matter of pay, that it had cheated them. (*OMWH* Dec. 7, 1890)

This passage foregrounds Lakota experiences and perspectives while reflecting La Flesche's "interaction with and investment in" Lakota communities in ways that introduce the role of conversation as a key methodology (Powell et al., "Our Story"; Jane in S. Wilson 113). Maintaining processes of alliance building ("In any community there are always some for and some against any proposition . . . "), La Flesche uses a measured language of commonality to highlight local contexts and Lakota points of view: "All this was inevitable from the very nature of things. To many of them the loss of their nationality is like the cutting off of a limb to save a life. To some of them the loss of their nationality is worse than death."

Specifically, La Flesche foregrounds Lakota perspectives on and feelings about the 1887 General Allotment Act—also called the Indian Severalty

Act, or Dawes Act—which, in legislating the allotment of reservation lands to Native Americans for the purpose of private property ownership, aimed "to break up the tribe as a social unit" and sell "'surplus land'" to fund boarding schools (Treuer 145–46). The 1889 Sioux Agreement that followed "called for the breakup of the Great Sioux Reservation into five smaller units, the cession of eleven million acres to the United States" and allotment of what remained (Hämäläinen 377). La Flesche draws attention to the devastation of land loss ("men there told me they would rather die than give up any more of their land to the government") and unscrupulous U.S. government practices ("it had cheated them") when referencing her prior interactions with the Lakota. Implicit in her presentation of such testimonies is a belief in the importance of conversation as a context-specific and "valid tool" for building and sharing knowledge (Jane qtd. in S. Wilson 113).

Striving to deepen readers' understanding, La Flesche continues by exposing further attacks on Lakota sovereignty, including a broken ration system and treaty violations. This is accompanied by a more extended critique of the U.S. government's propensity to cheat the Lakota. "We happened to be there during ration day," remembers La Flesche, "and White Thunder, who is now dead, showed us the amount given to a family of eleven persons, which consisted of a pint cup of coffee, the same of sugar and a few pounds of meat, on which they were expected to live for a week. He said the rations were getting less and less every year" (*OMWH* Dec. 7, 1890). Driven by a direct tone and precise details, this example again relays knowledge gained from conversation and close personal interaction—used here to confront *World-Herald* readers with clear evidence of injustice. Sovereignty violations are soon afterward punctuated with reference to treaty breaking when La Flesche states: "It was General Crook who said 'that in the course of twenty-five years' experience with the Indians and the government, I have never known the Indian to break a treaty or the government to keep one.'" Here, La Flesche appeals to her audience by way of resonating words from a prominent white general—indicating her cumulative ability to draw "link[ages]" with both the Lakota and "important and influential" Euro-Americans (Powell, "Rhetorics of Survivance" 421).

These "link[ages]" act as a bridge into La Flesche's articulation of the "causes" contributing to the development of the Ghost Dance movement among the Lakota: "that the government did not keep faith with them, that they really have suffered for food, owing to the system pursued in governing them by arbitrary authority and irregular proceedings of a bureau, instead of by law, as all the other citizens in the United States are governed, and their fear of the threatened loss of their nationality" (*OMWH* Dec. 7, 1890). La Flesche then critiques U.S. government interference in the Ghost Dance. She writes:

> These religious dances are common to every tribe of Indians and they are known under different names. In our tribe they are known under the name of "shell dances" and they take place in the spring and the fall of the year, sometimes lasting for weeks, the dancing going on almost every night. I do not approve of them, because being kept up so constantly and so long they tend to make the people neglect their crops; but I do not think the white people have any more right to go among them and break them up by force than the Indians have to go among the white people and break up their dances by force. (*OMWH* Dec. 7, 1890)

In this critique, La Flesche reproduces Euro-American beliefs about farming (a topic that her journalism would go on to complicate) to "authenticat[e] [her]self" by way of her audience's values and bolster this claim anchored in parallel logic: "I do not think the white people have any more right to go among them and break them up by force than the Indians have to go among the white people and break up their dances by force" (Powell, "Rhetorics of Survivance" 418, 421). To both cement this denunciation of forceful aggression and help safeguard Lakota survival, La Flesche then proposes that "educat[ion]" replace U.S. government attempts to "change the nature of a man by force." She thus employs purposeful strategies and a sustained emphasis on commonality ("the nature of a man") in "us[ing] the means available to her" to help keep the Lakota community "intact *as a community*"—anticipating her sister Susan La Flesche Picotte's 1891 medical writing about "her work among the Omahas," which similarly strove to ensure her community's preservation (Powell, "Down" 52, 54–55).[11]

La Flesche goes on to rebuke the ration system as a means of reimbursement for tribal lands and to censure U.S. governmental control of Lakota finances. First, La Flesche writes, "And for the ration system I think it is a very bad one. If the government owes them money for their lands it should pay it to them in cash per capita. The Indians would then have no cause for complaint. He is as just as the most of his fellow human beings and knowing that he was treated with justice would act accordingly." La Flesche here employs relationally based rational argument to insist that it is both logical and imperative to monetarily compensate the Lakota for their land. She posits a common understanding of justice to build identification with *World-Herald* readers and moreover suggests that upholding justice will inspire its reciprocation.

Second, La Flesche employs an analogy anchored in identification to critique governmental control of Lakota finances as both illogical and unjust:

> The government has no more right to say how their money shall be spent, or spend it for them, than it has to say how the salaries which it pays its employees shall be spent, or spend it for them in rations or clothing or things they do not want or need, in order that contractors shall have the chance of making some money. There are Indians who will spend their money foolishly, and so are there white men, but the government therefore does not claim the privilege of spending it for the latter on that account. On our reserve, two or three years ago, the government, under threat of withholding the coming installment of money from us, required us to give an account as to just how we had spent the last money, and the government was to say as to whether we had spent it well, in order to decide as to whether we should receive the next installment or not. Just imagine all the employees of the government and of all the state governments being compell[ed] to give an account of how they had spent their last installment of salary, the gentlemen, of just how much they had to give for their cigars, tobacco and neckties and the ladies of what they had paid for their bonnets, handkerchiefs, candles and ribbons. The Indians do not buy exactly the same things as the white people, but the principle is the same. (*OM WH* Dec. 7, 1890)

La Flesche again deploys a uniform "principle" of justice to build alliance with *World-Herald* readers and uphold the importance of Lakota sovereignty. Through catalogs of commonplace items ("cigars, tobacco and neckties" and "bonnets, handkerchiefs, candles and ribbons") and phrases such as "Just imagine . . . ," La Flesche tactically exposes the absurdity of governmental intrusion in Lakota finances and calls for their right to autonomous spending.

As "What Bright Eyes Thinks" approaches its conclusion, La Flesche advocates the establishment and application of fair laws after first relaying the need for critical newspaper reading by white audiences. She writes:

> The Indian is more intelligent than he seems. I am often sorry at the childish speeches attributed to them in the newspapers, but they are

frequently made silly by the fault of inadequate interpretation or the ignorance of the interpretor. I have no doubt that speeches translated literally from the French, German and other languages would sound as silly. I have often heard them talk as sensibly and wisely as anyone I ever heard among the white people. (*OMWH* Dec. 7, 1890)

Here, La Flesche promotes critical reading by white audiences. Spotlighting the prevalence of mistranslation in newspapers, she suggests that "inadequate interpretation or the ignorance of the interpretor" often fuels misperceptions of Indigenous peoples. Her point is amplified by this "equivalenc[y]": "speeches translated literally from French, German and other languages would sound as silly" (Powell, "Rhetorics of Survivance" 421). It is likely that La Flesche's call for accurate and nuanced translation stemmed additionally from her own experiences as a translator and her corresponding knowledge of the importance of reliability. Indeed, in addition to translating Chief White Eagle's 1879 statement, La Flesche served as an interpreter for Chief Standing Bear during their 1879-1880 lecture tour. She also interpreted his 1880 testimony during a U.S. Senate "inquiry into the circumstances of Ponca removal" (Mathes and Lowitt 88, 96–98). Overall, this passage calls for both translation accuracy in commercial journalism and critical newspaper reading attuned to ways in which mistranslation fuels misunderstanding.

In conclusion, La Flesche reaffirms the need for "a government of laws" in place of "arbitrary authority":

If the money question were settled as the land question is by the severalty bill and laws established on every reserve and enforced as they are among the white people there would soon be no more of the troubles incidental to all "class legislation." The Indian is more amenable to a government of laws than he is to one maintained by arbitrary authority, as are all "human beings."
BRIGHT EYES (Mrs. T. H. Tibbles)

Anchoring her conclusion in a reassertion of shared humanity, La Flesche advocates a system of fairly enforced laws. Intertwined with the suggestion that severalty has "settled . . . the land question" (complex in its presentation alongside Lakota testimonies opposing severalty), La Flesche's writing here appears to reflect her strategic attempts to help curb "arbitrary authority" attempting to undermine the financial sovereignty of the

Lakota. Her signature is moreover significant. By signing "BRIGHT EYES (Mrs. T. H. Tibbles)," La Flesche signals her ability to inhabit multiple roles simultaneously. She is an Omaha, a journalist spokesperson for the Lakota, and the wife of a veteran white journalist. This move may have been deliberate—a means of presenting herself as "a subject who can be heard inside Euroamerican discourses" and who is uniquely positioned to cross boundaries (Powell, "Rhetorics of Survivance" 418). Moreover, by constructing a signature intimately connected with her husband, La Flesche foregrounds their collaborative connection and invites audiences to read Tibbles's words as an extension of her own—maximizing possibilities for change.

COLLABORATIVE JOURNALISM WITH TIBBLES

The collaborative newswriting of La Flesche and Tibbles often appeared side by side in the pages of the *Omaha Morning World-Herald*. Two especially notable collaborative appeals occurred on December 14 and 25, 1890. Illuminating a diverse range of voices as knowledge sources, these appeals also model a relational and socially responsible form of news research and writing at a historical moment when press reformers were advocating greater attention to journalistic ethics by reporters. While the first set of articles highlights voices of white members of proximate communities, the second set shares Lakota knowledges. Both sets of articles reflect the role of conversation as a key methodology, and both function pedagogically by foregrounding the importance of dialogue and relationship building in commercial newspaper reporting (S. Wilson 79).

First, the collaborative appeal published on December 14, 1890, appeared under the headlines "Nothing Warlike There" and "Some Unvarnished Facts" (*OMWH* Dec. 14, 1890). This pair of articles by La Flesche and Tibbles attempted to quell unfounded rumors of war—including those indiscriminately circulated by commercial newspapers—by sharing the testimonies of both a white politician and former member of a proximate community and a school superintendent.

La Flesche's article "Nothing Warlike There" begins by immediately dismantling war rumors:

> Coming up on the train the only warlike signs were four gentlemen talking and gesticulating eagerly, each apparently giving his opinion on the existing state of things, with an air of laying down the law that

admitted of no question. One of them was a contractor, who looked pretty well satisfied with the existing state of things. He, however, asserted roundly that the whole agency system was a fraud.

Another was a prominent politician who had lived on the border of the Sioux reserve for years. He said he knew many of the Sioux personally and that they and the settlers were usually on friendly terms and that the troubles were not caused by any collisions with the settlers as was usually supposed, but from hard feeling against the government resulting from its management of their affairs. (*OMWH* Dec. 14, 1890)

La Flesche opens her article by allaying fears of war through satire and "tease"—characterizing the animated "talking" and "gesticulating" of four white men as "the only warlike signs" (Vizenor, *Literary Chance* 78). Contained within this opening is a clear critique of those who would characterize the Lakota in warlike terms. Statements by members of the "Euroamerican mainstream" then corroborate this point by turning readers' attention to the culpable role of the U.S. government in Indigenous "affairs." This corroboration is first revealed through the contractor, who despite "look[ing] pretty well satisfied with the existing state of things," nonetheless announces "that the whole agency system was a fraud." The "prominent politician"—a personal acquaintance of Lakota people—meanwhile dismantles war rumors ("the troubles were not caused by any collisions with the settlers as was usually supposed . . .") and catalogs "useless" machinery issued to the Lakota as his conversation with La Flesche and Tibbles continues. He tells them:

"When you go [to Pine Ridge Agency] ask some one to show you the machinery issued to the Sioux. Corn shellers that the Indians have no use for, as they raise no corn; implements for which they have no use, made of shoddy material; threshing machines, and they have no wheat to thresh, and all sorts of implements which they would not know how to use. All this useless stuff was bought for them while they were in a state of semi-starvation." He said also that more soap was issued to them than almost anything else, and that this year they had been doing what they had never done before, going to all the little towns on the border of the reservation and trading the clothing and soap that had been issued to them for something to eat. One might know they were pretty hard up when they went round selling clothing. One could see the force of this gentleman's remarks as to the corn shellers and machinery on coming into the reservation and seeing the bare, desolate country in every direction as far as the eye can see. (*OMWH* Dec. 14, 1890)

Like Santee Sioux intellectual Dr. Charles Alexander Eastman, La Flesche strategically demonstrates to readers through this passage her ability to "circulat[e] easily" among Euro-Americans and converse naturally with those she meets (Powell, "Rhetorics of Survivance" 422). Her conversational adeptness here elicits from the politician abundant evidence of the agency system "fraud[ulence]" of which the contractor speaks.

Notably, La Flesche's power as a conversationalist has strong roots in her earlier advocacy on behalf of the Poncas. An example from her February 1880 U.S. Senate testimony exemplifies this point. "I would like to say that when I was down at the Ponca Agency, in the Indian Territory, the white people there at the agency tried to make out that the Poncas did not suffer any," La Flesche begins.

> I was talking with a trader at the agency there . . . He said the agent was a very severe man—disposed to be very severe to the Indians; but he thought he was trying to do the best he could for the tribe. If Standing Bear had staid there, he said, he thought he would be satisfied now; he said the agent had issued wagons and reapers and mowers to the Indians, and was building them houses, and all that. After finishing our talk on such subjects we went to talking of other things, books and poetry and music, and such things. Among the rest we happened to get talking about the climate of the different States, and comparing that of the Indian Territory with other places, "And," said he, "do you know the Poncas have suffered terribly? A great many of them have been sick, and have had nothing to protect them but a canvas tent." This he said without intending to tell me anything. (*Removal* 31–32)

This example highlights La Flesche's ability to absorb her partners in conversation so as to reveal truth. During both her U.S. Senate testimony and Pine Ridge assignment, she not only invests herself with "authority in the colonizer's language" but also interacts in close connection with Euro-Americans to expose wrongs and practice survivance (Pratt 36).

Ultimately, she moves among white and Indigenous communities—assuming "the role of negotiator, someone who can cross boundaries and serve as guide and translator for Others" as Northern Paiute intellectual Sarah Winnemucca Hopkins does in her 1883 autobiography, *Life among the*

Piutes: Their Wrongs and Claims (Royster qtd. in Powell, "Rhetorics of Survivance" 415). The train on which La Flesche travels notably reinforces her mobility—indicating her ability to work across boundaries and anticipating work by Zitkala-Ša also set on a train.[12] Overall, La Flesche's use of white testimony and conversation as a methodology may be read as an effort to remedy injustices by "establishing a measure of identification" with her primarily Euro-American audience and by modeling the importance of attentive dialogue in journalistic practice (Stromberg 5).

Joining La Flesche's article is Tibbles's "Some Unvarnished Facts," which also draws on white testimonies after first setting the scene. "There is not a quieter village in all Nebraska than this town of Rushville," Tibbles begins. "One can walk about the streets and converse with the citizens for hours, and he will never hear one word about Indians or Indian wars, and yet this is the nearest railroad point to the Pine Ridge agency" (*OMWH* Dec. 14, 1890). Like La Flesche, Tibbles opens his article by foregrounding the disparity between rumors and reality. While La Flesche deems a lively debate "the only warlike" sign, Tibbles emphasizes the stillness of this Nebraska town. The remainder of the article uses local testimonies to confirm the pervasiveness of hunger at Pine Ridge. "I have, as I said, interviewed dozens of men in regard to what caused these troubles. On one thing they all agree. There is no exception to this among them, and that is that for more than eighteen months the Sioux have constantly suffered from hunger," Tibbles states. To illustrate this point more specifically, he references former Pine Ridge Indian school superintendent E. E. Van Buskirk, who documents inadequate rations:

> Mr. Van Buskirk says that . . . [t]he adult Indians had no vegetables and no pork. That it required the closest economy to make the rations last through the week, and the children would always have eaten more if he had had it to give to them. That a month or more before he was dismissed the beef ration, in this state of affairs, was cut down 1,000,000 pounds. (*OMWH* Dec. 14, 1890)

Tibbles supplements this testimony with further logos intended to appeal to his white audience's personal interests: "I got some figures from a gentleman who is in a position to know, and he says it has cost the government between $25,000 and $30,000 a day for the last thirty days" on account of unnecessary military presence among the Lakota. By underscoring wasted expenditure on military supplies and troops, Tibbles works to build common ground with potentially less receptive white readers by demonstrating negative consequences of U.S. governmental interference for both white and Indigenous peoples.

An additional set of articles by La Flesche and Tibbles published on December 25, 1890, highlights the crucial role of Lakota people in shaping their strongly "relational and community oriented" journalism (Flynn et al. 6). La Flesche's lead article "Ask Rational Treatment" first describes fear and anger resulting from troop interference in response to the Ghost Dance movement and catalogs with vivid, concrete imagery the responses of the Lakota:

> When the troops came here the Indians did not know why they had come. Some of them thought they had been sent here because they had complained of the rations and that the soldiers had come to compel them to accept the rations and to still further reduce them. There was one night when the Indians, who were camped all round here at the agency, and who had not joined in the ghost dances, sat up all night ready dressed, holding the bridles of their horses in their hands, believing that the soldiers would be on them at any moment. (*OMWH* Dec. 25, 1890)

The Lakota are here characterized as anxiously poised for flight—"holding the bridles of their horses" throughout the night in preparation for defense against an anticipated attack. To reinforce the needlessness of armed military intervention, La Flesche additionally characterizes the Lakota as perplexed by the U.S. Army's arrival ("the Indians did not know why they had come") and wary of a potential further decease in rations.

La Flesche's attempt to compel readers to critically reassess their perceptions of the Lakota in "Ask Rational Treatment" builds on her earlier article "Fleeing from Each Other: Indians and Whites Are Alike Alarmed for No Apparent Good Reason" (*OMWH* Dec. 11, 1890). In this piece, La Flesche focuses on a shared—yet mutually unwarranted—experience of fear in order to expose misunderstandings resulting from troop interference in the Ghost Dance movement:

> In traveling through the country I notice a condition of affairs for which it is not easy to account. Here on the one hand are hundreds of white people leaving their homes because they are afraid of the Sioux. On the other hand there are hundreds of Sioux fleeing to the Bad Lands because they fear the white people, troops having been sent among

them. No one has been killed, no blood shed, no assault made by the Indians on the whites and none on the Indians by the whites. Nothing has been proved which can justify the presence of the troops who have been moved at an expense of thousands of dollars, and the poor white settlers who have fled from their homes at this inclement season of the year call for all one's sympathies. It is a state of affairs that often has and always will result as long as the present system is in existence. I can assure my white friends there is no danger, and they can go quietly to their homes without any fear.

La Flesche posits fear as the impetus for both the flight of "white people" from "their homes" and the flight of "hundreds of" Lakota to the Bad Lands. Yet "[n]o one has been killed, no blood shed, no assault made by the Indians on the whites and none on the Indians by the whites. Nothing has been proved which can justify the presence of the troops" (*OMWH* Dec. 11, 1890). Both "Ask Rational Treatment" and "Fleeing from Each Other" thus debunk commercial newspapers' misrepresentations of the Lakota by portraying them not as preparing to initiate war but instead as frightened as much as whites for their safety. By refiguring the Lakota through an emphasis on mutual fear, La Flesche aims to redirect readers' attention to the troops' deleterious effects and to highlight the need for critical reassessment by white audiences.

"Ask Rational Treatment" also portrays the anger existing alongside fear—a direct result of military interference in the Ghost Dance:

> The coming of the troops made the Indians very angry. It is a very sore point with them. They feel insulted to think that they should have been considered so bad that it was considered necessary to send the troops to them. There is a distinct tone of resentment whenever they speak of the subject. It is a feeling which they would not have if they felt that the government had been justified in resorting to troops in actual self-defense against them. Even those Indians who are bitter against the hostiles for not coming in feel, as one of them expressed it, "there would not have been all this racket and row if that fool agent had not sent for the soldiers." (*OMWH* Dec. 25, 1890)

La Flesche here serves as a conduit for Lakota perspectives ("It is a very sore point with them. They feel insulted . . . ") while also providing direct Lakota testimonies such as the one above. This speaker rebukes the

misguided decision to increase military presence at Pine Ridge Reservation while several other speakers present comparisons used to uphold the
Lakota's right to religious sovereignty (Powell, "Rhetorics of Survivance"
421). One Lakota speaker asserts, "The Indians believe just as much in their
own religion as the white people believe in theirs, and the whites have no
more right to stop the Indians' sacred ceremonies than the Indians have
to stop the whites. I didn't believe in the ghost dances, but all the same I
never thought of interfering with them" (*OMWH* Dec. 25, 1890). Through
published firsthand comments such as these, the Lakota assert rhetorical
sovereignty in the *World-Herald*—a means of claiming their position as
"'knowing subjects'" within white commercial news discourse (García and
Baca 4). Their voices fortify claims by La Flesche and Tibbles regarding
the misuse of government troops, while contributing valuably to a dialogic
type of community-informed news discourse that reflects "interaction
with and investment in" Lakota communities (Powell et al. "Our Story").

Tibbles's adjoining piece "Crow Dog's Story" further reflects Lakota community investment by sharing Tibbles's communication of an account of
the Ghost Dance by the Sicangu (Brulé) Lakota medicine man Crow Dog.
This account, "told to me in the confidence of friendship," was confirmed
by "three different Indians who . . . have told the story in almost exactly the
same words, through different interpreters" (*OMWH* Dec. 25, 1890). The
phrase "confidence of friendship" affirms the centrality of relationships in
knowledge building, while the existence of several nearly identical rendi-
tions of the story is shared to project further credibility. Crow Dog's story,
told to Tibbles during a visit and recounted by the journalist in this piece,
describes the emergence of the Ghost Dance at Rosebud within the contexts
of a severe and dwindling ration system and the U.S. government's historical propensity to break treaties with Indigenous peoples. Refencing Crow
Dog's eventual agreement to, and signing of, a new treaty (presumably the
Great Sioux Agreement of 1889) on terms including the promise "that all
the old debts should be paid," Tibbles writes that Crow Dog "moved out
of the agency and selected a piece of land and waited a long time, but the
government never paid them any money and never sent them any wagons,
harness or anything at all." Rations soon "got less and less, and for a long time
when they gave rations for ten days, the food would all be eaten up in three
or four days, and the people were very hungry" (*OMWH* Dec. 25, 1890).

Tibbles goes on to relate Crow Dog's description of the development
of the Ghost Dance at Rosebud; the journalist also relates Crow Dog's

discussion of instructions by the Sicangu (Brulé) Lakota medicine man and Ghost Dance leader Short Bull that "[t]o their dances they must not take any weapon of war nor the smallest thing made of metal, not even a button." This detail resonates with words by the Oglala Lakota Chief Big Road, who notes in a reflection that "[t]he dance was not a war dance, for none that went to it were allowed to have one scrap of metal on his body" (qtd. in Coleman 57). Tibbles reinforces this point later in the article—relaying Crow Dog's statement that "not war dances but peace dances" occurred at Rosebud and that the Ghost Dance religion called Native peoples "to live in peace with the white people." Overall, Tibbles's article relates Crow Dog's story to affirm the nonviolent nature of the Ghost Dance and redirect white commercial press discourses that—like a December 12, 1890, *Chicago Tribune* article—declared it "Useless To Talk of Peace" (Dec. 12, 1890). The collaborative writing of La Flesche and Tibbles offers a corrective to reckless commercial newspaper discourses by modeling a form of reporting premised on relationally based understandings and local community knowledges.

Importantly, a December 16, 1890, article by La Flesche titled "What Bright Eyes Says" censures unsubstantiated commercial newspaper reporting:

> Yesterday being Sunday we went to the church, and so did a good many Sioux and some soldiers. The whole camp was quiet and serene and the idea of war and bloodshed was the one most distant from our thoughts. In the evening, as we were all quietly preparing for bed, telegrams began to arrive from Omaha to representatives of the papers here asking them to send full accounts of the battle or go out to where the fight occurred and send in the fullest details of the fight. There has been no fight and no bloodshed up to date and no movement of the troops from here, and those who send sensational dispatches when they don't know or are not sure of the truth ought to be—well, to put it mildly, ought to be treated as hostiles and inimical to the peace of the country. (*OMWH* Dec. 16, 1890)

La Flesche here inverts characterizations of Lakota Ghost Dancers as "hostiles" in presenting unprincipled journalists as the true threats to peace: "those who send sensational dispatches when they don't know or are not sure of the truth ought to be—well, to put it mildly, ought to be treated as hostiles and inimical to the peace of the country." Her strategy here builds on similar "language trick[s]" used by Indigenous journalists such as *Cherokee Phoenix* editor Elias Boudinot, who earlier in the nineteenth century "transformed the word *savage* in the paper by identifying Georgians who committed criminal acts against Cherokees as 'white savages'" (Gubele 108). For La Flesche, such a language trick is used to reinforce the crucial link between journalistic representation and policy in demanding accuracy in commercial news discourse. Tibbles echoes her call for accurate news reporting, writing, "I hope people will discontinue sensational dispatches about 5,000 per cent" (*OMWH* Dec. 19, 1890).

The collaborations of La Flesche and Tibbles to this end "t[each] by precept and example" by upholding and modeling relationally based ethics and measured writing during a period in which press reformers were calling for improvements in journalism education and journalistic "accuracy and conscience" (Pulitzer 646–47, 644). In modeling these values, their collaborative writing simultaneously promotes critical literacy among *Omaha Morning World-Herald* readers.

RELATIONALITY, STORY, AND SPEAKING FROM SILENCING

The relational nature of La Flesche's news research and reporting is further accentuated by two additional articles: "They Insulted the Sioux" and "Sunset Scenery" (prefaced by "Why They Are Starving"). The first article merges storytelling with further Lakota community dialogue to sustain critiques of U.S. government policies. The second article showcases La Flesche's powerful response to dialogic silencing when she is "told . . . not to talk to the Indians for a few days." Retaining an emphasis on relationality nonetheless, La Flesche strategically uses this constraint to "unvei[l] the logic of coloniality" and "contribut[e] to build[ing] a world in which many worlds will coexist" (Mignolo, *Darker Side* 54).

First, "They Insulted the Sioux" features Lakota community testimony that continues to illuminate Lakota "thought and feeling" while exposing injustices (García and Baca 3). La Flesche writes, for instance, that "[o]ne woman who had no husband and no man in the family told me that they had issued to her for her share a man's suit of clothes, and she said she did not know what on earth to do with them." This testimony depicts the indiscriminateness of government clothing distribution, reinforced by the additional detail that "[t]hey also issued a boy's suit of clothes to a little girl" (*OMWH* Dec. 24, 1890).

Later in the article, La Flesche relates the "story" of a Lakota widow whose dying husband requested that his favorite horse be shot. Doing as instructed, she was promptly stripped of the majority of her stock by a government farmer. "He took from her stock which had not been issued to her by the government, but was her individual property, bought with her own money. He gave it to other Indians." After sharing this Lakota woman's story, La Flesche proceeds to draw an analogy used to build alliance with *World-Herald* readers:

> As a counterpoint to this story, I will relate one I heard while I was in Boston. It seems there was a wealthy family who lived on the Back bay. The husband and father . . . had a beautiful horse ridden by no one but himself of which he was very fond. He died and the family rather than part with the animal and probably unable to bear the idea that the beautiful creature should pass into the hands of strangers and perhaps maltreated, had him shot. No one in Boston seemed to have the idea that because the family had made away with an expensive article, all that they possessed should therefore be taken from them. (*OMWH* Dec. 24, 1890)

Recalling the alliance-building strategies present in La Flesche's collaborations with Tibbles, this analogy repurposes the Euro-American value of individual ownership rights to protest attacks on Lakota sovereignty and to build identification with readers. Specifically, La Flesche emphasizes the Bostonian's emotional attachment to his horse through the repetition of the word "beautiful" and the threat of animal cruelty ("probably unable to bear the idea that the beautiful creature should pass into the hands of strangers and perhaps maltreated"). She thus encourages reader alliance with the Boston family and, by extension, the Lakota widow. Notably, these alliance-building practices are anchored in storytelling ("Here is the story of a widow"; "As a counterpoint to this story, I will relate one I heard . . ."). As Wilson relays in *Research Is Ceremony*, "[s]tories and metaphor are often used in Indigenous societies . . . as a teaching tool." The stories shared by La Flesche teach by "getting away from abstractions." They invite *World-Herald* readers "to see others' life experiences through [their] own eyes" in ways that accentuate connections between Euro-Americans and Lakota people (S. Wilson 17).

This article also contains a story told by La Flesche that reflects on her personal experience on the Omaha reserve. It is used alongside locally based facts to highlight the inadequacy of government farmers and forced farming among the Lakota. First, she reports that "[t]here are about five government farmers on the reserve, each receiving $75 a month for teaching the Indians to farm (?)" (*OMWH* Dec. 24, 1890). La Flesche then explicates the critique signaled by the parenthetical question mark: "[o]ne can judge quite well of their qualifications for farming when one knows that a clerk who had never farmed in his life was given the position of farmer." To intensify this critique, La Flesche shares:

> Having been brought up on a reserve and having borne the infliction of having farmers issued to us, who were paid salaries out of our tribal money, said farmers not even lifting a hand to teach an Indian to farm, I give my unqualified opinion that the government farmer is utterly useless to the Indians, especially on a reservation like this, where the soil is sandy and more fit for grazing purposes than for farming. (*OMWH* Dec. 24, 1890)

La Flesche here utilizes personal experience, combined with a strong declarative claim, to build reader knowledge. Her description of the sandy soil moreover recalls her view of "the bare, desolate country" seen from the train and reinforces the context of severe hunger experienced by the Lakota. Ultimately, the article's interwoven threads of conversation, storytelling, and locally based facts continue to reshape narratives about Lakota people in ways that rebuke and attempt to remedy unjust policies.

La Flesche's relational news research and reporting takes especially significant shape in the articles "Why They Are Starving" and "Sunset Scenery." The first reflects continued close conversation and relationship building as means of reinforcing the extreme hunger pervading Pine Ridge due to inadequate rations and forced farming on arid land. She writes:

> If they are not in by today, the soldiers are to be sent against them. This is literally forcing them to the fight. The Indian at whose house we are staying says that the tribe raised no crops at all this summer on account of dry weather, and that those who might have succeeded in raising a little in spite of that had their crops destroyed by being called in to the agency for fifteen days, while the commission was here last spring ... The Indians say that their rations have been entirely inadequate. One Indian woman had the curiosity to count the number of grains of coffee issued to her as her part of the rations, and the number of grains amounted to just thirty for two weeks. An Indian woman told me that she knew many that had died from a state of semi-starvation, and that

there had been an unusual number of deaths among them, the number of funerals amounting sometimes to five or six a day. They have not raised any crops to amount to anything for the last three years, and to cap the climax, after last summer's failure of crops the department cut down their rations. (*OMWH* Dec. 18, 1890)

This passage powerfully exposes the injustice of a planned military intervention by the U.S. government by bolstering depictions of acute hunger at Pine Ridge. In rebuking this planned military intervention, La Flesche draws intimately on her relationships with Lakota people—evident in both her lodging arrangement ("[t]he Indian at whose house we are staying says . . .") and continued dialogue with other Lakota people. La Flesche's stay with a Lakota host especially reflects the importance of relationships in knowledge formation—relationships "form[ed] . . . at a different level than we are accustomed to in our everyday lives" (S. Wilson 113). The remainder of the passage contains further Lakota testimonies ("The Indians say . . ."; "An Indian woman told me . . .") and locally based facts that underscore the misguidedness of forced farming, the devastating severity of hunger at Pine Ridge, and the injustice of planned troop interference among Lakota outside Pine Ridge.

The related and rhetorically masterful "Sunset Scenery" (written on December 14 but published on December 18, 1890) features La Flesche's skillful repurposing of silence when ordered to suspend community dialogue.[13] In doing so, she "confront[s] power . . . not with aggression or overt confrontation but with flexible, subtle, active responsiveness to the constraints and possibilities" of her altered context—including emerging possibilities for subversion (Flynn et al. 9–10). She opens:

General Brooke having told us not to talk to the Indians for a few days, obliges me to confine myself to the surface of things. Last night was a beautiful sunset, different from the usual run of sunsets, only two colors, blue and gold, all the various shades of each blended together as only the hand of nature could blend them, from the palest silvery blue to the deepest shade of that color, and the yellow so pale that one could hardly distinguish it from silver, to the deepest, most vivid gold. All this shining over a scene the like of which not to be seen anywhere in the world but here. (*OMWH* Dec. 18, 1890)

"[C]onfine[d] . . . to the surface of things," La Flesche immediately yet implicitly critiques the order to cease dialogue. She then proceeds to use this constraint in resilient ways. Without the benefit of community conversation, La Flesche assumes the challenge of using "surface[s]" to reveal deeper meanings and issue a potent call for justice. This process begins with rich descriptive imagery. Phrases such as "palest silvery blue" and "yellow so pale that one could hardly distinguish it from silver" bolster her writerly ethos and moreover subtly build toward tension between the "beautiful sunset" and "a scene the like of which not to be seen anywhere in the world but here."

La Flesche continues by describing this "scene" in ways that deconstruct the framing of differences "in terms of values of plus and minus degree of humanity" (Mignolo "Delinking" 499). She documents "white men in all the various stages of civilization (?) from the shabby, unkempt, roughbearded specimen up (or down) to the citified looking fellow with the invariable cigar in his mouth, and up, certainly, to the prim Presbyterian minister." Shortly thereafter, La Flesche describes

> Indians in the various stages, from the painted savage, wrapped in his Navajo blanket up or down (?) to the semi-civilized, who compromise by wearing a stove pipe hat in addition to the blanket, and up, certainly, to the full blooded Episcopalian Indian minister who officiates at the church yonder. Then here comes tripping by, bangs and all correct, a dainty little Indian maiden who would not look out of place on the streets of a city with school dress so simply and neatly made that it would give her an air of distinction anywhere. Yonder is a group of Indians surrounding a horseman, another Indian, whom I suppose we can term a western gentleman, as he is clothed correctly in the ordinary habiliments of a western white gentleman. (*OMWH* Dec. 18, 1890)

La Flesche's depiction of "the surface of things" reveals and critiques "the logic of coloniality" (Mignolo, *Darker Side* 53–54). Specifically, her strategic descriptions of white men and Lakota people indicate ways in which "colonial differences" are made and expose how "particular practices . . . are valued (or not)" within Euro-American cultural systems (Mignolo, "Delinking" 498; Powell et al., "Our Story"). To this end, her use of question marks destabilizes both classification schemas demarcating "various stages of civilization" as well as the very concept of "civilization" itself.

La Flesche, for instance, questions why a stovepipe hat should signal a higher stage of "civilization" than paint and a Navajo blanket. The phrase "whom I suppose we can term a western gentleman" reflects a similar rhetorical move at the end of the passage. Here, La Flesche again reveals "the instability of colonial . . . claims to dominance" by critiquing ways in which the category of "western gentleman" is constructed by certain "correct" practices of dress (Powell et al., "Our Story").[14]

Her critique notably echoes this related passage from her undated manuscript "The Omahas":

> I have sometimes had the question asked me, is your tribe civilized? And I have really not known what to answer. I have known men and women all my life who are brave, generous, truthful, honest, industrious, patriotic, and lovely in all the relations of life and yet if you were to see them you would call them savages because they can neither speak or read or write the English language or dress as you do. (S. Tibbles)

In this passage, La Flesche connects Euro-American practices such as English speaking and specific dress conventions to the maintenance of a colonial system in which "not all cultures are seen as equal—some are believed to be dominant/civilized while others are seen as marginal/savage" (Powell et al., "Our Story"). These dichotomies both informed and were perpetuated by much late nineteenth-century white commercial press discourse about Indigenous peoples—leading La Flesche to expose and critique in "Sunset Scenery" ways in which "Western categories of thoughts" impede the "ma[king]" of "[a] world in which many worlds could co-exist" (Mignolo, "Delinking" 499).

La Flesche continues:

> The cavalrymen going by on horseback make a fine appearance. There go two white young ladies who are gotten up as if they had just been shopping on Farnam street, probably the teachers at the government school. Here comes something cute, a little two-wheeled vehicle drawn by a tiny Indian pony and driven by two little Sioux boys, looking not much older than 8 or 9. As I stand at the gate of the Indian house where we are staying, looking alternately at the sunset and the varied scene, the bell of the Episcopal church begins to toll and I know that it is for the funeral of a little dead Indian baby. While the bell is still tolling, the band strikes up, and through all the stirring music I can still hear the

tolling. It was like the heartbreak underneath all this scene. I began to wonder what has brought all these things together here in this one spot. Ministers representing three different denominations, their churches, the government schools, the agent—all this paraphernalia of war, all apparently directed toward the one object of civilizing, taming and subduing a number of human beings, helpless, ignorant, and with hearts burning with a sense of injustice at being misunderstood by their more favored fellow men, who have brought all this machinery to bear on them for the purpose of quelling them, and all of which is ineffectual, because they are hungry and have not been treated with justice.

I think the merciful Father of us all must be looking in pity on the whole scene. (*OMWH* Dec. 18, 1890)

In this resounding call for relational understanding and justice, La Flesche reveals the devastation of "surface" interpretations, "colonial differences," and "all this paraphernalia of war . . . apparently directed toward the one object of civilizing, taming and subduing" those who are starving and "have not been treated with justice." Her article therefore takes readers beneath "the surface of things"—confronting them with "the funeral of a little dead Indian baby" through word choice that foregrounds her community knowledge ("I know that it is . . .")—and reverberates the testimony of the "Indian woman [who] told me that she knew many that had died from a state of semi-starvation, and that there had been an unusual number of deaths among them, the number of funerals amounting sometimes to five or six a day" (*OMWH* Dec. 18, 1890). Overall, "Sunset Scenery" strives to jolt *World-Herald* readers out of complacency, urging them to adopt new systems of knowledge and understanding anchored in relationships of "[r]espect, reciprocity and responsibility" (S. Wilson 77). From within this highly asymmetrical context of power, La Flesche calls on readers to critically reassess their misperceptions of Indigenous peoples, demand justice, and uphold the dignity of all people. She concludes by merging personal faith with a strong call for relationally centered justice expressed in a language of common humanity: "I think the merciful Father of us all must be looking in pity on the whole scene" (*OMWH* Dec. 18, 1890).

In the December 27, 1890, article "Disarming The Red Men: Bright Eyes Declares It a Senseless and Harmful Injustice Without Cause," La Flesche enacts one of her last efforts to teach her readership prior to the Wounded Knee Massacre. In this article, La Flesche calls on her Euro-American audience to pursue discursive public participation in response to the planned disarmament of Spotted Elk's band of Lakota by the Seventh Cavalry on Wounded Knee Creek (Treuer 5–6). "I wish some attempt could be made to protest against the taking away from the Indians of their ponies and arms. This protest should come from the white people as it would be to the interest of the white people themselves," she writes. "If it is done it will fail in its purpose and only create feelings which may last for years. In all this so-called war and with all the arms the Indians are supposed to possess, there has been no white man shot and not a single white man's or woman's life taken" (*OMWH* Dec. 27, 1890). The disarmament nonetheless proceeded. On December 29, 1890, attempts by the Seventh Cavalry to disarm the Lakota led to the brutal massacre of more than 150 (and likely 300 or more) men, women, and children (Treuer 6; Lee 130; Hopson 266).[15] Recalling the horrendous aftermath of the Wounded Knee Massacre in his later autobiography, Dr. Charles Alexander Eastman wrote, "we found them scattered along as they had been relentlessly hunted down and slaughtered while fleeing for their lives" (111).

La Flesche's journalistic writing following the Wounded Knee Massacre underscored its brutality while also "dismantl[ing]" narratives of the massacre as "the end of Indian life"—seen, for instance, in commercial newspaper headlines such as "Redskins All Wiped Out," "All Murdered In A Mass: Big Foot [Spotted Elk] and All His Followers Shot Down Without Regard to Sex," and "Completely Wiped Out" (Lee 132; Treuer 1; qtd. in Andersson 237; *OMWH* Dec. 30, 1890; *OMWH* Dec. 31, 1890). La Flesche's continued practices of rhetorical sovereignty and survivance and her sustained emphasis on Lakota testimony and social protest to this end reflect renewed rhetorical resilience that "recogniz[es] and seiz[es] opportunities even in the most oppressive situations" (Flynn et al. 8).

Ongoing Practices of Survivance and Rhetorical Resilience

In one sense indicative of the devastating limitations of journalistic pedagogy for this Omaha writer addressing a white audience, this chapter also highlights La Flesche's sustained, powerful practices of rhetorical sovereignty and survivance as well as her rhetorical resilience in "continually recreat[ing] possibilit[ies]" for change (Flynn et al. 8). Following the Wounded Knee Massacre, La Flesche maintained and vigorously asserted "an active sense of presence over absence, deracination, and oblivion" through work reflecting "the continuance of native stories, not just a reaction, however pertinent, or the mere right of a survivable name" (Vizenor, *Literary Chance* 13). This is apparent in an article published on January 2, 1891, titled "Horrors of War" (*OMWH* Jan. 2 1891).

In this article, La Flesche reports from a reservation church where wounded Lakota lie on mattresses of hay:

> Hay thrown on the floor for mattresses and the wounded lying on the hay. There had been no time to get pillows as yet. There was a woman sitting on the floor with a wounded baby on her lap and four or five children around her, all her grand children. Their father and mother were killed. There was a young woman shot through both thighs and her wrist was broken. Mr. Tibbles has had to get a pair of pinchers to get her rings off. There was a little boy with his throat apparently shot to pieces. (*OMWH* Jan. 2, 1891)

This stark catalog challenges *World-Herald* readers to confront the scene through bare facts that communicate the atrocity of the Wounded Knee Massacre. La Flesche then extends her description of the little boy:

> He was a horrible sight, having nothing around him but a blanket, and his little bare, lean arms looked pitiful. They were all hungry, and when we fed this little boy we found he could swallow. We gave him some gruel, and he grabbed with both his little hands a dipper of water. When I saw him yesterday afternoon he looked worse than the day before, and when they feed him now the food and water come out of the side of his neck. (*OMWH* Jan. 2, 1891)

Bluntness drives this description as La Flesche, through participatory involvement ("when we fed this little boy . . . "), foregrounds the boy's "little hands" and "little bare, lean arms"—attempting to awaken affective responses in *World-Herald* readers.

The voices of Lakota children contribute powerfully to this strategy. This is emblematized in the following passage:

> One little girl was wounded in several places and her leg was broken, and her mother was wounded in the leg. The little girl, who did not seem to be more than 7 years old, lay there saying over and over, of course, in Sioux:

"The soldiers are bad. I saw them kill my father. They killed my father." (*OMWH* Jan. 2, 1891)

Driven by a resilient commitment to foregrounding Lakota perspectives, La Flesche interweaves the stark firsthand testimony of this Lakota girl with her own firsthand observations of the violent aftermath of Wounded Knee. She writes of her approach: "I have been thus particular in giving horrible details in the hope of rousing such an indignation that another such causeless war shall never again be allowed by the people of the United States." Exemplifying La Flesche's rhetorical resilience, this statement calls on "the people of the United States" to prevent "causeless" future violence through opposition fueled by "indignation" over attacks on Indigenous sovereignty.

She continues shortly afterward:

The conviction is slowly forcing itself into my mind that this war has been deliberately brought about. The hostile Sioux firmly believe now that it has been brought about because their land was wanted. If the white people want their land and must have it, they can go about getting it in some other way than by forcing it from them by starving them or provoking them to war and sacrificing the lives of innocent women and children, and through the sufferings of the wives and children of officers and soldiers. Cannot the white people see that by making the government keep its agreements with the Indians to the letter, and treating them with justice, I do not say kindness or mercy, but justice, that the Indians might feel inclined of their own accord to let the most of their lands go when they know that they will surely be paid for it and all agreements kept with them. They are a notoriously generous people and I think in some cases would give their land if they felt sure the white people were just to them and were their friends.

Through this acute "renunciatio[n]" of "victimry," La Flesche asks readers to confront the violent implications of settler colonialism: "The conviction is slowly forcing itself into my mind that this war has been deliberately brought about (Vizenor, *Manifest Manners* vii). La Flesche denounces the licensing of starvation and violence—urging her white readership to join in her demands for justice. In simultaneously referencing the "sufferings of the wives and children of officers and soldiers," La Flesche's appeal here resembles Sarah Winnemucca Hopkins's similar articulation of "the damage done to 'two races'" by the violence of colonization in *Life among the Paiutes* (Powell, "Rhetorics of Survivance" 409).

Her call for justice, just relations, and peace is then sustained by her suggestion that "the Indians might feel inclined of their own accord to let the most of their lands go when they know that they will surely be paid for it and all agreements kept with them. They are a notoriously generous people and I think in some cases would give their land if they felt sure the white people were just to them and were their friends" (*OMWH* Jan. 2, 1891). Read in the context of La Flesche's undated manuscript "The Omahas" that reflects on the principle of generosity, these words take on additional significance. La Flesche writes in this manuscript:

> A man is considered great according to what he has given away and not according to what he has. Every year we had a harvest feast lasting three days. Whoever chose to do so gave a horse or as many horses as he wished to give, and these horses were given to the poorest man in the tribe. When a calamity occurs to a family all the members of his band make up to them what they have lost. A family on our reserve was burnt out by a prairie fire and a house and barn were lost and the value of them was made up to him by his band. Another family camped in a valley was struck by a water-spout and the tent was swept away and the grandmother was drowned. His band gave him seven horses where he had had none before. Sometimes I think you white people do not know how to love each other as we Indians do, but then you see we have nothing in the world but each other. (S. Tibbles)

La Flesche describes generosity as both a measure of character ("A man is considered great according to what he has given away and not according to what he has") and an outgrowth of relational ways of being ("we have nothing in the world but each other"). By interconnecting in her article "Horrors of War" a reflection on generosity with both a demand for justice and a call for relationality ("They are a notoriously generous people and I think in some cases would give their land if they felt sure the white people were just to them and were their friends"), La Flesche practices a form of survivance intended to build just, relational alliances and uphold Indigenous self-determination and survival.

◈ ◈ ◈

In closing, it is possible to adopt what Jacqueline Jones Royster and Gesa E. Kirsch have termed "critical imagination" to consider ways in which La Flesche's journalistic teaching and rhetorical influence may have helped prevent additional violence directed at the Lakota after the Wounded Knee Massacre (19–20). This possibility is indicated by La Flesche's January 1, 1891, description of the U.S. military response to those Lakota who had fled Pine Ridge Reservation immediately following the Wounded Knee Massacre, fearing they, too, would be shot. "General Brooke has been severely criticized because he did not fire on the Indians when they were leaving the reservation," La Flesche reports, "but if he had there would have been a general fusillade, as all the agency buildings and spaces around were packed with us women and children" (*OMWH* Jan. 1, 1891). While it is difficult to ascertain La Flesche's precise impact on General Brooke's decision, this example invites us to imagine powerful ways in which her rhetorical influence may have helped avert further violence—both in this instance and beyond. Ultimately, La Flesche's relational news reporting embodies a determination to respond proactively with hope and powerfully with literacy through the pages of the late nineteenth-century mass-circulating press (Flynn et al. 1). Continuing to attend closely to histories of Indigenous rhetorics in journalism will further illuminate the instrumental pedagogical and activist work of journalists like La Flesche.

Conclusion: Public Memory and the Pan-extracurriculum

In recent years, public memory studies in rhetoric has dynamically grown as Jessica Enoch, Jordynn Jack, Kendall Phillips, Kristy Maddux, Carol Mattingly, and other scholars have directed increased attention to "the rhetorical practice of remembering" (Enoch, "Releasing Hold" 60). For Enoch, remembering within feminist historiography entails "working within *while expanding* the boundaries of historiographic recovery" (60; italics mine). This convergence of feminist and public memory scholarship invites us to examine "the rhetorical work that goes into remembering women" by posing a question: "'How have women been remembered and to what rhetorical purpose has their memory been put?'" (62). I conclude this study by exploring how the rhetorical careers of Black, Mossell, and La Flesche have been inscribed in public memory. Specifically, I examine the sustained influence of these three journalists on extracurricular literacy practices and rhetorical education. Their influence is evident in the various ways that a diverse range of individuals and groups have remembered these newspaperwomen and their meaningful work.

I first analyze Winifred Black Bonfils's ongoing influence on extracurricular literacy practices among clubwomen, junior high school students, children hospital patients, nursing students, musicians, and other San Franciscans decades after "Annie Laurie's Appeal" was published in 1894. Interrelatedly, I examine how the remarkable rhetorical influence of Black's "Little Jim" campaign spurred public memory practices that came to intimately link the reporter with the "Little Jim Ward"—which itself became an enduring "monument to Annie Laurie" for over eighty years (*SFE* Oct. 8, 1936).

Second, I discuss collection-based, spatial, and digital extracurricular literacy practices relevant to the public memory of Gertrude Bustill Mossell and a constellation of other African American rhetors. This discussion covers the extensive collection practices of librarian Jessie Carney Smith, author of *Notable Black American Women* (1992), and the African

American historical marker program headed by Dr. Charles Blockson in Philadelphia during the 1990s, which memorialized Mossell with a cast aluminum marker posted outside her former home. I analyze not only this marker's history but also the diverse literacy practices inspired by markers such as Mossell's—ranging from photo taking, conversation, and self-sponsored research to digital proficiencies such as waymarking and online cataloging.

Finally, I address extracurricular literacy endeavors related to Susette La Flesche Tibbles and her nomination and eventual entry into the Nebraska Hall of Fame: a 1975 *Lincoln Evening Journal* article by International Women's Year celebrant Betty Loudon that remembers La Flesche and endorses her Hall of Fame induction, and a 2016 "Nebraska Story" by Princella Parker (Omaha Nation) that celebrates La Flesche—one of five women inducted into the Nebraska Hall of Fame—as a role model. As part of this discussion, I analyze ways in which public memory of La Flesche has been both enmeshed within the "continuing rhetorical legacy of colonialism" and delinked from this legacy by Indigenous-led rhetorical practices of remembering (Kelly and Black 5; Mignolo, "Delinking").

I close the conclusion by proposing takeaways for future scholarship at the intersection of women's rhetorical historiography, public memory, and rhetoric and composition's extracurriculum.

Remembering Winifred Black: The Ongoing Extracurricular Influences of "Annie Laurie's Appeal"

On March 2, 1932, Edna J. Shirpser wrote Winifred Black a letter inviting her to a meeting of the "Little Jim Club"—an organization inspired by Black's 1894 story and for which Shirpser served as president. "The children would be interested in knowing you," Shirpser explained, "because you really knew and still remember Little Jim." The remainder of the letter detailed the purpose of the group. Founded "to bring cheer and happiness" to young patients, the "Little Jim Club" was supervised by women and open to any child under the age of eighteen years old. The organization undertook various projects for the "Little Jim Ward" including sponsoring occupational therapy, supplying Christmas presents, and redecorating the premises. It also threw holiday parties for the young patients. The club funded these projects through bazaars, children's plays, and private donations—and members relied heavily on extracurricular literacy.

Female organizers of the "Little Jim Club" held meetings, kept minutes, and created bylaws. They defined positions and wrote letters that they revised for content, style, and format. An undated letter (circa 1932) from Edith Slack, "Little Jim Club" supervisor and Children's Hospital board member, begins:

> My dear Miss Shirpser: –
>
> While double spacing looks better, don't you think that a letter of this length should be single spaced in order to get it on one page? Here it is retyped and even with a narrow margin, it should not look crowded.
>
> You have done all the hard work in composing a really fine letter and I have had the easy job of using all your ideas but changing the wording here and there and condensing it a little so that we would have a rather different letter and "set up" from those read at the Auxiliary and Board meetings.

Slack explains her revisions to Shirpser's draft. In the first paragraph, she justifies deviating from double spacing on account of the letter's length. Yet she is simultaneously aware that a single-space format must not repel readers—"even with a narrow margin, it should not look crowded," she reasons. Slack goes on to commend Shirpser for drafting "fine" content, which she deems to be the most difficult part of the writing process. She revises the letter for style and concision, while also considering the rhetorical context in which it will be received. Wanting it to stand out against "those read at the Auxiliary and Board meetings," Slack makes revision choices that will produce "a rather different letter."

Importantly, in addition to writing and revising letters to members, patrons, and the hospital board, the club also published the *Little Jim Clarion*—a newsletter featuring club news, meeting announcements, and creative writing by young hospital patients. The March 1932 *Clarion*, for instance, included a poem by a ward resident, Stella, in praise of Mrs. Lowell, a club supervisor who taught children "all the things they can do to fill in those empty long hours" at the hospital.

In the poem, Stella applauds Mrs. Lowell in creative form. She playfully employs rhyme, alliteration, and musical conventions to share her delight—evident also in the exclamation mark that ends the chorus ("Oh!"). Importantly, Stella's piece signals the role of the *Little Jim Clarion* in

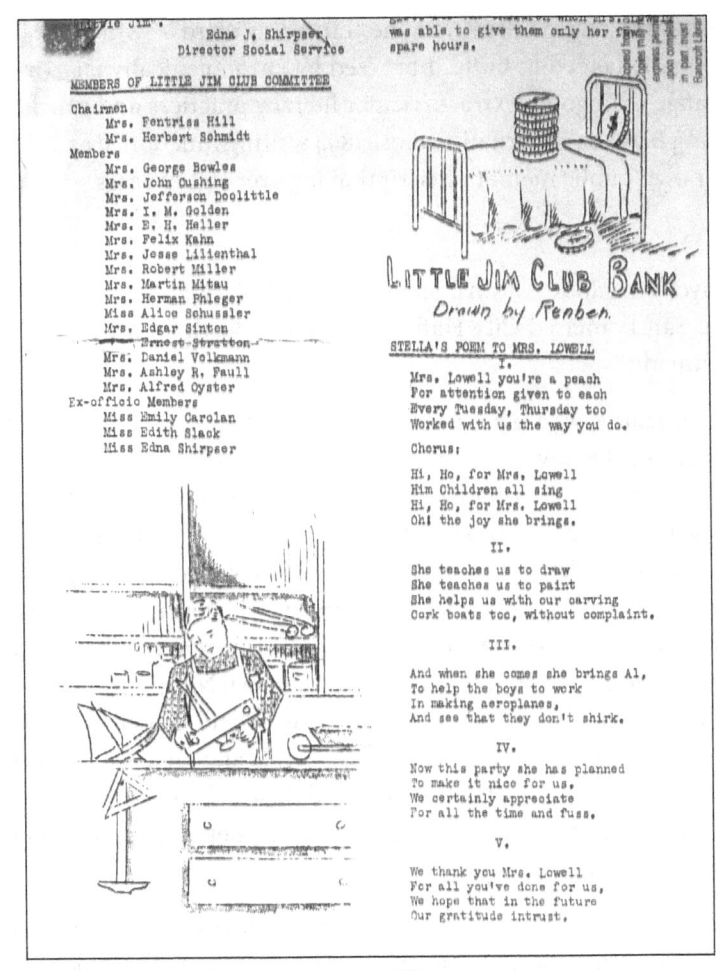

C.1. "Stella's Poem to Mrs. Lowell." *Little Jim Clarion*, Mar. 1932,
Children's Hospital of San Francisco records, BANC MSS 89/87 c,
The Bancroft Library, University of California, Berkeley.

providing a space for a child patient to become "rhetorical in [her] own right" by articulating her own voice and perspective in public writing (Cedillo, "What Does It Mean").

The literacy practices of both Stella and the "Little Jim" clubwomen attest to the endurance of Black's influence on extracurricular writing decades after her 1894 publication of "Annie Laurie's Appeal." Indeed, the rhetorical power of her article precipitated a wide range of continuing extracurricular literacy practices ranging from musical composition to children's radio drama, while furthermore linking Black intimately in San

Franciscan public memory with the "Little Jim Ward"—which she had so influentially helped to build. I proceed by chronologically charting this rich range of ongoing extracurricular literacy practices and conclude by situating Black as a journalist whose 1894 writing functioned as a channel for her own public memory inscription for over eighty years.

In Mayor Angelo Rossi's tribute to Winifred Black at her memorial service in San Francisco City Hall following her death on May 25, 1936, he proclaimed:

> Annie Laurie, we are privileged to accord you here the highest tribute our city can bestow. We bring you here, where the spirit of San Francisco lives, as a recognition of what you have done for those you loved and for those who loved you. In a humble way we acknowledge by this simple ceremony the debt San Francisco owes you for your unfailing interest in the public good—a debt that can never be repaid. You adopted and were adopted by San Francisco. You mothered our fire and police departments, our South of Market Boys, our own Ninety-first Division and other veteran groups, and in the realm of your chosen profession you were the foremost lady—and I believe that although your requiem will soon have been sung, these men and their womenfolk will parade down the avenue of time singing your praises, not in requiem—but in jubilee. (*SFE* May 26, 1936)

Notably, many San Franciscans did "parade down the avenue of time" not only "singing [Black's] praises" but engaging, too, in a wide range of ongoing extracurricular literacy practices instigated by Black's 1894 "Little Jim" campaign. And while still other San Franciscans pursued literacy practices that remembered "Little Jim" but (to varying degrees) erased Black herself, this cumulative body of writing, speaking, and musical composing points to the rich trails of extracurricular literacy influence that a rhetor can sustain over time—even when the rhetor herself becomes less visible in such practices.

One early yet unique extracurricular outgrowth of Black's "Little Jim" campaign was Noah Brandt's 1895 musical composition "Little Jim: A Ballad" with words by J. F. Fleming. "Respectfully dedicated to Annie Laurie," this ballad "was sent to all contributors to the Little Jim hospital," according to a note penciled on the verso.

C.2a & C.2b. "Little Jim: A Ballad." Words by J. F. Fleming; music by Noah Brandt. 1895. California Sheet Music Digital Collection. UC Berkeley. Jean Gray Hargrove Music Library.

The cover of the ballad notably reprints the *San Francisco Examiner*'s December 9, 1894, illustration featuring children's "Little Jim" letters in an outdoor public setting—letters that depart from prevailing late nineteenth-century standards of grammar, mechanics, and spelling. The reprinting of these letters on this "souvenir . . . sent to all contributors to the Little Jim hospital" indicates ways that children's activist writing continued to circulate and contribute to public rhetorical education by promoting values of sincerity and social conscience. Black's inspiration of the ballad itself is moreover significant in indicating how the reporter's extracurricular influence extended into musical composition. "Little Jim, Little Jim, weary and sore; / Little Jim, Little Jim, sorrow no more; / Loving thee, shielding thee, helping thee stand / Charity cheering thee, holding thy hand" begins the chorus,[1] as the ballad overall praises "Bonnie Annie Laurie" for her kindhearted appeal—one that both spurred the construction of the "Little Jim Ward" and inspired Noah Brandt and J. F. Fleming to compose music and lyrics for voice and piano.

A second example offers further evidence of Black's ongoing influence on San Franciscans' literate practices: the *Annual of the Children's Hospital Training School for Nurses*. Composed "in the border space" between school and the extracurriculum, this yearbook-like serial—later titled "Little Jim"—was published annually by San Francisco student nurses from at least 1924 to 1930 (Schultz 10).[2] It contained student photographs, alumnae reports, editorials, poetry, bits of humor, and other writings primarily (but not exclusively) written by student nurses. Two issues of this annual are especially notable in featuring essays that explicitly discuss "Little Jim." The first appears in 1925. Composed by Dr. George McChesney, this essay recounts the history and describes the growth of the "Little Jim Ward." Of the ward's origins, McChesney describes "a reporter" at a city intersection who "overhear[s]" the conversation of a boy and his mother. "They had just been to the hospital, asking for admittance for the boy, but because of the lack of room the boy was not admitted. Mother and child were both crying. The reporter wrote the 'Little Jim' story very pathetically and the result was the building of the 'Little Jim Ward'" (25).

This passage reveals both a unique rewriting of the "Little Jim" story and erasure of Black's name from the rewritten events. No longer is the story related to Black by Dr. Overacker within the hospital; Black is now positioned on a street corner as a firsthand witness of the conversation between mother and son. Moreover, she is simply referred to as "a reporter"—

marking emerging ways in which the "remembering" of "Little Jim" would at times eclipse the "remembering" of Black as the journalist who first disseminated his story. McChesney's essay also indicates how various San Franciscans—through their active extracurricular literacy practices—would come to circulate reimagined narratives about "Little Jim."

The second example (from 1928) is an award-winning essay titled "The Legend of 'Little Jim'" by nursing student Aileen G. Crowley—the first-prize finisher of the annual's literary contest. This essay also creatively rewrites the "Little Jim" story without reference to Black or even "a reporter." Significantly, however, it alludes to the relevant dynamics of public formation. Crowley begins: "In ancient days there stood away out in the sand dunes of San Francisco a small wooden structure capable of housing only a few of those children who were so unfortunate as to be sick . . . This building was well equipped for that time but lacked sufficient funds for maintenance, thereby causing many needy poverty stricken patients to be turned from its doors" (34). She soon introduces "Little Jim" and his mother—"wending their weary way westward" toward the hospital while "[t]he child talked gaily, for was he not going to this great place to be cured?" The hospital, however, could not accommodate "Little Jim," and the two were "seen leaving the hospital, obviously brokenhearted and low in spirits":

> The outlook was dark and dreary for this disconsolate mother, who realized only too well that there was no place to care for this child nor for many others afflicted. As she turned toward the street she was moved to tears, and likewise the child who seemed also to sense the tragedy already at hand. A passerby was attracted by the unhappy looking couple and talking with the boy learned of the unfortunate incident . . . Soon the boy limped breathlessly back to his mother, his sweet childish voice ringing out in excited tones—"Don't cry, Mother, don't cry! The 'Public,' whoever that is, will build a place for me." (Crowley 34)

In this essay, Crowley employs various conventions of storytelling such as retrospection (e.g., "In ancient days . . . "), alliteration (e.g., "wending their weary way westward"), and a narrative arc that proceeds from the protagonists' goal to a conflict to an eventual resolution: "In the year that followed," Crowley concludes, "a round, towerlike building was erected by the 'Public' of San Francisco, directly on the spot where the influential passerby had met the child." Here, Crowley highlights "Public" formation and agency—a notable choice given Black's mobilization of a powerful counterpublic during the "Little Jim" campaign. If we interpret the "passerby" as a symbolic stand-in for this "public," the story then also suggests how intimacy can propel publics toward social action. As Crowley writes, "[a] passerby was attracted by the unhappy looking couple and talking with the boy learned of the unfortunate incident." This moment underscores the centrality of dialogue in prompting social action and calls to mind both Black's conversation with Dr. Overacker in the hospital and her subsequent correspondence with San Francisco children through their intimately "public" letters about "Little Jim." Overall, these two examples point to the continued trail of extracurricular influence that a rhetor can sustain over time—even when the rhetor herself becomes less visible in such literacy practices.

Despite Black's erasure from these 1920s "Little Jim" annual essays, she remained not only regionally but nationally known at this time. As Katherine H. Adams and Michael L. Keene confirm, during "a career in which she wrote perhaps ten thousand short pieces and three books," Black "reach[ed] a nationwide audience that learned from her and respected her work" (6). She notably remained "in the harness" of journalism until her death on May 25, 1936, when she was remembered by San Franciscans as "America's best known newspaper woman" (*SFE* May 26, 1936). Even outside the United States, Black was heralded in Ontario, Canada's *Windsor Star* as a "veteran newspaper woman whose columns signed 'Annie Laurie' were read by millions" (May 29, 1936). Notably, many tributes following her death—including those published in the *San Francisco Examiner, Windsor Star*, and Pittsburgh *Sun-Telegraph*—highlighted Black's work in the "Little Jim" campaign. As the *Sun-Telegraph* put it, "[h]er active interest in the Children's Hospital came through a chance meeting with 'Little Jim' . . . In the *Examiner* Mrs. Bonfils conducted a vigorous campaign through which the 'Little Jim' fund was raised and a ward for incurables made available in the hospital" (May 26, 1936). Such tributes were broadcast in both newspapers and on radio, another site of Black's ongoing influence on extracurricular literacy.

On October 8, 1936, students from Roosevelt Junior High School paid tribute to Black over radio by "dramatiz[ing] [the] story of 'Little Jim,' a classic in Annie Laurie's humanitarian writings." In this "'Little Jim' Story Told over Air," students relayed that, thanks to Black's journalistic appeal, "the little boy was cured, and enough funds were raised to establish the 'Little Jim Ward' of the Children's Hospital, which will be a lasting memorial to Annie Laurie and the kindness of the people of San Francisco" (*SFE* Oct. 9, 1936). Over forty years after the publication of "Annie Laurie's Appeal" (1894), the story of "Little Jim" inspired these children to practice extracurricular elocution skills that simultaneously contributed to rhetorical processes of remembering both Black and the social action campaign spurred by her journalism.

THE SAN FRANCISCO EXAMINER:

ANNIE LAURIE TRIBUTE
High School Pupils in Radio Drama

FOR COMMUNITY CHEST—In a tribute to Annie Laurie, late feature writer for The Examiner, pupils of Roosevelt Junior High School dramatize story of "Little Jim," a classic in Annie Laurie's humanitarian writings. Grouped about the microphone in Station KYA are, left to right, Billy Bakestraw, Leona Asmussen and Sophie Sclar. Held aloft is an enlarged photograph of Annie Laurie.

—International News Photo by San Francisco Examiner.

C.3. "Annie Laurie Tribute: High School Pupils in Radio Drama."

San Francisco Examiner, 9 Oct. 1936.

On August 19, 1941, over forty-five years after the publication of "Annie Laurie's Appeal" (1894), public memory of Black and "Little Jim" continued with the publication of this letter in the *San Francisco Examiner* from an original child participant in the 1890s campaign:

> To The San Francisco Examiner:
>
> Quite some years ago, in San Francisco, there was an organization started by your paper, called "The Order of Mercy" whose badge emblem was a heart (silver) with Swinnerton's Bear and the name as above, on it. Members were those who had contributed toward a fund for the "Little Jim Ward" of the Children's Hospital. What I would like to do is have them contact me, if possible, through your paper and renew our work. I believe the late Annie Laurie was the organization's head. I have my pin and other credentials such as programs, tickets and a Swinnerton Bear Cut, used for the entertainment we gave as a benefit.
>
> MRS. ELLA A. CHASE
Colma, Calif

In her 1941 letter, Mrs. Ella A. Chase recounts her 1890s participation in "The Order of Mercy," an organization that was part of Black's "Little Jim" social action efforts. Remarkably, Chase refers not only to her preserved "pin and other credentials" but also to "the entertainment" she performed almost fifty years earlier as a fund-raising benefit for the new ward. Present-day extracurricular literacy practices (the published letter) are here the vehicle for both remembering those of the past (the entertainment) and inviting those of the future ("What I would like to do is have them contact me, if possible, through your paper")—driven by the purpose of "renew[ing]" social action work. It remains uncertain if anyone responded to Chase and, if so, whether her efforts were connected with the revival of the "Little Jim Club" after World War II. (The club had grown in size and influence until World War II, during which the organization was inactive.) Regardless, Chase's letter stands as a remarkable example of Black's enduring influence on extracurricular literacy in connection with San Franciscans' interest in social action.

Importantly, interwoven past and present literate practices (as reflected in Chase's letter) again surface meaningfully in the *Examiner* during the late 1940s and early 1950s, indicating vibrant ways in which San Franciscan public memory came to intimately link Winifred Black with the "Little Jim Ward"—an enduring site for public memory of Black and her activist work. Several articles cumulatively reveal the workings of this process. The first, a 1945 article by Hazel Holly titled "New Wing Needed at Children's Hospital: $750,000 Sought to Replace Crowded and Outmoded Department" begins: "Tattered and yellow, in the clipping files of *The Examiner*, is a story written by the late, beloved writer, Annie Laurie, the 'story that raised $30,000.' It's time to tell that story again." Holly continues: "[the Little Jim Ward] is almost as old and worn as the clipping that tells about its creation" (*SFE* Apr. 21, 1945). The remainder of Holly's article describes fund-raising efforts for the new wing—efforts enthusiastically supported by an original "Little Jim Ward" contributor and San Franciscan Arthur A. Smith, whom the *Examiner* describes like so: "Mr. Smith read Annie Laurie's famed 'Little Jim' story in *The Examiner*, and rushed downtown to contribute the first dollar to the fund which eventually built the Little Jim Ward. Mr. Smith wants the present day building fund committee to know that he wants to help this time too" (*SFE* May 20, 1945).

Work began on this modern replacement ward in the early 1950s. On March 24, 1952, an *Examiner* article titled "Wing to Bear 1895 Plaque" not only sustained the public memory connection between Black and "the famed 'Little Jim' building" but also reprinted a portion of her 1894 appeal:

> At the moment, the famed "Little Jim" building at Children's Hospital is nothing more than a hole in the ground. Workmen . . . began excavating for the $2,000,000 wing that will better care for the ailing children of the future.
>
> PLAQUE SAVED.
> They dumped the wood and bricks and the metal work but they saved one item from the trash heap. That was the plaque which went up with the building in 1895—the plaque that told how The Examiner readers had flooded the newspaper office with contributions so a little boy named Jim and others like him could be cared for. That plaque will be put on the front of the modern building. Annie Laurie was responsible for the plaque, in the sense that she was responsible for the building itself.

VISITS HOSPITAL.

The famed feature writer for The Examiner paid a visit to Children's Hospital one day in 1895 and heard about Jim . . . His mother brought him to the hospital, but as Annie Laurie wrote:

> "Little Jim couldn't stay there to be cured. There was no room for him—not even an inch of room. No place for a cot where he could lie . . . so Little Jim and his mother who had left their dark little room that morning with such light and hopeful hearts, crept back again into the dark and cold and hunger—alone.

BOY PICTURED.

> "And there was nothing to do about it, not a thing—and Little Jim's back hurt him so when he got home that he cried all night, though he did his best to cry quietly so that his mother couldn't hear it. And there was no hope for Poor Little Jim—not a hope in the world."

Right in the center of the front page was a drawing . . . captioned "Nobody Wants Him." The next day, seemingly everyone in San Francisco wanted Jim. (*SFE* Mar. 24, 1952)

This 1952 *Examiner* article attests to Black's enduring place in San Francisco's public memory and signals the rhetorical power her writing exerted almost sixty years after the 1894 publication of "Annie Laurie's Appeal." It notably concludes in this way: "The [original] building is no more, but the spirit that created it and kept it going for more than fifty years is still here, ready to start a modern wing going in July of 1953" (*SFE* Mar. 24, 1952).

Overall, then, this 1952 *Examiner* article sustains the intimate link between Black and the "Little Jim Ward." Its sentiments moreover echo prior articulations of public memory such as the *Macon Republican*'s 1908 characterization of "The Little Jim Ward" as "a monument to the girl reporter [Winifred Black] . . . It is built of enduring stone and carved deep over the entrance are the words, "Little Jim Hospital." Can there be a finer monument?" (Dec. 5, 1908). In 1936, Darrell Donnell of the *Examiner* similarly described the ward as "a monument to Annie Laurie, and the innate kindliness of San Franciscans" (*SFE* Oct. 8, 1936). It is significant that even in 1952, when "the famed 'Little Jim' building" became "nothing more than a hole in the ground," Black's memory is preserved through the retaining of the 1895 plaque and the reprinting of her influential 1894 story.

Further into the second half of the twentieth century, San Franciscan public memory of Black continued—as did extracurricular literacy practices related to her 1890s "Little Jim" campaign. In 1975, for instance, an *Examiner* article covered the Mardi Gras Ball of the "Little Jim Club," an event "sponsored annually by the Little Jim Club as a benefit for Children's Hospital." It proclaimed in "A Ball to Warm the Heart of Annie Laurie" that "Annie Laurie would have felt right at home at Tuesday night's Mardi Gras Ball." And in 1976, the candidate for Mardi Gras queen, Nancy Vineburgh, sponsored an evening discussion on "[s]olar energy and your lifestyle"—reflecting Black's still ongoing influence on extracurricular literacy. "I wanted to do something a bit different than the usual cocktail party,' Vineburgh said, "and with solar energy so much a concern now, it seemed like a natural" (*SFE* Jan. 25, 1976).

Today, the "Little Jim Club" remains an active nonprofit fund-raising organization "supporting neo-natal, child development, speech and language pathology and other important pediatric programs at California Pacific Medical Center." In these programs, children are treated "regardless of a family's insurance status or ability to pay"—surely as Black would have intended. The reporter is not, however, referenced in the "History" section of the club's website, which describes the original *Examiner* "story of 'Little Jim'" (and the corresponding social action efforts that "raise[d] $30,000" for the ward) but does not mention Black by name (Little Jim Club). This is perhaps reflective of broader trends of "collective forgetting," which have in many ways erased women reporters like Black from both popular and critical attention (qtd. in Adams and Keene 5–6). As Adams and Keene have noted,

> Although Black's reputation suffered because she did not generally write "hard" news, in fact few journalists from the beginning of the century have received much critical attention. Those that worked on newspapers labeled as yellow journalism . . . did not always get taken seriously. And even front-page reporters at more traditional newspapers did not sign their work and did not achieve the respect ceded to novelists, biographers, and historians . . . Given multiple prejudices, against women in newspaper careers, against the writing that they would be allowed to do, and against any reporter as less consequential than the author of other genres, it is not surprising that even the best women journalists—the most prolific, respected, and influential—largely go unnoticed in histories of American writing. (5–6)

Yet even today—over 125 years after the publication of "Annie Laurie's Appeal"—devotion to "Little Jim" has carried on. Winifred Black continues to influence the active civic involvement of members of "[t]he oldest pediatric philanthropic organization in San Francisco" and their corresponding literacy practices that sustain the legacy of Black's journalistic social action in connection with "Little Jim" (Little Jim Club).

Remembering Gertrude Bustill Mossell: Continuing Collection Practices, Mapping Public Memory, and Engaging the Digital Extracurriculum

After a rich and abundant career as a journalist, author, and teacher, Gertrude Bustill Mossell was widely memorialized following her death on January 21, 1948, at the age of 92. Evi Heilbrunn affirms that "[a]s a member of one of the most elite 19th-century African American families, and as both a prolific journalist and social activist, Gertrude was memorialized in an obituary printed in countless American newspapers, including the Philadelphia Tribune and the New York Times" (*PI* Jan. 27, 2013). Over the decades, however, barriers of racism and sexism rendered Mossell less visible in public memory, leading Amanda Wray to observe in 2007 that "Mossell is noticeably absent from contemporary discourse" (435). Royster has written that

> African American women have been persistently subjected to measures of value and achievement that have been set and monitored by others, who have not had their interests or potential in mind and who have been free historically to discount, ignore, and disempower them. These barriers, though variable, are socially, politically, and culturally defined, and the impact of them in this case is that they have cast the lives of African American women in shadow. (3–4)

As one seminal corrective to the shadowing of African American women's dynamic literacy practices, *Traces of a Stream* (2000) illuminated "the stream that is visible as evidence of the sea" of "African American women's achievements as language users" (Royster 5).

Around the turn of the twenty-first century, two other related correctives took shape that disseminated stories of African American women of the past with "important political and ethical implications for the present" (VanderHaagen 11): (1) the collection practices of librarian Jessie

Carney Smith that led to her publication of the "1,200-plus-page" *Notable Black American Women* in 1992 and (2) the commemoration practices of Dr. Charles Blockson, whose efforts during the 1990s resulted in sixty-six historical markers—including one dedicated to Gertrude Bustill Mossell—recognizing important sites of Philadelphia's Black history (*PI* Apr. 19, 1992). I first discuss the extracurricular literacy purpose motivating Smith's project and the intimate ties between her collection practices and those practiced and promoted by Mossell in "Our Woman's Department." Second, I turn to the diverse extracurricular literacy practices embodied within, and instigated by, Blockson's public memory work in Philadelphia.

In the 1992 *Philadelphia Inquirer* article "A Librarian Who Saved Her Lives," Kimberly J. McLarin describes the "6-pound tome" that constituted librarian Jessie Carney Smith's "all-consuming passion for the last four years" (Apr. 19, 1992). McLarin goes on to describe the origins of Smith's *Notable Black American Women* (1992), "the result of 20 years of hoarding":

> Smith saved every article and every note, every book and every paper, every sliver of information she came across on the lives of America's notable, if not noted, black women. Saving things is not unusual for a librarian, Smith said. And being a black, female librarian working at historically black Fisk University in Tennessee made it all the more likely that she would come across intriguing bits of history. She saved notes on famous women such as civil rights activist Rosa Parks and freedom fighter Harriet Tubman, and on less-famous women such as Gertrude Bustill Mossell, an early 19th-century Philadelphia journalist, educator and feminist. She saved clippings on singers, teachers, doctors, activists, seamstresses and sharecroppers. Sometimes Smith picked up bits of information about women while reading about their more famous husbands, such as freedom fighter Anna Murray Douglass, without whose help Frederick Douglass might never have reached such stirring heights. "Sometimes you run across the name of someone you didn't know or maybe this person had done something that was really outstanding," she said. "I didn't want that to get lost. I didn't know what I would do with it, but when I saw it, I collected it."

Smith's collection practices not only led to her contributions toward a recovery of Mossell; they bear an intimate resemblance as well to those performed and advocated by the editor a century earlier in "Our Woman's Department." Specifically, Smith's efforts to "sav[e] every article and every note, every book and every paper, every sliver of information she came across on the lives of America's notable, if not noted, black women" recall Mossell's promotion of various collection projects aimed at assembling "unwritten histor[ies]"—including both the Frederick Douglass scrapbook, an idea inspired by the editor's own clipping practices, and the Historical Association collection containing "all publications of interest to us" (*PI* Apr. 19, 1992; *NYF* July 31, 1886). They moreover echo the construction of Mossell's "Our Woman's Department" column itself, which in many ways resembled a collection of gathered materials.

The collective spirit of "Our Woman's Department" is also replicated in Smith's work. As McLarin describes, "Smith started with a list of more than 1,000 names, then sent the list to friends, colleagues and members of a 10-person advisory committee she had assembled for the project. In the end, more than 200 people contributed to the 500 biographies in the book" (*PI* Apr. 19, 1992). These collective literacy practices united Smith with friends, colleagues, and advisory committee members in the shared project of producing a "1,200-plus-page" book intended for extracurricular learning:

> What does she see as the future of this mammoth, $75 book? Certainly not languishing on the dusty shelves of some library reference section. No offense to libraries. "I want it to be in homes the way *Roots* was in homes," said Smith, who's on a promotion tour. "I realize it's more costly, but I think if people knew how much research went into it, they'd understand." (*PI* Apr. 19, 1992)

Reflecting again on her purpose at the close of the article in ways that suggest both a curricular and extracurricular place for *Notable Black American Women*, Smith comments: "'We need to start in the elementary grades . . . and make it a greater part of our lives . . . It's important not only to instill this knowledge in black youth, but to let other groups know about what we've done.' That, Smith said, is where her book comes in" (*PI* Apr. 19, 1992). Overall, Smith's book and its collaborative, collection-based production uphold values key to "Our Woman's Department," while aspiring through processes of historical reconstruction to exert a similar robust influence on learning and literacy by circulating stories of influential Black women and the important "values that animate th[e]se stories" (VanderHaagen 2).

A second 1990s historical reconstruction project aimed at reviving public memory of Mossell and other African American writers, activists, musicians, artists, and religious leaders central to Philadelphia's Black history is Dr. Charles Blockson's historical marker installation program. Blockson, a Pennsylvania-born Black historian, collector, and author initiated this project when "it became apparent that Philadelphia, like other American cities, was losing places of historical significance through gentrification and neglect. It is our hope," he continued, "that through the installation of the African-American historical markers, we can preserve the remaining sites and revive memories of past events and citizens who lived before us and made positive contributions to our nation" (qtd. in F. Anderson). As a result of Blockson's efforts and advocacy of "what should be remembered . . . as part of a community's heritage," the number of markers associated with African American history in Philadelphia increased from two to sixty-eight during the 1990s—and Mossell's marker was one of them (Rose and Gaillet 242).[3]

Located at 1423 Lombard Street in Philadelphia, the historical marker posted outside Mossell's former home reads:

> Teacher and journalist lived here. Wrote for many publications on race and feminism. Her books included "The Work of the Afro-American Woman." Fundraiser for Frederick Douglass Hospital; her husband was its founder. ("Gertrude E. H. Bustill Mossell")

Mossell is not the only member of her family who has been commemorated by this marker program. Cyrus Bustill (1732–1806) and David Bustill Bowser (1820–1900) also have markers in Philadelphia—the former for his founding of the Free African Society and a school for Black children and the latter for his career as "[a] self-taught Black artist" whose portrait paintings "include[d] several of Lincoln and one of the abolitionist John Brown" ("Historical Markers Database"). Beyond Philadelphia, a third relative in Harrisburg—Joseph Bustill, a fugitive slave protector—is also commemorated in a marker for Tanner's Alley, part of the Underground Railroad. These markers are significant for the fact that they "'pas[s] on'" historical understanding of African American lives and events by "taking up residence in vernacular spaces" within Philadelphia (and Pennsylvania more broadly) (VanderHaagen 7; Rose and Gaillet 242).[4] More so, such important sites of remembering are (and have been) dynamically linked to various forms of extracurricular literacy development. Students,

C.4. Historical marker for Gertrude E. H. Bustill
Mossell. Author's collection.

historians, and travelers have advocated for, learned from, conducted research on, and shared knowledge gained from Pennsylvania historical markers such as Mossell's.

The Pennsylvania Historical Marker Program, initiated in 1913 with the formation of the Pennsylvania Historical Commission, aims to "capture the memory of people, places, events, and innovations" central to state history (Robinson and Galle; "Historical Markers"). Over two thousand cast aluminum markers currently populate the state ("Historical Markers"). Notably, such markers have facilitated extracurricular literacy development since the program's early days. As John K. Robinson and Karen Galle recount in "A Century of Marking History: 100 Years of the PA Historical Marker Program," a report by Pennsylvania Historical Commission Chairman Henry W. Shoemaker described the popularity of marker dedication ceremonies during the 1920s—for which "speeches were given" and "schools were closed and pupils brought to the site" ("A Century").

Later in the century, new opportunities for extracurricular literacy emerged when the marker nomination process "bec[a]me exclusively public-driven" in the 1990s. "[A]ny group or individual" could now nominate a marker, prompting a surge of interest among Pennsylvania residents and reflecting ways in which public memory structures "are often rhetorically chosen" and "lobbied for" (Robinson and Galle; Rose and Gaillet 242). This process involves the completion of a marker nomination and adherence to approval criteria for state historical markers. Notably, the nomination process promotes extracurricular and information literacy development by requesting nominations grounded in diligent research and documentation. The first approval criterion specifies that nominations must "includ[e] thorough documentation (with selected photocopies and bibliographies from reliable primary and secondary sources) and verification of the facts claimed" ("Nominate a Historical Marker"). Nomination of a historical marker entails further extracurricular literacy practices in asking nominators to "specify fully the historical significance of the person, event, innovation, or site," "propose a draft of the text for the marker" (followed by collaboration with Pennsylvania Historical and Museum Commission [PHMC] staff on the final text), and "describe the proposed location and its connection [to] the subject being marked" (Historical Marker Nomination Form). The opportunity to help compose marker text is especially significant. By extending to the public primary responsibility for drafting and collaborative responsibility in revising and producing the final text, the PHMC offers residents active roles in shaping the language that will in turn shape the historical learning of tourists and passersby.

This is not to suggest that the Pennsylvania Historical Marker Program is free of power asymmetries. First, it is the PHMC (not the public) that makes final decisions about markers. It is thus the PHMC that ultimately determines if "[t]he person, place, event, or innovation" indeed "had a significant impact" on statewide or national history ("Nominate a Historical Marker"). Second, African American history is significantly underrepresented among Pennsylvania markers. Of more than 2,500 total markers, only 242 commemorate people, places, or events in African American history.[5] The marker program as a whole is, therefore (despite its democratic dimensions), also enmeshed in "relations of power that circulate in the publics of interest" (Enoch, "Releasing Hold" 62).

Of the 242 Pennsylvania markers that recognize African American history, 106 are located in the city of Philadelphia. It was here that public memory efforts by Blockson and Dr. Bernard C. Watson, William Penn Foundation president, succeeded in establishing sixty-six new markers in the 1990s that commemorated important sites of Black history (Palmore-Lewis 47).[6] Aside from Mossell's, other markers established by Blockson and Watson include a Philadelphia Museum of Art tribute to architect Julian Abele and a Penn's Landing marker designating Pennsylvania's participation in the slave trade by way of its Delaware River port. Blockson notably "took money from my own pocket" to erect the latter marker—an especially potent reminder of the asymmetrical relations of power underlying much public memory construction. Reflecting on his commitment to map Philadelphia Black history, Blockson pointed to an early interest in reading and in learning through his grandfather about his family's connections to the Underground Railroad. According to Blockson, this interest surfaced despite "what my teacher told me—that we didn't have a history" ("Conversation with Charles L. Blockson").[7] Philadelphia's more robust representation of Black history through its markers (compared with Pennsylvania as a whole) is thus substantially rooted in the extracurricular literacy practices of Dr. Charles Blockson.

Today, markers such as Mossell's have gained further significance in fueling new types of digital literacy proficiencies. These build on the long-standing role of markers as conversation starters and inducements to self-sponsored research. As Robinson and Galle have observed, "[o]nce they appear in the landscape, conversations arise and further research takes place. People actually talk to each other about the markers and what they mean to them." Former Luzerne County Historical Society executive director Jessie Teitelbaum similarly asserts that "[m]arkers . . . encourage readers to go beyond the brief text and learn more by visiting local historical societies, museums, libraries or online research sites" (qtd. in Robinson and Galle). Digital forums such as the Historical Marker Database and Waymarking. com have now taken such literacy practices in a fresh direction. These forums act as dynamic venues for historical marker aficionados to connect with one another and share photographs, information, and commentary.

First, the Historical Marker Database (HMdb.org) emerged in 2006 as "an illustrated searchable online catalog of historical information viewed through the filter of roadside and other permanent outdoor markers, monuments, and plaques." Brimming with "photographs, inscription transcriptions, marker locations, maps, additional information and commentary, and links to more information," The Historical Marker Database has for sixteen years fostered global digital literacy practices by inviting users to add or update marker pages with "photographs, links, information and commentary" ("Historical Marker Database"). Of the 178,944 publicly contributed entries to HMdb.org, a page featuring Gertrude Bustill Mossell's marker is one of them. It contains two photographs of the marker taken by page creator Don Morfe as well as the marker's inscription text, year of origin, location and coordinates (with a link to a map), and information on "nearby markers." This page—originally created in March 2015 and last revised by another user in February 2022—has accumulated 432 views since its initial posting. Social media links at the bottom of the entry next to "Share this page" offer other possibilities for digitally circulating information about Mossell. Overall, then, the Historical Marker Database points to notable ways in which "the rhetorical practice of remembering" and related extracurricular literacy practices have dynamically entered the digital realm (Enoch, "Releasing Hold" 60).

A second venue for digital literacy development anchored in "remembering" is Waymarking.com. This website invites users to "mark unique locations on the planet and give them a voice" by providing "the toolset for categorizing and adding unique information" to locations around the globe ("Waymarking FAQ"). Mossell's marker also appears on this site (the entry again contributed by Morfe) along with pages for relatives Cyrus Bustill

(Philadelphia) and Joseph Bustill (commemorated by the Underground Railroad marker in Harrisburg). These pages feature photographs, factual information, descriptive commentary, and a hyperlinked visitor log. One notable visitor's comment about the Underground Railroad marker recognizing Joseph Bustill and fellow fugitive slave protector William Jones reads: "Was in the area today. Once again I have learned more doing waymarking and geocaching than I did in history class" ("Waymark Visit"). Ultimately, both the Historical Marker Database and Waymarking.com demonstrate ways in which processes of remembering Gertrude Bustill Mossell and her relatives have helped fuel the rich dynamics of the digital extracurriculum.

Remembering Susette La Flesche: Extracurricular Advocacy, Contexts of Settler Colonialism, and Indigenous-Led Public Memory Practices

On April 8, 1975, an article appeared in the *Lincoln Evening Journal* by local resident Betty Loudon advocating for Susette La Flesche's entry into the Nebraska Hall of Fame. "As we celebrate International Women's Year and look forward to Bicentennial activities," the article begins, "there could be no better time for the Hall of Fame Commission to consider Susette La Flesche for induction into Nebraska's Hall of Fame" (Loudon). This opening notably endorses La Flesche's induction by way of a timely connection to International Women's Year (IWY): a 1975 global initiative to raise "World-Wide Awareness of Women's Worth" by concentrating "attention on the situation of women, and on the means to improve it" ("Goals of International Women's Year").

To this end, Loudon connects specific IWY commitments with those embodied by La Flesche: "The official emblem for International Women's Year symbolizes equality and peace," she writes. "In her lifetime Susette La Flesche or 'Bright Eyes' exemplified both. In justice, she would be a fitting candidate for the first Indian woman to be inducted into the Nebraska Hall of Fame." Loudon here references IWY's dove and Venus symbol to connect her nomination of La Flesche to key IWY values. Characterized by the *New York Times* as a "peace dove with the mathematical equal sign where its tail feather should sprout," this emblem is referenced by Loudon to emphasize La Flesche's exemplifi[cation] of activist efforts for equality and peace (qtd. in Peril). In striving to diversify Nebraska's Hall of Fame,

Loudon moreover aligns La Flesche's career with contemporary global efforts to promote women's advancements through cross-cultural dialogue, for 1975 marked not only International Women's Year but also the inaugural World Conference on Women. This conference—held in Mexico City—served as a capstone for the IWY's commitment to "Equality, Development and Peace" and resulted in "a global plan of action to improve the status of women" ("United Nations Commission"). By situating La Flesche's Hall of Fame nomination within this cross-cultural exigence, Loudon uses extracurricular literacy in ways that aim to "shift the ground" of the Nebraska Hall of Fame—enhancing visitors' "capacity to see and appreciate a different vista, and mak[ing] room for human variety" (Royster and Kirsch 113). Ultimately, La Flesche was inducted into Nebraska's Hall of Fame in 1983–1984, joining the Ponca chief Standing Bear, who had been inducted six years earlier in 1977–1978. She is now one of twenty-six individuals, among them three Native Americans including Oglala Lakota chief Red Cloud, commemorated by way of sculpted busts located "on the second floor of the Nebraska State Capitol" ("Nebraska Hall of Fame").

In *Legible Sovereignties: Rhetoric, Representations, and Native American Museums*, Lisa King has argued that "museums and cultural centers remain sites of both friction and potential in their endeavors to represent Native cultures and sovereignties" (2). The presence of La Flesche's bust in the Nebraska Hall of Fame and processes of her nomination and commemoration reflect related "potential" with regard to recognitions of her activism but also significant "friction" inherent to the context of settler colonialism. The potential of La Flesche's presence in the Hall of Fame includes both public recognition of her influence as a writer and lecturer on Indigenous rights and the possibility that the presence of her bust in the Hall of Fame will incite further learning, self-sponsored research, or digital extracurricular literacy practices that sustain or enrich public memory of La Flesche. Further potential is suggested by Loudon's 1975 *Lincoln Evening Journal* article, which discusses the Omaha as the longstanding inhabitants of the land and thereby inscribes La Flesche as a "foundational voic[e]": "The Omaha have been in Nebraska perhaps since 1650," she writes. "The very name of our state is taken from an Omaha Indian word meaning "'flat water'" (King et al, "Introduction" 9; Loudon).[8]

Yet this article, La Flesche's Hall of Fame presence, and additional public memory narratives related to her induction are also enmeshed within the "continuing rhetorical legacy of colonialism" (Kelly and Black 5). Foremost,

La Flesche's bust is located in the Nebraska State Capitol—itself a re-sounding reflection and outgrowth of colonization. Emily Robinson has recently drawn attention to ways in which "public memory practices and the resulting narratives" depend closely "on the context constructed with the surrounding built environment" (103). In this case, the potential of La Flesche's bust to significantly disrupt settler colonial histories is limited by a context that significantly sustains a "dominant historical conscious-ness" (104). Additionally, discourses related to La Flesche's Hall of Fame induction to various degrees articulate versions of the idealized, romantic public image of La Flesche present in many late nineteenth-century rep-resentations of the journalist. In 1983, for instance, a speech delivered for La Flesche's Hall of Fame induction highlighted her rhetorical activism alongside Chief Standing Bear and noted that "her beauty and sincerity convinced the people that the Indians should be respected and admired for their traditions and their culture" ("Betty Lagdon Speaks"). Loudon's article contains a similar discourse of remembering: "Susette helped publi-cize the plight of the Ponca. Standing Bear was released in accordance with District Judge Elmer Dundy's historic decision that 'an Indian is a person'"; thereafter La Flesche "became a spokeswoman for Indian rights, charming American and European audiences with her beauty and sincerity."

Journalistic discourses predating La Flesche's Hall of Fame nomina-tion also focused on her activist work on behalf of the Poncas when re-membering her past rhetorical activities. An October 22, 1914, Camden *Courier-Post* article titled "'Bright Eyes' Plea Saved This Tribe" explained, for instance, how "Standing Bear, the Chief of the Poncas, together with Bright Eyes, the daughter of Joseph La Flesche, formerly Chief of the tribe, changed the policy of the Government relative to the Indians" following "the removal of the Poncas from their reservation in Nebraska."[9] Later in the century, a Beatrice *Daily Sun* article from August 27, 1961, titled "Out of Old Nebraska: Inshtatheamba, 'Bright Eyes' One of Talented Nebraskans" described the forced Ponca removal as "[a] dramatic and tragic occurrence [that] brought national attention to the young Indian girl." It continued:

> Susette La Flesche helped with articles and speeches to publicize the plight of the Ponca. Thomas H. Tibbles and W. L. Carpenter of the Omaha World Herald interested themselves in the case and hired able legal assistance. District Judge Elmer Dundy found in favor of Standing Bear in a historic decision that an Indian was a person in the eyes of the

law. Under Tibbles' management, Susette, her brilliant brother Francis, and Standing Bear toured the East speaking for Indian rights. Bright Eyes charmed the audiences with her beauty and sincerity. It is said that Henry Wadsworth Longfellow stated upon meeting her, 'This is Minnehaha.' (*BDS* Aug. 27, 1961)

These examples demonstrate ways in which such public memory discourses both remember La Flesche's influential activism on behalf of the Poncas (oftentimes reflecting continued sentimentalizing tendencies) and yet elide complexities and acknowledgment of sustained attacks on sovereignty faced by the Poncas and other Indigenous peoples. The Camden *Courier-Post*, for instance, states that "[p]ublic sentiment became aroused" by La Flesche's "clear, dispassionate" speeches. "The Senate of the United States named a committee to investigate the story told by Standing Bear and Bright Eyes," it continues, and "[a]n effort was made to right the wrong as far as possible." Yet the corresponding reform movement connected with these events "culminated . . . in the passage of the General Allotment Act, or Dawes Act," a legislative act that La Flesche came to complicate and critique after initially advocating for "titles to our lands."

La Flesche expresses this critique in a political speech:

When I grew old enough to think, I saw that there was no help for us Indians unless we were made citizens, and titles to our lands were given us so that we could not be torn from our homes any more by the government. If we were citizens we could vote and our lives and property would be protected by the laws of the land. There were others who thought so too, and an opportunity occurring, we started an agitation on the subject throughout the Country. Eventually, and after having the whole Interior Department to fight against, we succeeded in having laws passed which changed the old conditions of things, and gave the Indians the same chance to live that white men had. My tribe was one of the first to become citizens, and get titles to lands in severalty. Hitherto the Indians had acted on the principle that God had given the land to everybody, and that the land was as free to every human being as the air and water. They would as soon have thought of individual ownership to air and water as individual ownership of land; but when they saw how the white people put a price on land, they became eager to own land individually. After we had passed the laws we wanted I went to our reservation to live. I watched the experiment, for those who fought against the passage of our bills said an Indian wouldn't work, and that he could neither be civilized nor educated.

Indians who had never been taught to harness a horse or hold a plow began to farm and put up little homes, and build stables. They carried their wheat to the railroad elevators to sell. They farmed more and more every year. They voted; and voted the old party tickets, as the new party was not yet organized. So far they exceeded all expectations, but there it seemed to end. Where was the practical result of their labor? They barely received enough for their work to keep them decently clothed and fed. They lived in a state of semi-starvation as before, and yet, they were working harder than they ever worked before. (La Flesche, "Political Speech")

As this speech makes clear, rhetorical remembering of La Flesche's activist work has oftentimes elided complexities, "establishe[d] selective historical narratives," and insufficiently acknowledged sustained injustices faced by Indigenous peoples (Robinson 96). Yet public memory of La Flesche has also "br[ought] to the foreground" other ways of knowing and understanding by means of Indigenous-led rhetorical practices of remembering (Mignolo, "Delinking" 453).

One significant example is a 2016 "Nebraska Story" by Princella Parker (Omaha Nation) titled *Bright Eyes* that celebrates the rhetorical sovereignty and activism of La Flesche. The Nebraska Stories project, a compilation of online-accessible video journals, aims to share "feature-oriented content produced by a variety of talented storytellers who travel statewide to bring [viewers] a celebration of our culture, history, arts, science, nature . . . and more" ("Nebraska Stories"). Parker launched her own "Nebraska Story" video project to commemorate La Flesche and served as both producer and narrator in this extracurricular endeavor. Her short film opens by relaying her admiration of La Flesche as a role model. As Parker states:

No matter who you are, everybody needs a role model. As a Native American woman, I admire activist Winona LaDuke, filmmaker Valerie Red-Horse, attorney Danelle Smith, and police officer Darla Black. Even better, I've discovered a leader from my own tribe, a woman who lived over a hundred years ago. Susette La Flesche was the first Native woman to speak to national audiences about Indian rights. My name is Princella Parker and I'm a member of the Omaha tribe of Nebraska. (Parker, *Bright Eyes*)

After next recounting her family's struggles with poverty and home-lessness, Parker goes on to describe her emerging admiration of La Flesche upon learning of her advocacy for the Ponca Tribe and support of Standing Bear as he fought "to be recognized as a person in the eyes of the law."

Importantly, Parker's "Nebraska Story" reflects a "commitment to centering Native and Indigenous voices"—indicating parallels with other responsible public memory narratives such as the exhibition *Remembering Our Indian School Days* (analyzed by Robinson in "Objects, Documentation, and Identification: Materiality and Memory of American Indian Boarding Schools at the Heard Museum") that "counte[r] the silencing of Native and Indigenous voices in dominant histories" (107). Aside from her own richly communicated storytelling, Parker features Ponca community testimonies in her presentation of La Flesche's activism. These testimonies include that of Ponca activist Casey Camp-Horinek, who speaks solemnly of the Ponca Trail of Tears: "It was our march to the concentration camps that the United States government had created, and we knew it. And we knew our way of life was gone." Parker's video also features Louis Head-man, an elder of the southern Ponca, who says of La Flesche: "She wasn't a person to sit back where social issues were concerned, you know. She wanted to get involved, and maybe she was one of the first Indian feminists who stuck her neck out and did what she was supposed to do." The film concludes with Parker's summation of her own activist and familial commitments inspired by La Flesche and leaves viewers with final shots of La Flesche's and Chief Standing Bear's busts in the Nebraska Hall of Fame. Parker concludes:

> Learning about Susette's life has inspired me. When I drive through the reservation where my mother grew up, I feel a need to help. I want to bring awareness and pride to the Omaha people. My dream is for Native children to be able to see positive reflections of themselves in media. As the eldest daughter of my family, I try to set a good example for my siblings. Just like Susette did for her family. Her youngest sister, Susan, went on to become the first Native American woman doctor. Dr. Susan Picotte has been nominated to the Nebraska Hall of Fame. Chief Standing Bear and Bright Eyes are already there. (Parker, *Bright Eyes*)

Parker's concluding words remember La Flesche's inspirational life, reestablish her as a role model, and crucially "locat[e] the continual existence of" Omaha people "within and throughout the present" (Robinson

104). Furthermore, Parker's desire for "Native children to be able to see positive reflections of themselves in media" echoes a driving motivation of La Flesche's 1890 journalistic work to reshape press misrepresentations of Lakota people. And while Parker does not specifically reference La Flesche's relationally based journalism written from Pine Ridge, her "Nebraska Story" is an extracurricular literacy endeavor reflecting important decolonial memory work and indicative of sustained rhetorical resilience across time (Flynn et al. 1).

These three case studies suggest several takeaways for scholarship conducted at the intersection of women's rhetorical historiography, public memory, and the extracurriculum.

First, rhetorical practices of remembering "Little Jim" reveal the remarkable longevity with which a rhetor can influence extracurricular literacy practices. Even in instances of Winifred Black's erasure from such discourses (including both the "Little Jim" annual essays and the current website of the "Little Jim Club"), related literacy practices persisted for a range of individuals on account of the rhetorical power of Black's 1894 writing, which positioned "Little Jim" for a long-lasting place in public memory and extracurricular influence. Scholars working at the convergence of feminist rhetorical studies and public memory might therefore ask not only "[h]ow have women been remembered, and to what rhetorical purpose has their memory been put?" (by attending especially to "the rhetorical work that goes into remembering women and, consequently, examining how women's memories are composed, leveraged . . . and erased") *but also* (as in the case of "Little Jim") ask how women have left powerful rhetorical legacies that inspire remembering *despite* their full or partial erasure from the landscape of public memory. Moreover, what vestiges of a female rhetor's career continue to influence the extracurricular literacy practices and public participation of those who sustain the rhetor's legacy (even without substantial knowledge of the rhetor herself)?

Second, consideration of Jessie Carney Smith's collection practices and collaborative construction of *Notable Black American Women*, alongside Charles Blockson's African American historical marker program, illuminates not only how sites of public memory are "subject to and reflective of . . . relations of power" but also how "counterpublic memories" emerge from resistant extracurricular endeavors as well as drive extracurricular learning and literacy development among those for whom "counterpublic memories" offer knowledge absent from formal curriculums (as expressed by "PaHawkeye") (Enoch, "Releasing Hold" 62). To this end, more extensively integrating considerations of rhetoric and composition's extracurriculum into the already fruitful convergence of feminist rhetorical studies and public memory may further enrich scholarship in this area.

Third, Princella Parker's "Nebraska Story"—a digital extracurricular project that disrupts the "continuing rhetorical legacy of colonialism" and that also sustains La Flesche's rhetorical commitments—meaningfully reflects both Shawn Wilson's assertion that "all knowledge is cultural and based in a relational context" and Flynn, Sotirin, and Brady's affirmation that resilience is "relationally embedded" (Kelly and Black 5; Wilson 95; Flynn et al. 12).[10] Parker's processes of remembering La Flesche involve community investment, assert "the ongoing presence" of Indigenous peoples, and reveal her own commitment to helping "Native children . . . see positive reflections of themselves in media" (King et al., "Introduction" 7; Parker, *Bright Eyes*). Her "Nebraska Story" is indeed one such iteration of the type of media discourse that La Flesche both modeled and advocated over a hundred years earlier. This example invites scholars to follow trails of feminist rhetorical resilience far beyond a rhetor's historical moment and into the future—attending especially to ways in which the commitments of Indigenous rhetors have been not only remembered but simultaneously readopted (or adapted) by Indigenous peoples who now sustain their legacies through expressions of extracurricular literacy and rhetorical sovereignty (Lyons, "Rhetorical Sovereignty" 449).

Overall, these three case studies highlight the productive scholarly possibilities of investigating the dynamic operations of extracurriculums across time. Debra Hawhee and Christa J. Olson have notably already called for increased engagement in "pan-historiography": "writing histories whose temporal scope extends well beyond the span of individual generations. Pan-historiography," they continue, "can also refer to studies that leap across geographic space, tracking important activities, terms, movements, or practices" (90). Hawhee and Olson do not advocate this approach "over and against more focused histories" but instead contend that *both* "wide-ranging" studies (concerned with "big-picture questions") and "focused" (or "fine-grained") studies add complementary value to our discipline (91).

I conclude therefore by proposing that greater scholarly attention be paid to what I call the "pan-extracurriculum." Building on Hawhee and

Olson, I suggest that studies of extracurricular operations across time—anchored in "focused" examinations of the teachers or "literacy sponsors" who initiated them—offer us a compelling way to simultaneously "'go small'" *and* embrace "the choice to span" (Brandt 169; Hawhee and Olson 92). Continuing efforts to examine the remarkable rhetorical work of women journalists and other writers for periodicals can not only deepen our knowledge of the role of newspapers, magazines, and journals as vibrant extracurricular literacy sites and vehicles for social action at particular historical moments but perhaps can also enrich our unfolding understandings of the pan-extracurriculum.

NOTES

WORKS CITED

INDEX

Notes

Preface

1. I draw on language used by Cheryl Glenn in *Rhetorical Feminism and This Thing Called Hope* to refer to members of "provisionally yet systematically marginalized" groups with whom these journalists built relationships and collectively worked for change (64).

Introduction

1. As Ellen Gruber Garvey documents in *Writing with Scissors: American Scrapbooks from the Civil War to the Harlem Renaissance*, "[c]ities often supported a dozen or more dailies, and the largest of them had half a million readers each by 1900" (6).

2. In May 2020, Ida B. Wells was awarded a Pulitzer Prize citation for her powerful and rigorous anti-lynching journalism.

3. Enoch's *Refiguring Rhetorical Education* (2008) explores the subversive instructional practices of Lydia Maria Child, Zitkala-Ša, Jovita Idar, Marta Peña, and Leonor Villegas de Magnón.

4. Gold's *Rhetoric at the Margins: Revising the History of Writing Instruction in American Colleges, 1873–1947*, for instance, illuminates complex instructional practices at women's, working-class, and historically Black colleges. His study builds on important work by Robin Varnum, Charles Paine, Susan Kates, and Lucille Schultz.

5. Ramírez also coedited with Enoch *Mestiza Rhetorics: An Anthology of Mexicana Activism in the Spanish-Language Press, 1887–1922* (2019).

6. In their 2006 article "The Rise of Periodical Studies" (in *PMLA*), Sean Latham and Robert Scholes similarly deemed periodicals to be "ideal sites for studies of the rise of an intellectual public sphere in which many kinds of literacy were encouraged or enabled" (518–19).

7. My understanding of Susette La Flesche Tibbles's relational form of news reporting draws on understandings of the term relational as discussed

by a number of scholars: Shawn Wilson in *Research Is Ceremony: Indige-nous Research Methods*; Malea Powell, Daisy Levy, Andrea Riley-Mukavetz, Marilee Brooks-Gillies, Maria Novotny, and Jennifer Fisch-Ferguson in "Our Story Begins Here" (*Constellations*); and Elizabeth A. Flynn, Patricia Sotirin, and Ann Brady in *Feminist Rhetorical Resilience*. I discuss the in-fluential work of these scholars in more detail in Chapter 3. These scholars' works, along with Glenn's *Rhetorical Feminism and This Thing Called Hope*, have also contributed to my thinking about the meanings of relationality in connection to the work of all three journalists in this study.

8. As in the preface, I again draw on language used by Cheryl Glenn in *Rhetorical Feminism and This Thing Called Hope* in referring to members of "provisionally yet systematically marginalized" groups with whom these journalists interacted dialogically (64).

9. Johnson's submission was rejected by *Youth's Companion*, to whom she identified herself as "a colored woman, and proud of it." Even when Johnson persuaded publishers to accept the story, it never ran (qtd. in Wagner 99).

10. In *The Work of the Afro-American Woman* (1894), Mossell wrote, "In this century, sometimes called the 'Nineteenth Century,' but often the 'Wom-en's Century,' there has been a yielding of the barriers that surround her life. In the school, the church, the state, her value as a co-operative is being widely discussed. The co-education of the sexes, the higher education of woman, has given to her life a strong impetus in the line of literary effort. Perhaps this can be more strongly felt in the profession of journalism than in any other" (98).

11. Olin reflects on this "wholly feminine standpoint" in the context of women's writing about murder trials for the penny press (51).

12. Peyer here draws on Daniel Littlefield Jr. and James Parins's *American Indian and Alaska Native Newspapers and Periodicals, 1826–1924* (1984).

13. The Progress resumed publication over a year after its first issue, fol-lowing "a subcommittee testimony and favorable hearing in federal court" (Vizenor, "Aesthetics" 7).

14. In a letter to Thomas Henry Tibbles dated April 29, 1879, Susette La Flesche wrote, "Dear Sir, Mr. Dorsey requested me to send you the inclosed copy of a statement made by the Ponca chiefs at my house on their return from Indian Territory about two years ago. We had it published at their desire in one of the Sioux City papers at the time . . ." (La Flesche, Letter). The Sioux City newspaper La Flesche references is likely the Sioux City Daily Journal, which published an almost identical copy of the statement on March 31, 1877 (in addition to a copy of a related telegram sent by the Ponca chiefs to

President Rutherford B. Hayes). I feature the version of the statement from La Flesche's letter, which, as La Flesche explains, was "made by the Ponca chiefs at my house on their return from Indian Territory." La Flesche refers to this version as "the original" (La Flesche, Letter).

15. The full statement is available through the Smithsonian Online Virtual Archives at https://sova.si.edu/details/NMAI.AC.066?s=0&n=10&t=C&q=tibbles&i=0#ref25.

16. As Shawn Wilson writes in *Research Is Ceremony: Indigenous Research Methods*, "with all of these knots of being/relationships as our reality, we can go one step further and ask, 'How can I find out more about this other being, or idea, or whatever you decide to call a particular knot?' The answer, which is our methodology, seems obvious—the more relationships between yourself and the other thing, the more fully you can comprehend its form and the greater your understanding becomes . . . So the methodology is simply the building of more relations" (79).

17. bell hooks focuses particularly on film and TV, writing, "[b]oth African and Native Americans have been deeply affected by the degrading representations of red and black people that continue to be the dominant images projected by movies and television. Portrayed as cowardly, cannibalistic, uncivilized, the images of 'Indians' mirror screen images of Africans" (186).

18. Peterson writes that "both de Tocqueville and Anderson emphasize the importance of the newspaper as an institution that connects people by articulating a sameness of purpose and providing a common means of executing designs. Thus, the newspaper, and other cultural forms as well, helps create 'imagined community.' For, if it is impossible for each member of the nation to know all the other members, these vehicles now make possible that 'in the minds of each lives the image of their communion,' a communion 'conceived as a deep horizontal comradeship'" (11). The journalism of Black, Mossell, and La Flesche, however, forges not merely imagined but, in fact, actual connections among readers and local communities as I go on to discuss.

19. Other scholars have also analyzed intimate interplay in nineteenth-century U.S. magazines. Amy Aronson, for instance, argues that, in general, "the American magazine was unusually amenable to a relatively open and dynamic exchange of reader voices and views" (315). Women's magazines were especially participatory and often intimate. This is evident, for instance, in Sarah Josepha Hale's 1829 invitation for *Godey's* readers to respond to a male contributor's charge that women are as superficial as men. A female reader's subsequent rebuttal is prefaced by this acknowledgment:

"Mrs. Hale—had you not so kindly invited me . . . in your last Magazine, to answer the curious epistle, I do not think I ever should have summoned resolution to appear in print" (qtd. in Aronson 317).

20. In *Feminist Rhetorical Resilience*, Elizabeth A. Flynn, Patricia Sotirin, and Ann Brady use this term when summarizing work by feminist therapist Judith Jordan as a foundation for their concept of feminist rhetorical resilience. I borrow this term because Black, Mossell, and La Flesche similarly privilege "meaning making" through the "relational dynamics" that drive their newspaper writing (12).

21. Carla L. Peterson defines "the ethnic public sphere" as "a set of broader institutions designed to provide intellectual and political leadership to the African-American population as a whole" (10). As chapter 2 addresses, the New York Freeman was one such institution that provided this type of leadership. While Peterson posits the elite character of the ethnic public sphere (writing that African American urban elites "did separate [themselves] out to some degree, working, speaking, and writing from within the ethnic public sphere"), I show how Mossell's "Our Woman's Department" functions as a democratic type of "ethnic public sphere" that values collaborative literacy practices across class lines (10).

22. I acknowledge that within these counterpublics, certain power asymmetries existed. For instance, Black and the Examiner appear to have selected from among the many letters they received, giving voice to some readers but leaving other letters unpublished (see "Methods, Methodologies, and Further Contributions" for a discussion of unpublished letters). Yet, on the whole, the three writers I discuss demonstrate a commitment to "foster[ing] a relational dynamic of mutual empowerment" as they interacted with readers and local communities (Flynn et. al 12).

23. Schultz has observed that children's "amateur writing provided a site for self-expression and for resistance that was not ordinarily available in classroom-based writing" (134). As further clarification, *The Young Composers* (1999) overall contends "that nineteenth-century writing instruction in the schools was a site for tremendous pedagogical innovation" (more so than prior scholarship had acknowledged); Schultz nonetheless emphasizes the greater freedom offered by extracurricular sites (147). She explains: "For all the educational reform that occurred in the century, schools replicated the culture's dominant values," and "[e]ven the experience-based writing that students did in school was framed by the restrictions of school." Her examination of out-of-school letters and diaries, however, shows that children "use[d] those scenes of writing to contest received wisdom" (134).

24. Even now, digitization of certain nineteenth-century newspapers is not fully accessible or optimal. The historical San Francisco Examiner, for one, has been recently digitized by the San Francisco Public Library but is available only to California residents and not to outside researchers. The *Examiner* is also available through a paid subscription to newspapers.com, which would benefit from an enhanced search engine for comprehensive research. As more nineteenth-century newspapers are digitized and search engines optimized, our exploration of the rhetorical and pedagogical work of women's journalism during this period will become even more enriched.

25. I use the term "activist" in characterizing children's public writing during the "Little Jim" campaign (chapter 1) and elsewhere in other chapters. Like Patricia Bizzell and Lisa Zimmerelli, I "realize that applying activist to nineteenth-century rhetoric is anachronistic, but [I] do not think it is inaccurate. The period abounded with diverse intellectual, social, and civic issues with which people across race, creed, class, and gender were passionately engaged" (1).

26. Although Susette La Flesche is largely absent from rhetorical and other secondary scholarship, Malea Powell has analyzed the rhetorical practices of her sister, Susan La Flesche Picotte, in "Down by the River, or How Susan La Flesche Picotte Can Teach Us about Alliance as a Practice of Survivance" (2004).

1. Winifred Black Bonfils's "Little Jim" Campaign

1. As Katherine H. Adams and Michael L. Keene have noted in *Winifred Black/Annie Laurie and the Making of Modern Nonfiction*, "Martha Winifred Sweet Black Bonfils wrote as Annie Laurie at the *San Francisco Examiner* and in her advice columns but otherwise as Winifred Black" (176). Like Adams and Keene, I have therefore also chosen to use the name Winifred Black in this book, except in the first occurrence of her name in a chapter.

2. I borrow the phrase "symbolic motherhood" from Mari Tonn, whose essay "Militant Motherhood: Labor's Mary Harris 'Mother' Jones" in the *Quarterly Journal of Speech* analyzes Harris's symbolic and militant motherhood in the context of agitation in the industrial labor movement.

3. New journalism of the late nineteenth century was defined by conventions such as attention-grabbing headlines, "bold-faced type," plentiful illustrations, and "vivid accounts" (Fahs 3–4; Britton 27; Lutes, *Front-Page Girls* 14). The term *yellow journalism* is also associated with journalism of this period, though the term itself "was not coined until at least 1897" (Edelstein 116). In this study, I have chosen to use the term *new journalism*.

4. The Thaw murder trial of 1907 tried Harry Thaw, "heir to a coal-mining fortune," for the murder of Stanford White, an architect. See chapter 3, "The Original Sob Sisters: Writers on Trial," in Jean Lutes's *Front-Page Girls: Women Journalists in American Culture and Fiction, 1880–1930* (68).

5. Additional testimonials also support this claim. At a January 1936 luncheon in Black's honor, South of Market Boys president Thomas W. Hickey proclaimed, "thanks be to God for women of this type who stand for the old traditions and . . . stand for the home, which is the very cornerstone of the community, which stands for the sanctity of marriage and the welfare of the child" (*SFE* Jan. 26, 1936). On May 28, 1936, Judge Deasy similarly commemorated Black for championing motherhood: "[s]he joined hands at the altar of home and fireside to declare the eternal virtues of duty, honor, and chastity to the children and mothers of the country" (*SFE* May 28, 1936).

6. The work of other scholars such as Robin Bernstein has more briefly addressed the subject of late nineteenth-century children's writing stimulated by large newspapers. In her *PMLA* article "Children's Books, Dolls, and the Performance of Race; or, The Possibility of Children's Literature," Bernstein demonstrates how commercially interdependent literary and material cultures "coscripted" patterns of violence inflicted on African American dolls in part by pointing to a set of white children's letters published in the *Minneapolis Journal* responding to a writing prompt asking them to describe their play with toys (167).

7. In this chapter, I argue that Black promotes a distinctive kind of rhetorical education that privileges moral principles over prescriptive grammatical and mechanical standards. Although children's letters published in the "Letter-Box" of the "Boys and Girls' Page" during Black's editorship appear to reflect greater adherence to prevailing grammatical and mechanical conventions than do the "Little Jim" campaign letters, departures from normative conceptions of correctness are also represented in children's "Letter-Box" contributions. Their presence suggests that children's public writing was not merely continually encouraged by Black and the *Examiner*; it was valued whether or not it conformed with prevailing conceptions of correctness and eloquence.

8. Black's analysis of these three letters points to ways that the reporter contributed to the late nineteenth-century creation of childhood. As children came to be recognized as more than "miniature adults," women were encouraged "to discover the innate qualities of a child's nature, and their gentle influence was supposed to draw out and shape these undeveloped elements into the child's character" (Husband and O'Loughlin 121). Black's

journalism operates within this tradition by offering children freedom from grammatical and mechanical regulations. She encourages children like Joey, Ralph, and Alexander to embrace their "innate qualities" and in turn develop their natural character through sincere, civically motivated writing.

9. In this section, Black also remarks on a letter with "a pretty feminine hand. The letter was so thick that I knew it was full of good advice." Nonetheless it was the "little crumply" child's letter, representing a vast improvement over the embellished "business-like" letter, that proved "the bright spot in the day had come" (*SFE* Dec. 9, 1894).

10. Denman here draws on Halloran's "From Rhetoric to Composition," which charts the shift from late eighteenth-century neoclassical rhetoric to late nineteenth-century composition courses. Denman, summarizing Halloran, notes: "In place of a rich array of stylistic forms and techniques was the flat voice of mechanical correctness. The greatest loss was the sense of a large social purpose for writing, a social role for which rhetorical art was necessary equipment" (Denman 10).

11. Throughout the "Little Jim" campaign, Black published a relatively equal number of contributions from boys and girls. It is difficult to determine, though, whether girls and boys contributed equally to the total number of letters received (many of which were likely not published).

12. Although Black's teacherly ethos enabled important inroads for male and female children's discursive public participation across socioeconomic class, there is no indication of racial diversity among these children writers. San Francisco census records suggest that the majority were presumably white, but ultimately their racial demographics are unknown (*Bay Area Census*).

13. According to Russell Quinn, the *Examiner* used 42–50 percent of its space for advertising in 1890, 39–40 percent of its space for advertising in 1900, and 49–56 percent of its space for advertising in 1910 (21).

2. Gertrude Bustill Mossell's "Helpful Sisterhood"

1. Jacqueline Jones Royster has similarly observed that periodical publications such as newspapers "have served as a constant forum for the voices of African Americans to be heard" (219).

2. Mossell references this teaching experience in the first column of "Our Woman's Department," prefacing a claim about children's development with the phrase, "[a]fter seven years experience in primary, and secondary teaching we are led to believe . . ." (*NYF* Dec. 26, 1885).

3. Zackodnik here draws on work by Hazel Dicken-Garcia.

4. The *Work of the Afro-American Woman* (1894) "celebrated the various works of Black women of the nineteenth century in the fields of literature, medicine, education, activism, and more" (M. Wright 225).

5. Despite her different tactics, Mossell had high praise for Wells. In 1889, Mossell wrote in the *Indianapolis Freeman* that "Miss Wells has already made her non-de-plume Iola a power, and her articles are much sought after. She writes with a vim and sparkle that holds the attention. One always reads her articles to the end and never casts aside the humblest publication after seeing her signature, until one finds what she has to say" (qtd. in McMurry 112). In 1892, after hearing a lecture by Wells titled "Darkest America," Mossell reported: "This lecture cannot fail to be of value to the race and serve as a source of enlightenment to many of our people in the north who have not as yet grasped the difficulties of the southern problem" (*IW* Sept. 24, 1892).

6. Readers of "Our Woman's Department" would have connected education to racial uplift through statements such as M. E. L.'s "[t]he time has surely come when our young people require thorough education in order to move in the best grade of society" (*NYF* Oct. 16, 1886).

7. I am not arguing that white women did not participate in public life but rather that the cult of true womanhood may have ideologically restricted them to a greater degree than the ideology of Black female moral leadership did African American women.

8. While not all white middle-class women found the ideology of true womanhood restraining, they generally had less control over the terms of "true womanhood" than did Black women during this period.

9. Wright confirms that Mossell was "one of the first black women journalists to edit an advice column for black women and girls in the early black press" (116).

10. This passage from a selection titled "Domestic Training of Girls" was quite possibly written by Mossell. It is also possible that this selection is an unattributed exchange publication. If the latter, I treat this reprint (and others like it) as an extension of Mossell's own pedagogical practices. As Shirley Wilson Logan notes in *Liberating Language* when discussing the nineteenth-century Black press, "[w]here articles appear as reprints from other papers, I consider that the editors made the choice to include them and thus functioned as agents of any rhetorical education that such articles contained" (99).

11. Shirley Wilson Logan describes *Woman's Era* as a "vital" instrument for "community-building among black clubwomen as the first newspaper published by and for African American women" (*Liberating Language* 117).

12. It is sometimes challenging to decisively identify the authorship of particular selections in "Our Woman's Department." In the case of "Equal Rights at the Fireside," it appears that Mossell wrote this selection, which contains a quotation from E. B. B.'s letter. It is unlikely that E. B. B. composed the entire selection (despite the location of her initials in the column) because the selection's opening points to Mossell: "A letter lately received by us contained the following . . ." (*NYF* Mar. 12, 1887). It is also unlikely that this is an exchange publication because a different letter from E. B. B. (with an explicit address to Mossell) appears elsewhere in the column. Ultimately, then, while not definitive, there is sufficient reason to believe this selection was written by Mossell, who opened it by quoting from E. B. B.'s letter.

13. Douglass himself created scrapbooks in the late nineteenth century. *New York Freeman* editor Timothy Thomas Fortune (or his wife) also "kept a scrapbook on his activities" (Garvey 132).

14. For a more extensive treatment of the role of journals and diaries in African American extracurricular education, see Shirley Wilson Logan's chapter "Private Learners: Self-Education in Rhetoric" in *Liberating Language* (2008).

15. Ellen Gruber Garvey analyzes this passage, as well as the Frederick Douglass assignment, in the context of African American scrapbooking practices. See chapter 4 in *Writing with Scissors*.

16. Carla Peterson explains that in the nineteenth century, "[u]rban blacks . . . sought to engage in skilled crafts and trades in which in-house production or self-employment would be possible, in the process offering service to the black community rather than a white clientele" (9–10).

17. Eliza Archard Connor was an influential late nineteenth-century white journalist and literary editor of the *World*. She held a master of journalism degree from Antioch College and has been described by Cheryl Crowell as "one of the most educated females of the time" (41).

18. I again approach reprints such as Archard's paper in keeping with Logan's claim that if the editor "made the choice to include them," she "thus functioned as [an] agen[t] of any rhetorical education that such articles contained" (*Liberating Language* 99).

19. Importantly, domestic and journalistic roles were not mutually exclusive paths for Mossell. As she affirms in the first installment of the "Women and Journalism" series, "the majority of our most successful female writers were married women, and had attained a greater part of their success after marriage" (*NYF* May 8, 1886).

20. It is possible that readers may have suggested to Mossell that she share advice from her own experience or that of other African American journalists (as opposed to texts by white female journalists such as Archard and Cooke). Mossell writes in the fourth installment: "Thinking that some of our less hopeful readers may say, All this is the work of the dominant race, but what can we hope for? we have decided to give a few extracts from our own notebook, hoping they may be of some value" (*NYF* June 5, 1886). Although Mossell does not explicitly state that reader input guided this decision, it remains possible that readers influenced her notebook sharing given this allusion and the volume of communications received on the subject.

3. Susette La Flesche's Relational Journalism and Literacy Teaching

1. David Treuer writes that "more than 150 Lakota" were killed at Wounded Knee, though "[t]he actual number of dead is still in dispute, with some putting the number at more than three hundred" (6). Kimberli Lee, for instance, writes that "at least three hundred Lakota men, women, and children were shot down" (130). Susannah Hopson meanwhile states that "[a]round 300 Sioux were killed" (266).

2. Extending scholarly work by Malea Powell in "Down by the River, or How Susan La Flesche Picotte Can Teach Us about Alliance as a Practice of Survivance," King utilizes this phrase when discussing "[r]hetorical alliance" "in terms of its broader applications for cross-cultural discourse" (7). I draw on both King and Powell to understand alliance building as a rhetorical practice involving relationally based language operating "across cultures and communities" that foregrounds connections among human beings (King 7). Powell relatedly writes, when reflecting on the field of rhetoric and composition, that "[w]e need a new language, one that doesn't convince us of our unutterable and ongoing differences . . . We need a language that allows us to imagine respectful and reciprocal relationships that acknowledge the degree to which we need one another (have needed one another) in order to survive and flourish" (41). Through her relational journalism and practices of alliance building, La Flesche similarly models and invites the cultivation of "respectful and reciprocal relationships" (41).

3. In her anthology *Native American Women's Writing*, Karen Kilcup writes that "[f]or cultures valuing community and authorizing communal voices . . . individualism may be a negative value, in contrast to mainstream

culture" (4). The collaborative journalism of La Flesche and Tibbles similarly prioritizes communal activism rather than "mainstream" individualism.

4. Jason Edward Black builds on work by Frederick Hoxie in writing that "Native groups 'talked back,' which helped them reconstitute their own identities, rebuke governmental policies, and reconfigure US identities in the rhetorical process" (6).

5. See Powell's "Down by the River, or How Susan La Flesche Picotte Can Teach Us about Alliance as a Practice of Survivance" (2004) for an analysis of the rhetorical practices of Susette La Flesche's sister Susan La Flesche Picotte.

6. Both David Treuer and Joe Starita identify General George Crook, the military official who arrested Standing Bear's party upon orders, as the person who contacted Tibbles after experiencing a "change of heart" (Treuer 123; "Ancestry").

7. "The solution of the Indian problem, as it is called, is citizenship," La Flesche emphasized in a speech delivered in Boston in 1880 ("Lecture Delivered by Bright Eyes"). Her introduction to William Justin Harsha's *Ploughed Under: The Story of an Indian Chief* (1881) similarly argued for citizenship. Later in life, La Flesche complicated her arguments about citizenship and critiqued the General Allotment Act. See this book's conclusion, "Public Memory and the Pan-extracurriculum," for further discussion.

8. John M. Coward, referencing La Flesche's biographer Dorothy Clarke Wilson, similarly claims that La Flesche "wanted to be known by her formal name, Susette LaFlesche, but 'the newspapers would not let her'" (216).

9. Ernest Stromberg has similarly argued that "[w]hile exceptions to . . . negative representations of Indians exist within the historical record, the general trend was toward a discourse of Indianness that had the rhetorical effect of persuading a non-Indian audience of the inherent inferiority of America's indigenous peoples" (95).

10. Coleman states that "[t]he report of the massacre of seven white men was false. It may have been a rehash by a reporter of the erroneous report of a massacre a few days earlier" (101).

11. See Powell's "Down by the River, or How Susan La Flesche Picotte Can Teach Us about Alliance as a Practice of Survivance" for a further discussion of ways in which Susan La Flesche Picotte encouraged readers of her 1891 Women's National Indian Association report "to see her people as willing and able to engage in dominant notions of 'civilization' because she kn[ew] their lives, literally, depend[ed] upon it" (55).

12. See both "School Days of an Indian Girl" (*Atlantic*, January 1900) and also Zitkala-Ša's 1919 discussion of another incident on a train in *American Indian Magazine*.

13. Notably, this exigence is also referenced in "Why They Are Starving" when La Flesche reports that General Brooke "says that the Indians have been talked to too much" (OMWH Dec. 18, 1890).

14. Malea Powell, Daisy Levy, Andrea Riley-Mukavetz, Marilee Brooks-Gillies, Maria Novotny, and Jennifer Fisch-Ferguson here draw on De Certeau's *The Practice of Everyday Life*.

15. The *New York Times* affirmed that "[t]he trouble came when the soldiers attempted to disarm the Indians" (Dec. 30, 1890).

Conclusion

1. These lyrics reflect another clear example of a sentimental rhetoric of disability, present in not only the visual rhetoric and journalistic discourse of the "Little Jim" campaign but also in this lyrical composition. See chapter 1 for a discussion of limiting representations of disability during the "Little Jim" campaign.

2. Publication of the annual may have preceded or extended beyond this time frame, but archival records of this yearbook (from Archives and Special Collections at the University of California, San Francisco) are only available for volumes published 1924–1930.

3. See the "Origins" section of Charles Blockson's *Philadelphia's Guide: African-American State Historical Markers*. Blockson discusses the origins of (and his contributions to) "the installation of markers identifying historic African-American sites throughout the city" (12). Of the sixty-six markers listed in the guide, Gertrude E. H. Bustill Mossell's marker is one.

4. Sara VanderHaagen here draws on work by children's literature scholar Dianne Johnson in observing that "African American communities have long used stories to transmit an appreciation of the past" (7).

5. These data were gathered from searching the Pennsylvania Historical Marker Database and were last updated in September 2022. To identify the number of African American markers in both Philadelphia and the rest of the state, I selected the keywords *African American* from the category search filters. (It is possible, of course, that this database is not entirely up to date.)

6. Charlene Palmore-Lewis writes, "Charles Blockson, collector and retired curator of the African-American exhibit at Temple University" had been

"engaged by the William Penn Foundation in 1990 to head the Philadelphia portion of the African-American Pennsylvania State Marker Project." As of 2007, "[o]f approximately 2,200 historical markers in Pennsylvania, only 180 refer[ed] to the African American Experience, and invaluable Charles Blockson is responsible for sixty-six of them" (47).

7. In the same interview, Blockson also noted, "I never had an African American teacher in my life" ("Conversation with Charles L. Blockson").

8. King, Gubele, and Anderson here draw on work by Craig Womack: "as Craig Womack asserts," they write, "indigenous voices should not be thought of as an addition to the canon but rather as the foundational voices, the foundational stories on and of these lands (Womack 1999)" (9).

9. Joseph La Flesche was Principal Chief of the Omaha Tribe (not Chief of the Poncas as implied in this newspaper quotation).

10. Flynn, Sotirin, and Brady here draw directly on the work of feminist therapist Judith Jordan. See their collection's introduction, "Feminist Rhetorical Resilience—Possibilities and Impossibilities," for a further discussion of ways in which Jordan informs their concept of "rhetorical resilience."

Works Cited

Abernathy, Penelope Muse. *The Expanding News Desert*. Center for Innovation and Sustainability in Local Media / U of North Carolina P, 2018.

———. *Saving Community Journalism: The Path to Profitability*. U of North Carolina P, 2014.

Adams, Katherine H., and Michael L. Keene. *Winifred Black/Annie Laurie and the Making of Modern Nonfiction*. McFarland & Company, 2015.

"Ancestry." *Constitutional*, podcast created by Lillian Cunningham, episode 2 with guests Joe Starita, Larry Wright Jr., and Lindsay Robertson. *Washington Post*, 7 Aug. 2017, https://www.washingtonpost.com /news/on-leadership/wp/2017/08/07/episode-2-of-the-constitutional -podcast-ancestry/.

Anderson, Benedict. *Imagined Communities: Reflections on the Origin and Spread of Nationalism*. Verso, 2006.

Anderson, Faye. "Unmarking African American History in Philadelphia." *Anderson@Large*, 11 Feb. 2019, https://andersonatlarge.type-pad.com/andersonlarge/social-media/.

Andersson, Rani-Henrik. *The Lakota Ghost Dance of 1890*. U of Nebraska P, 2008.

Aronson, Amy. "Everything Old Is New Again: How the 'New' User-Generated Women's Magazine Takes Us Back to the Future." *American Journalism: A Journal of Media History*, vol. 31, no. 3, 2014, pp. 312–28.

Batker, Carol J. *Reforming Fictions: Native, African & Jewish American Women's Literature and Journalism in the Progressive Era*. Columbia UP, 2000.

Bay Area Census: San Francisco City and County [website], MTC-ABAG Library, http://www.bayareacensus.ca.gov/counties/SanFrancisco County40.htm.

"Beauties of the Reservation System." *Iapi Oaye*, 1 Nov. 1881.

Bederman, Gail. *Manliness and Civilization: A Cultural History of Gender and Race in the United States, 1880–1917.* U of Chicago P, 1995.

"Betty Lagdon Speaks." Audio recording. Library of Congress, Omaha Powwow Project collection (AFC 1986/038), 13 Aug. 1983, https://www.loc.gov/item/omhbib000027/.

Bird, S. Elizabeth. *Dressing in Feathers: The Construction of the Indian in American Popular Culture.* 1996. Routledge, 2018.

Bizzell, Patricia, and Lisa Zimmerelli. "Introduction." *Nineteenth-Century American Activist Rhetorics*, edited by Patricia Bizzell and Lisa Zimmerelli, Modern Language Association of America, 2020, pp. 1–12.

Black, Winfred. "Annie Laurie's Experience." *San Francisco Examiner*, 13 July 1890.

Blockson, Charles L. "Marking History in Philadelphia." Video interview with Blockson. *Voices of the Civil Rights Movement*, Comcast / NBC Universal, https://voicesofthecivilrightsmovement.com.

———. *Philadelphia's Guide: African-American State Historical Markers.* Charles L. Blockson Afro-American Collection / William Penn Foundation, 1992.

Bly, Nellie. *Ten Days in a Madhouse.* 1887. University of Pennsylvania Digital Library, https://digital.library.upenn.edu/women/bly/madhouse/madhouse.html.

Bolden, Tonya. "Biographies." *Digital Schomburg African American Women Writers of the 19th Century*, https://libguides.nypl.org/african-american-women-writers-of-the-19th-Century/Mattison-Plato.

Brandt, Deborah. "Sponsors of Literacy." *College Composition and Communication*, vol. 49, no. 2, 1998, pp. 165–85.

Brazeau, Alicia. *Circulating Literacy: Writing Instruction in American Periodicals, 1880–1910.* Southern Illinois UP, 2016.

Brereton, John C. *The Origins of Composition Studies in the American College, 1875–1925.* U of Pittsburgh P, 1995.

Britton, John A. *Cables, Crises, and the Press: The Geopolitics of the New Information System in the Americas, 1866–1903.* U of New Mexico P, 2013.

Camp, E[ugene] M. "Journalists: Born or Made?" Paper read before the Alumni Association of the Wharton School, University of Pennsylvania. Philadelphia: Philadelphia Social Science Association, 1888. YA Pamphlet Collection, Library of Congress, DLC. *HathiTrust*, https://catalog.hathitrust.org/Record/001438915.

Campbell, Karlyn Kohrs. "Consciousness-Raising: Linking Theory, Criticism, and Practice." *Rhetoric Society Quarterly*, vol. 32, no. 1, Winter 2002, pp. 45–64.

———. "Feminist Rhetoric." *Encyclopedia of Rhetoric and Composition: Communication from Ancient Times to the Information Age*, edited by Theresa Enos, Garland Publishing, 1996, pp. 262–65.

Carlson, Shirley J. "Black Ideals of Womanhood in the Late Victorian Era." *Journal of Negro History*, vol. 77, no. 2, 1992, pp. 61–73.

Carr, Jean Ferguson, et al. *Archives of Instruction: Nineteenth-Century Rhetorics, Readers, and Composition Books in the United States.* Southern Illinois UP, 2005.

Cedillo, Christina V. "What Does It Mean to Move? Race, Disability, and Critical Embodiment Pedagogy." *Composition Forum*, vol. 39, Summer 2018.

Chambers, Deborah, et al. *Women and Journalism.* Routledge, 2004.

Coleman, William S. E. *Voices of Wounded Knee.* Bison Books, 2001.

Collier, Price. *America and the Americans.* Charles Scribner's Sons, 1897.

Conaway, Carol B. "Mary Ann Shadd Cary: A Visionary of the Black Press." *Black Women's Intellectual Traditions: Speaking Their Minds*, edited by Kristin Waters and Carol B. Conaway, U of Vermont P, 2007, pp.216–48.

"Conversation with Charles L. Blockson" Video recording with Stephanie Renée. *Slought*, 12 July 2018, University of Pennsylvania, https://slought.org/resources/charles_l_blockson.

Coward, John M. *The Newspaper Indian: Native American Identity in the Press, 1820–90.* U of Illinois P, 1999.

Crowell, Cheryl. *New Richmond.* Arcadia Publishing, 2012.

Crowley, Aileen G. "The Legend of 'Little Jim.'" *Little Jim.* San Francisco, 1928. Register of the Children's Hospital School of Nursing Alumnae Association Papers, 1905–1987. Archives and Special Collections, University of California, San Francisco.

Cushman, Ellen, et al. "Decolonizing Projects: Creating Pluriversal Possibilities in Rhetoric," *Rhetoric Review*, vol. 38, no. 1, 2019, pp. 1–22.

Dabel, Jane E. *A Respectable Woman: The Public Roles of African American Women in 19th-Century New York.* New York UP, 2008.

Dando-Collins, Stephen. *Standing Bear Is a Person: The True Story of a Native American's Quest for Justice.* Da Capo Press, 2004.

Dann, Martin E. *The Black Press, 1827–1890: The Quest for National Identity.* Putnam, 1971.

DeFrance, Charles Q. "Some Recollections of Thomas H. Tibbles." *Nebraska History Magazine*, vol. 13, no. 4, 1932, pp. 238–47.

Denman, William N. "Rhetoric, the 'Citizen-Orator,' and the Revitalization of Civic Discourse in American Life." *Rhetorical Education in America*, edited by Cheryl Glenn et al., U of Alabama P, 2004, pp. 3–17.

DePastino, Todd. *Citizen Hobo: How a Century of Homelessness Shaped America*. U of Chicago P, 2003.

Dolmage, Jay Timothy. *Disability Rhetoric*. Syracuse UP, 2014.

Dorr, Rheta Childe. *A Woman of Fifty*. Funk & Wagnalls, 1924.

Duniway, Abigail Scott. "Women in Journalism." *"She Flies with Her Own Wings": The Collected Speeches of Abigail Scott Duniway* [website], edited by Randall A. Lake, https://asduniway.org/"woman-in -journalism"-circa-february-september-1897/.

Eastman, Charles Alexander. *From the Deep Woods to Civilization: Chapters in the Autobiography of an Indian*. Little, Brown, 1916.

Edelstein, Sari. *Between the Novel and the News: The Emergence of American Women's Writing*. U of Virginia P, 2014.

Engbers, Susanna Kelly. "With Great Sympathy: Elizabeth Cady Stanton's Innovative Appeals to Emotion." *Rhetoric Society Quarterly*, vol. 37, no. 3, 2007, pp. 307–32.

Enoch, Jessica. "Changing Research Methods, Changing History: A Reflection on Language, Location, and Archive." *Composition Studies*, vol. 38, no. 2, 2010, pp. 47–73.

———. *Refiguring Rhetorical Education: Women Teaching African American, Native American, and Chicano/a Students, 1865–1911*. Southern Illinois UP, 2008.

———. "Releasing Hold: Feminist Historiography without the Tradition." *Theorizing Histories of Rhetoric*, edited by Michelle Ballif, Southern Illinois UP, 2013, pp. 58–73.

Erisman, Fred. "St. Nicholas." *Children's Periodicals of the United States*, edited by Gordan R. Kelly, Greenwood Press, 1984.

Fahs, Alice. *Out on Assignment: Newspaper Women and the Making of Modern Public Space*. U of North Carolina P, 2011.

Fehler, Brian. "Put It in the Papers: Rhetorical Ecologies, Labor Rhetorics, and the Newsboys' Strike of 1899." *Nineteenth-Century American Activist Rhetorics*, edited by Patricia Bizzell and Lisa Zimmerelli, Modern Language Association of America, 2020, pp. 149–62.

Fleckenstein, Kristie S. "Aesthetic Daughter and Civic Mother: Collective Identity and the Visual-Verbal Rhetorics of the New Negro Woman." *Nineteenth-Century American Activist Rhetorics*, edited by Patricia Bizzell and Lisa Zimmerelli, Modern Language Association of America, 2020, pp. 249–64.

Flynn, Elizabeth A., et al. "Introduction: Feminist Rhetorical Resilience—Possibilities and Impossibilities." *Feminist Rhetorical Resilience*, edited by Elizabeth A. Flynn et al., Utah State UP, 2012, pp. 1–29.

Foster, Frances Smith. "A Narrative of the Interesting Origins and (Somewhat) Surprising Developments of African-American Print Culture." *American Literary History*, vol. 17, no. 4, 2005, pp. 714–40.

Fraser, Nancy. "Rethinking the Public Sphere: A Contribution to the Critique of Actually Existing Democracy," *Social Text*, vols. 25/26, 1990, pp. 56–80.

Frost, John. *Easy Exercises in Composition: Designed for the Use of Beginners.* E. H. Butler, 1843.

García, Romeo, and Damián Baca. *Rhetorics Elsewhere and Otherwise: Contested Modernities, Decolonial Visions.* National Council of Teachers of English, 2019.

Garland-Thomson, Rosemarie. "The Politics of Staring: Visual Rhetorics of Disability in Popular Photography." *Disability Studies: Enabling the Humanities*, edited by Sharon L. Snyder et al., Modern Language Association of America, 2002, pp. 56-75.

Garvey, Ellen Gruber. *Writing with Scissors: American Scrapbooks from the Civil War to the Harlem Renaissance.* Oxford UP, 2013.

Gatewood, Willard B. *Aristocrats of Color: The Black Elite, 1880–1920.* Indiana UP, 1990.

Gere, Anne Ruggles. "An Art of Survivance: Angel DeCora at Carlisle." *The American Indian Quarterly*, vol. 28, no. 3-4, 2004.

———. *Intimate Practices: Literacy and Cultural Work in U.S. Women's Clubs, 1880–1920.* U of Illinois P, 1997.

———. "Kitchen Tables and Rented Rooms: The Extracurriculum of Composition." *College Composition and Communication*, vol. 45, no. 1, 1994, pp. 75–107.

"Gertrude E. H. Bustill Mossell." *Historical Marker Database*, last revised 5 Feb. 2022, https://www.hmdb.org/m.asp?m=81928.

Glenn, Cheryl. *Rhetoric Retold: Regendering the Tradition from Antiquity through the Renaissance.* Southern Illinois UP, 1997.

———. *Rhetorical Feminism and This Thing Called Hope*. Southern Illinois UP, 2018.

"Goals of International Women's Year 1975." *College Teaching*, vol. 23, no. 1, 1975, p. 64.

Gold, David. *Rhetoric at the Margins: Revising the History of Writing Instruction in American Colleges, 1873–1947*. Southern Illinois UP, 2008.

Goldsby, Jacqueline. *A Spectacular Secret: Lynching in American Life and Literature*. U of Chicago P, 2006.

Gooding-Williams, Robert. *In the Shadow of Du Bois: Afro-Modern Political Thought in America*. Harvard UP, 2009.

Gray, Paige. *Cub Reporters: American Children's Literature and Journalism in the Golden Age*. SUNY P, 2019.

Guarneri, Julia. *Newsprint Metropolis: City Papers and the Making of Modern Americans*. U of Chicago P, 2017.

Gubele, Rose. "Unlearning the Pictures in Our Heads: Teaching the Cherokee Phoenix, Boudinot, and Cherokee History." *Survivance, Sovereignty, and Story: Teaching American Indian Rhetorics*, edited by Lisa King et al., Utah State UP, 2015, 96–115.

Guy-Sheftall, Beverly, editor. *Words of Fire: An Anthology of African-American Feminist Thought*. New Press, 1995.

Habermas, Jurgen. *The Structural Transformation of the Public Sphere: An Inquiry into a Category of Bourgeois Society*. Translated by Thomas Burger, MIT P, 1989.

Hämäläinen, Pekka. *Lakota America: A New History of Indigenous Power*. Yale UP, 2019.

Harris, Sharon M., editor. *Blue Pencils and Hidden Hands: Women Editing Periodicals, 1830–1910*. Northeastern UP, 2004.

Hauser, Gerald A. *Vernacular Voices: The Rhetoric of Publics and Public Spheres*. U of South Carolina P, 1999.

Hawhee, Debra, and Christa J. Olson. "Pan-historiography: The Challenges of Writing History across Time and Space." *Theorizing Historiography in Rhetoric*, edited by Michelle Ballif, Southern Illinois UP, 2013, pp. 90–105.

"Historical Marker Database." *HMdb.org*, https://www.hmdb.org/about.asp.

"Historical Marker Nomination Form," Pennsylvania State Historic Preservation Office, Pennsylvania Historical and Museum Commission, updated April 2020, https://www.phmc.pa.gov/Preservation/Historical-Markers/Documents/Marker_Nomination_Form_reference.pdf.

"Historical Markers: Pennsylvania Historical Marker Program." *Pennsylvania Historical & Museum Commission*, https://www.phmc.pa.gov/Preservation/Historical-Markers/Pages/default.aspx.

hooks, bell. *Black Looks: Race and Representation*. Routledge, 2015.

Hopson, Susannah. "Religious Sovereignty and the Ghost Dance in Native American Fiction." *The Routledge Companion to Native American Literature*, edited by Deborah L. Madsen, Routledge, 2015, pp. 260–72.

Husband, Julie, and Jim O'Loughlin. *Daily Life in the Industrial United States, 1870–1900*. Greenwood Press, 2004.

Hutelmyer, Laura L. *Gertrude Bustill Mossell and "Our Woman's Department": Advocating Change through a Weekly Advice Column, 1885–1887*. 2007. Villanova U, MA thesis.

Johnson, Nan. *Gender and Rhetorical Space in American Life, 1866–1910*. Southern Illinois UP, 2002.

Kaestle, Carl F. "Seeing the Sites: Readers, Publishers, and Local Print Cultures." *Print in Motion: The Expansion of Publishing and Reading in the United States, 1880–1940*, edited by Carl F. Kaestle and Janice Radway. *A History of the Book in America*, vol. 4, U of North Carolina P, 2009, pp. 22–48.

Kaestle, Carl F., and Janice A. Radway. "A Framework for the History of Publishing and Reading in the United States, 1880–1940." *Print in Motion: The Expansion of Publishing and Reading in the United States, 1880–1940*, edited by Carl F. Kaestle and Janice Radway. *A History of the Book in America*, vol. 4, U of North Carolina P, 2009, pp. 7–21.

Keller, J. W. "Journalism as a Career." *Forum*, vol. 15, Aug. 1893, pp. 693–94.

Kelly, Casey Ryan, and Jason Edward Black, editors. *Decolonizing Native American Rhetoric: Communicating Self-Determination*. Peter Lang, 2018.

Kilcup, Karen L. *Native American Women's Writing, 1800–1924: An Anthology*. John Wiley & Sons, 1991.

King, Lisa. *Legible Sovereignties: Rhetoric, Representations, and Native American Museums*. Oregon State UP, 2017.

———. "Sovereignty, Rhetorical Sovereignty, and Representation: Keywords for Teaching Indigenous Texts." *Survivance, Sovereignty, and Story: Teaching Indigenous Rhetorics*, edited by Lisa King et al., U of Utah P, 2015, pp. 17–34.

King, Lisa, et al. "Introduction—Careful with the Stories We Tell: Naming Survivance, Sovereignty, and Story." *Survivance, Sovereignty, and*

Story: Teaching Indigenous Rhetorics, edited by Lisa King et al., U of
Utah P, 2015, pp. 3–16.

Kirsch, Gesa E., and Liz Rohan. "Introduction: The Role of Serendipity,
Family Connections, and Cultural Memory in Historical Research."
Beyond the Archives: Research as a Lived Process, edited by Gesa E.
Kirsch and Liz Rohan, Southern Illinois UP, 2008.

Klapper, Melissa R. *Jewish Girls Coming of Age in America, 1860–1920*.
New York UP, 2005.

Krupat, Arnold. *"That the People Might Live": Loss and Renewal in Native
American Elegy*. Cornell UP, 2012.

"La Flesche Family" [RG2026.AM]. Series 14: Papers of Susette La Flesche
Tibbles, 1880-1896. Box 3. Autograph book, 1880-1896. Nebraska State
Historical Society.

La Flesche, Susette. "Bright Eyes." 1881. *Emory Women Writers Resource
Project* [website].

———. Introduction. *Ploughed Under: The Story of an Indian Chief, Told
by Himself*, by William Justin Harsha, [New York:] Fords, Howard &
Hulbert, 1881.

———. Introduction. *Standing Bear and the Ponca Chiefs*. Thomas Henry
Tibbles, 1880.

———. Letter to T. H. Tibbles. 29 Apr. 1879. NMAI_AC066/Box_001
/Folder_04, Thomas Henry Tibbles Papers, National Museum of the
American Indian, Smithsonian Institution.

———. "Political Speech Given by Bright Eyes." NMAI-066_001_05_013,
Thomas H. Tibbles Papers, National Museum of the American Indian,
Smithsonian Institution.

Latham, Sean, and Robert Scholes. "The Rise of Periodical Studies."
PMLA, vol. 121, no. 2, Mar. 2006, pp. 517–31.

Leahy, Elizabeth. "'Their Voice Should Be Allowed to Be Heard': The
Rhetorical Power of the University of New Mexico's Bilingual Student
Newspaper." *Rhetoric Review*, vol. 39, no. 2, 2020, pp. 127–41.

"Lecture Delivered by Bright Eyes." Boston, MA, 1880. NMAI-066_001
_05_001, Thomas H. Tibbles Papers, National Museum of the American Indian, Smithsonian Institution.

Lee, Kimberli. "Heartspeak from the Spirit: Songs of John Trudell, Keith
Secola, and Robbie Robertson." *Survivance, Sovereignty, and Story: Teaching Indigenous Rhetorics*, edited by Lisa King et al., U of Utah P, 2015, pp.
116–37.

Libertz, Daniel. "Amplification by Counterstory in the Quantitative Rhetoric of Ida B. Wells." *Rhetoric Society Quarterly*, vol. 51, no. 4, Summer 2021, pp. 309–24.

Lindey, Sara. "Boys Write Back: Self-Education and Periodical Authorship in Late-Nineteenth-Century Story Papers." *American Periodicals: A Journal of History, Criticism, and Bibliography*, vol. 21, no. 1, July 2011, pp. 72–88.

Littlefield, Daniel F., Jr., and James W. Parins. *A Bibliography of Native American Writers, 1772–1924: A Supplement*. Scarecrow Press, 1985.

Little Jim Club of California Medical Center. "Home" and "History." https://ljc.clubexpress.com/content.aspx?page_id=0&club_id =631323.

Logan, Shirley Wilson. *Liberating Language: Sites of Rhetorical Education in Nineteenth-Century Black America*. Southern Illinois UP, 2008.

———. *"We Are Coming": The Persuasive Discourse of Nineteenth-Century Black Women*. Southern Illinois UP, 1999.

Loudon, Betty. "Bright Eyes Fit for Hall of Fame." *Lincoln Evening Journal*, 8 Apr. 1975.

Luo, Michael. "How Can the Press Best Serve a Democratic Society?" *New Yorker*, 11 July 2020.

Lutes, Jean Marie. "Beyond the Bounds of the Book: Periodical Studies and Women Writers of the Late Nineteenth and Early Twentieth Centuries." *Legacy*, vol. 27, no. 2, 2010, pp. 336–56.

———. *Front-Page Girls: Women Journalists in American Culture and Fiction, 1880–1930*. Cornell UP, 2006.

Lyons, Scott Richard. Foreword. *Plateau Indian Ways with Words: The Rhetorical Tradition of the Tribes of the Inland Pacific*. U of Pittsburgh P, 2014, pp. viii–xvi.

———. "Rhetorical Sovereignty: What Do American Indians Want from Writing?" *College Composition and Communication*, vol. 51, no. 3, 2000, pp. 447–68.

"Marriage of 'Bright Eyes.'" *The Valley Sentinel*, 19 Aug. 1881.

Marshall, Joseph M., III. *Crazy Horse Weeps: The Challenge of Being Lakota in White America*. Fulcrum Publishing, 2019.

Marzolf, Marion. *Up from the Footnote: A History of Women Journalists*. Hastings House, 1977.

Masur, Kate. *An Example for All the Land: Emancipation and the Struggle over Equality in Washington, D.C.* U of North Carolina P, 2010.

Mathes, Valerie Sherer, and Richard Lowitt. *The Standing Bear Controversy: Prelude to Indian Reform.* U of Illinois P, 2003.

Mattingly, Carol. *Well-Tempered Women: Nineteenth-Century Temperance Rhetoric.* Southern Illinois UP, 1998.

McChesney, George. "The Care of Crippled Children in the Little Jim Ward." *Little Jim.* San Francisco, 1925. Register of the Children's Hospital School of Nursing Alumnae Association Papers, 1905–1987. Archives and Special Collections, University of California, San Francisco.

McHenry, Elizabeth. *Forgotten Readers: Recovering the Lost History of African American Literary Societies.* Duke UP, 2002.

———. "Reading and Race Pride: The Literary Activism of Black Clubwomen." *Print in Motion: The Expansion of Publishing and Reading in the United States, 1880–1940,* edited by Carl F. Kaestle and Janice Radway. *A History of the Book in America,* vol. 4, U of North Carolina P, 2009, chap. 25.

McKee, Heidi A., and James E. Porter. "The Ethics of Archival Research." *College Composition and Communication,* vol. 64, no. 1, 2012, pp. 59–81.

McMurry, Linda O. *To Keep the Waters Troubled: The Life of Ida B. Wells.* Oxford UP, 1998.

Mignolo, Walter D. *The Darker Side of Western Modernity: Global Futures, Decolonial Options.* Duke UP, 2011.

———. "Delinking: The Rhetoric of Modernity, the Logic of Coloniality and the Grammar of De-coloniality." *Cultural Studies,* vol. 21, no. 2, 2007, pp. 449–514.

Miller, Karen Li. "'Heart Talk': Chinese Schoolgirls' Letters to American Girls." *Saving the World: Girlhood and Evangelicalism in Nineteenth-Century Literature,* edited by Allison Giffen and Robin L. Cadwallader, Routledge, 2017, pp. 19–37.

Mitchell, Michele. *Righteous Propagation: African Americans and the Politics of Racial Destiny after Reconstruction.* U of North Carolina P, 2004.

Monroe, Barbara. *Plateau Indian Ways with Words: The Rhetorical Tradition of the Tribes of the Inland Pacific.* U of Pittsburgh P, 2014.

Mooney, James. *The Ghost-Dance Religion and the Sioux Outbreak of 1890.* Government Printing Office, 1896.

Moss, Beverly. *A Community Text Arises: A Literate Text and a Literacy Tradition in African-American Churches*. Hampton Press, 2003.

Mossell, Gertrude Bustill. *The Work of the Afro-American Woman*. Introduction by Joanne Braxton, Oxford UP, 1988.

Nachbar, Jack, and Kevin Lause. *Popular Culture: An Introductory Text*. Bowling Green State University Popular Press, 1992.

"Nebraska Hall of Fame." *History Nebraska*, https://history.nebraska.gov/nebraska-hall-fame.

"Nebraska Stories." *Nebraska Public Media*, https://nebraskastories.org.

"Nominate a Historical Marker." *Pennsylvania Historical & Museum Commission*, https://www.phmc.pa.gov/Preservation/Historical-Markers/Pages/Nominate.aspx.

Odem, Mary E. *Delinquent Daughters: Protecting and Policing Adolescent Female Sexuality in the United States, 1885–1920*. U of North Carolina P, 1995.

Olin, Charles H. *Journalism: Explains the Workings of a Modern Newspaper Office, and Gives Full Directions for Those Who Desire to Enter the Field of Journalism*. Penn Publishing, 1906.

"Omaha, Neb." *The Kansas City Times*, 26 July 1881.

Palmore-Lewis, Charlene. *Multiculturalism in Twenty-First Century Philadelphia*. 2007. U Pennsylvania, MA thesis.

Parker, Princella, producer and narrator. *Bright Eyes. Nebraska Public Media*, 2016, https://nebraskastories.org/videos/bright-eyes/.

Peril, Lynn. "Behind the Symbol of 'International Women's Year,' 1975." *Bust*, Dec./Jan. 2017.

Peterson, Carla L. *"Doers of the Word": African-American Women Speakers and Writers in the North (1830–1880)*. Oxford UP, 1995.

Peyer, Bernd. "Non-fiction Prose." *The Cambridge Companion to Native American Literature*, edited by Joy Porter and Kenneth M. Roemer, Cambridge UP, 2005, pp. 105–24.

Pflieger, Pat. *Letters from Nineteenth-Century Children to Robert Merry's Museum Magazine*. Edwin Mellen Press, 2001.

Pittman, Coretta M. "To Labor with Dignity: Alberta Hunter's Respectability and Resistance Rhetoric." *Women at Work: Rhetorics of Gender and Labor*, edited by David Gold and Jessica Enoch, U of Pittsburgh P, 2019, pp. 144–57.

Powell, Malea. "Down by the River, or How Susan La Flesche Picotte Can Teach Us about Alliance as a Practice of Survivance." *Rhetorics from/of Color*, special issue of *College English*, vol. 67, no. 1, 2004, pp. 38–60.

———. "Rhetorics of Survivance: How American Indians Use Writing." *College Composition and Communication*, vol. 53, no. 3, 2002, pp. 396–434.

Powell, Malea, et al. "Our Story Begins Here: Constellating Cultural Rhetorics." *Enculturation*, Oct. 25, 2014, https://www.enculturation. net/our-story-begins-here.

Pratt, Mary Louise. "Arts of the Contact Zone." *Profession*, vol. 91, 1991, pp. 33–40.

Price-Groff, Claire. *Extraordinary Women Journalists*. Scholastic, 1998.

Pulitzer, Joseph. "The College of Journalism." *North American Review*, vol. 178, 1904, pp. 641–80.

Quinn, Russell. *Trends in Size, Circulation, News and Advertising in San Francisco Journalism, 1870–1938. The History of San Francisco Journalism*, vol. 4, San Francisco: W.P.A., 1939.

Ramírez, Cristina. *Occupying Our Space: The Mestiza Rhetorics of Mexican Women Journalists and Activists, 1875–1942*. U of Arizona P, 2015.

Redcay, Anna M. "'Live to Learn and Learn to Live': The St. Nicholas League and the Vocation of Childhood." *Children's Literature*, vol. 39, no. 1, 2011, pp. 58–84.

Removal of the Ponca Indians. Senate of the United States. 46th Congress, 2d Session. Report No. 670, 31 May 1880.

Rhodes, Jane. *Mary Ann Shadd Cary: The Black Press and Protest in the Nineteenth Century*. Indiana UP, 1998.

Richardson, Darcy G. *Others: Third Parties during the Populist Period*. Vol. 2, Universe, 2007.

Ringel, Paul B. *Commercializing Childhood: Children's Magazines, Urban Gentility, and the Ideal of the Child Consumer in the United States, 1823–1918*. U of Massachusetts P, 2015.

Robbins, Hollis, and Henry Louis Gates Jr., editors. *The Portable Nineteenth-Century African American Women Writers*. Penguin Books, 2017.

Robinson, Emily. "Objects, Documentation, and Identification: Materiality and Memory of American Indian Boarding Schools at the Heard Museum." *Rhetoric Society Quarterly*, vol. 51, no. 2, Spring 2021, pp. 94–108.

Robinson, John K., and Karen Galle. "A Century of Marking History: 100 Years of the Pennsylvania Historical Marker Program." *Pennsylvania*

Heritage, vol. 40, no. 4, Fall 2014, http://paheritage.wpengine.com
/article/century-marking-history-100-years-pennsylvania-historical
-marker-program/.

Rogers, Will. *The Papers of Will Rogers*. Edited by Arthur Frank Wert-
heim and Barbara Bair. Vol. 1, *The Early Years, November 1879–April
1904*, U of Oklahoma P, 1996.

Rose, Jessica A. and Lynée Lewis Gaillet. "Archiving Our Own Historical
Moments: Learning from the Disrupted Public Memory of Temperance." *Nineteenth-Century American Activist Rhetorics*, edited by
Patricia Bizzell and Lisa Zimmerelli, Modern Language Association
of America, 2020, pp. 234–48.

Ross, Ishbel. *Ladies of the Press: The Story of Women in Journalism by an
Insider*. 1936. Arno Press, 1974.

Rothermel, Beth Ann. "A Sphere of Noble Action: Gender, Rhetoric,
and Influence at a Nineteenth-Century Massachusetts State Normal
School." *Rhetoric Society Quarterly*, vol. 33, no. 1, Winter 2003, pp.
35–64.

Royster, Jacqueline Jones. "The Long Nineteenth Century and the Bend
toward Justice." *Nineteenth-Century American Activist Rhetorics*,
edited by Patricia Bizzell and Lisa Zimmerelli, Modern Language
Association of America, 2020, pp. 318–32.

———. *Traces of a Stream: Literacy and Social Change among African
American Women*. U of Pittsburgh P, 1994.

Royster, Jacqueline Jones, and Gesa E. Kirsch. *Feminist Rhetorical Practices: New Horizons for Rhetoric, Composition, and Literacy Studies*.
Southern Illinois UP, 2012.

Schilpp, Madelon Golden, and Sharon M. Murphy. *Great Women of the
Press*. Southern Illinois UP, 1983.

Schultz, Lucille M. *The Young Composers: Composition's Beginnings in
Nineteenth-Century Schools*. Southern Illinois UP, 1999.

Seidel, Chalet K. "Professionalizing the Study Body: Uptake in a Nineteenth Century Journalism Textbook." *Linguistics and the Human
Sciences*, vol. 3, no. 1, 2007, pp. 67–85.

Shaw, Stephanie J. *Woman Ought to Be and to Do: Black Professional
Women Workers during the Jim Crow Era*. U of Chicago P, 1996.

Shott, Brian. *Mediating America: Black and Irish Press and the Struggle
for Citizenship, 1870–1914*. Temple UP, 2019.

Shuman, Edwin Llewellyn. *Steps into Journalism: Helps and Hints for
Young Writers*. Correspondence School of Journalism, 1894.

Smith, Jessie Carney, and Joseph M. Palmisano, editors. *Reference Library of Black America*. Vol. 2, Gale Group, 2000.

Smith, Linda Tuhiwai. *Decolonizing Methodologies: Research and Indigenous Peoples*. Zed Books, 1999.

Sonneborn, Liz, editor. *A to Z of American Indian Women*. Infobase Publishing, 2007.

Sorby, Angela. "A Visit from *St. Nicholas*: The Poetics of Peer Culture, 1872–1900." *American Studies*, vol. 39, no. 1, Spring 1998, pp. 59–74.

Steffens, J. Lincoln. "The Business of a Newspaper." *Scribner's Magazine*, edited by Edward Livermore et al., Charles Scribner's Sons, 1897.

Street, Douglas. "La Flesche Sisters Write to *St. Nicholas Magazine*." *Nebraska History*, vol. 62, no. 4, Winter 1981, pp. 515–23.

Streitmatter, Rodger. *Raising Her Voice: African-American Women Journalists Who Changed History*. UP of Kentucky, 1994.

Stromberg, Ernest. "Rhetoric and American Indians." *American Indian Rhetorics of Survivance: Word Medicine, Word Magic*, U of Pittsburgh P, 2006, pp. 95–109.

Sumpter, Randall S. "'Practical Reporting': Late Nineteenth-Century Journalistic Standards and Rule Breaking." *American Journalism*, vol. 30, no. 1, 2013, pp. 44–64.

Theriot, Nancy M. *Mothers and Daughters in Nineteenth-Century America: The Biosocial Construction of Femininity*. UP of Kentucky, 1996.

Thorne, Tanis C. *The Many Hands of My Relations: French and Indians on the Lower Missouri*. U of Missouri P, 1996.

Tibbles, Susette La Flesche. "The Omahas." NMAI-066_001_03_075, Thomas H. Tibbles Papers, National Museum of the American Indian, Smithsonian Institution.

Tibbles, Thomas. "Bright Eyes in England." Chapter 6 of *Law Is Liberty*, a typescript of collected writings by Bright Eyes. Compiled and edited by Anna C. Smith Pabst, 1958. NMAI-066_001_03_001, Thomas H. Tibbles Papers, National Museum of the American Indian, Smithsonian Institution.

——. *Buckskin and Blanket Days: Memoirs of a Friend of the Indians*. 1905. Doubleday, 1957.

Tonn, Mari. "Militant Motherhood: Labor's Mary Harris 'Mother' Jones." *Quarterly Journal of Speech*, vol. 82, no. 1, Feb. 1996, pp. 1–21.

Treuer, David. *The Heartbeat of Wounded Knee: Native America from 1890 to the Present*. Riverhead Books, 2019.

"United Nations Commission on the Status of Women." *United Nations. Division for the Advancement of Women,* https://www.un.org/women watch/daw/CSW60YRS/index.htm.

VanderHaagen, Sara. *Children's Biographies of African American Women: Rhetoric, Public Memory, and Agency.* U of South Carolina P, 2018.

VanHaitsma, Pamela. "An Archival Framework for Affirming Black Women's Bisexual Rhetorics in the Primus Collections." *Rhetoric Society Quarterly,* vol. 51, no. 1, Winter 2021, pp. 27–41.

———. *Queering Romantic Engagement in the Postal Age: A Rhetorical Education.* U of South Carolina P, 2019.

———. "Romantic Correspondence as Queer Extracurriculum: The Self-Education for Racial Uplift of Addie Brown and Rebecca Primus." *College Composition and Communication,* vol. 69, no. 2, 2017, pp. 182–207.

Van Horn, Catherine. "Turning Child Readers into Consumers: Children's Magazines and Advertising, 1900–1920." *Defining Print Culture for Youth: The Cultural Work of Children's Literature,* edited by Anne H. Lundin and Wayne Wiegand, Libraries Unlimited, 2003, pp. 121–38.

Vizenor, Gerald. "Aesthetics of Survivance: Literary Theory and Practice." *Survivance: Narratives of Native Presence,* edited by Gerald Vizenor, U of Nebraska P, 2008, pp. 1–24.

———. *Literary Chance: Essays on Native American Survivance.* Universitat de València, 2007.

———. *Manifest Manners: Narratives on Postindian Survivance.* U of Nebraska P, 1999.

Wagner, Wendy. "Black Separatism in the Periodical Writings of Mrs. A. E. (Amelia) Johnson." *The Black Press: New Literary and Historical Essays,* edited by Todd Vogel, Rutgers UP, 2001, pp. 93–103.

Washburn, Patrick S. *The African American Newspaper: Voice of Freedom.* Northwestern UP, 2006.

Waters, Kristin. "Some Core Themes of Nineteenth-Century Black Feminism." *Black Women's Intellectual Traditions: Speaking Their Minds,* edited by Kristin Waters and Carol B. Conaway, U of Vermont P, 2007, pp. 365–92.

Watson, Elmo Scott. "The Last Indian War, 1890–91: A Study of Newspaper Jingoism." *Journalism Quarterly,* vol. 20, no. 3, Sept. 1943, pp. 205–19.

"Waymarking FAQ." *Waymarking,* accessed 29 Aug. 2018, https://www.waymarking.com/help/faq.aspx.

"Waymark Visit—PaHawkeye Visited Underground Railroad." "Underground Railroad—Pennsylvania Historical Markers on Waymarking.
com." *Waymarking*, https://www.waymarking.com/waymarks/wm62R
_Underground_Railroad.

Wells, Ida B. *Crusade for Justice: The Autobiography of Ida B. Wells*. Edited by Alfreda M. Duster, 2nd ed., U of Chicago P, 2020.

Wells-Barnett, Ida B. *Selected Works of Ida B. Wells-Barnett*. Introduction
by Trudier Harris, Oxford UP, 1991.

Welter, Barbara. *Dimity Convictions: The American Woman in the Nineteenth Century*. Ohio UP, 1976.

Whitburn, Merrill D., et al. "Elocution and Feminine Power in the First
Quarter of the Twentieth Century: The Career of Carolyn Winkler
(Paterson) as Performer and Teacher." *Rhetoric Review*, vol. 30, no. 4,
2011, pp. 389–405.

White Eagle. "Statement by White Eagle." Transcribed by and with a
preface and afterword by Susette La Flesche. 20 May 1879. NMAI
-066_001_06_001, Thomas H. Tibbles Papers, National Museum of
the American Indian, Smithsonian Institution.

Wilson, Francille Rusan. *The Segregated Scholars: Black Social Scientists
and the Creation of Black Labor Studies, 1890–1950*. U of Virginia P,
2006.

Wilson, Shawn. *Research Is Ceremony: Indigenous Research Methods*.
Fernwood Publishing, 2008.

Wray, Amanda. "Gertrude Bustill Mossell (1855–1948)." *Encyclopedia of
African American Women Writers*, edited by Yolanda Williams Page,
Greenwood Press, 2007.

Wright, Michelle Diane, editor. *Broken Utterances: A Selected Anthology
of 19th Century Black Women's Social Thought*. Three Sistahs Press,
2007.

Wright, Nazera Sadiq. *Black Girlhood in the Nineteenth Century*. U of
Illinois P, 2016.

Zackodnik, Teresa. *Press, Platform, Pulpit: Black Feminist Publics in the
Era of Reform*. U of Tennessee P, 2011.

Zuckerman, Faye B. "Winifred Black (Annie Laurie)." *American Newspaper Journalists, 1901–1925*, edited by Perry J. Ashley, *Dictionary of
Literary Biography*, vol. 25, Gale Research, 1985.

Index

GRACE WETZEL is an associate professor of English, writing, and journalism at Saint Joseph's University, where she serves as first-year course coordinator. Her essays have appeared in *Composition Studies*, *Journal of the Assembly for Expanded Perspectives on Learning*, *Rhetoric Society Quarterly*, and *Reflections: A Journal of Community-Engaged Writing and Rhetoric*.

Studies in Rhetorics and Feminisms

Studies in Rhetorics and Feminisms seeks to address the interdisciplinarity that rhetorics and feminisms represent. Rhetorical and feminist scholars connect rhetorical inquiry with contemporary academic and social concerns, exploring rhetoric's relevance to current issues of opportunity and diversity. This interdisciplinarity is transforming the rhetorical tradition as we have known it (upper-class, agonistic, public, and male) into regendered, inclusionary rhetorics (democratic, dialogic, collaborative, cultural, and private). Our intellectual advancements depend on such ongoing transformation.

Rhetoric, whether ancient, contemporary, or futuristic, always inscribes the relation of language and power at a particular moment, indicating who may speak, who may listen, and what can be said. The only way we can displace the traditional rhetoric of masculine-only, public performance is to replace it with rhetorics that are recognized as being better suited to our present needs. We must understand more fully the rhetorics of the non-Western tradition, of women, of a variety of cultural and ethnic groups. Therefore, Studies in Rhetorics and Feminisms espouses a theoretical position of openness and expansion, a place for rhetorics to grow and thrive in a symbiotic relationship with all that feminisms have to offer, particularly when these two fields intersect with philosophical, sociological, religious, psychological, pedagogical, and literary issues.

Books in the series both examine and extend rhetoric through examination of sexes, disciplines, cultures, ethnicities, and sociocultural practices as they intersect with the rhetorical tradition. After all, the recent resurgence of rhetorical studies has been not so much a discovery of new rhetorics as a recognition of existing rhetorical activities and practices, of our newfound ability and willingness to listen to previously untold stories.

Professor Emerita Shirley Wilson Logan
University of Maryland

Cheryl Glenn
Penn State University

Other Books in the Studies in Rhetorics and Feminisms Series